THE FORGOTTEN HOMELAND

This report was commissioned by The Century Foundation as part of its major Homeland Security Project. The project began with a working group cochaired by former Governors Thomas Kean and Richard Celeste. Some components of the project are supported in part by the John S. and James L. Knight Foundation, the Carnegie Corporation of New York, the Robert Wood Johnson Foundation, and the John D. and Catherine T. MacArthur Foundation. The task force was assembled and chaired by Richard A. Clarke and Rand Beers. More information on this project can be found at www.homelandsec.org or The Century Foundation's main Web site, www.tcf.org.

THE FORGOTTEN HOMELAND

A Century Foundation
Task Force Report

RICHARD A. CLARKE AND RAND BEERS, CHAIRS

The Century Foundation

THE CENTURY FOUNDATION PRESS ◆ NEW YORK

Library of Congress Cataloging-in-Publication Data

Library of Congress Cataloging-in-Publication Data

The forgotten homeland : a Century Foundation task force report / Richard A. Clarke and Rand Beers, Chairs.
    p. cm.
  Includes bibliographical references and index.
  ISBN-13: 978-0-87078-498-9 (pbk. : alk. paper)
  ISBN-10: 0-87078-498-6 (pbk. : alk. paper)
  1. Civil defense--United States. 2. United States--Defenses. I. Century Foundation. II. Title.

  UA927.F67 2006
  363.325'170973--dc22

2006016988

FOREWORD

We are approaching the fifth anniversary of the attacks of September 11, 2001. Over that time, the United States has led the effort to overthrow the Taliban from Afghanistan, invaded Iraq, and is still fighting in both nations. Congress enacted and renewed the Patriot Act. It put in place a new Department of Homeland Security and a new National Directorate of Intelligence as major components of an even wider reorganization of government intended to increase our capacities for fighting terrorism and coping with emergencies. We have spent several hundred billion dollars on activities labeled as part of the "war on terrorism," in effect drastically altering budget priorities. In the process, domestic surveillance has been radically increased, challenging the way we judge basic issues of liberty and privacy. The American base at Guantanamo in Cuba was transformed into an open-ended prison facility from which international monitors have been barred.

The list could be extended almost indefinitely, but the importance of these developments is clear. American policymakers have been reshaping the role of government, foreign policy, and everyday life. In the past, such sweeping changes only took place when we were engaged in a full-scale war, which required mobilization of people and resources. But the current situation is different: there has been no conscription into military service and no explicit and immediate rationing or trade-off of private resources for military and security purposes. Tax cuts have gone forward and deficits continue to build up. The cost and consequences, in other words, still are accumulating. Moreover, the probability that there will be additional terrorist actions means that the changes set in motion on September 11 are probably far from final.

In this context, it is a matter of considerable urgency that we continue to ask basic questions about how effectively we are responding to the threat posed by suicidal terrorists. Have we made the most of our chances to shape a national and international response to terrorism? Have we made the right choices in terms of how we spend money and allocate resources to defend the homeland? Have we strengthened or created the institutions we need to protect us? Have we struck a sensible balance between security and liberty? These sorts of questions are crucial to attaining a necessary level of transparency and accountability. They may seem obvious, but they have been, in large measure, unanswered. Obtaining and examining the facts with a critical eye has been proven over and over again to be the best method for testing and improving performance. We know from the experience of other government activities, from the routine exposure of problems in the private sector, and even from reports of serious problems in such nongovernmental institutions as the Catholic Church and the United Way, that no institution can be expected to perform well consistently without the discipline provided by outside scrutiny and advice.

For a time after September 11, there was a rare potential for unity. American leadership, perhaps, had an opportunity not only to bridge political divisions within the United States, but also to organize a vast global coalition against terrorism. Normal partisanship and nationalism, in a sense, were suspended as almost everyone felt the desire and need to come together and find ways to contain and eliminate the dangers made apparent by the attacks. Some had warned for years that the violence perpetrated around the world was hard evidence of a growing and unprecedented threat. But it took the shock of the massive casualties and damage on September 11 to awaken most people to the necessity to act.

This is not to say that it was obvious what the right decisions were after the attacks. But the opportunity was unique. Perhaps most important, because it is simply impossible to do every conceivable thing that might add to homeland security, we must examine closely the actual choices that have been made. And we must judge the effectiveness of what has ensued not just in conventional terms but also in light of the "opportunity costs" of following the road chosen by the current administration versus other possible responses.

To help all of us sort through these questions, The Century Foundation was delighted to work again with Richard Clarke, chairman of Good Harbor Consulting and former national coordinator for security and counterterrorism, among other senior White House positions, and to work with Rand Beers, president of the Valley Forge Initiative and former director for counterterrorism and counternarcotics on the National Security Council staff. Messrs. Clarke and Beers assembled an exceptional team of experts to work collaboratively on this volume. Their knowledge and judgment are reflected in the depth of understanding and scope of this report. Just a sampling of the chapter titles provides a sense of how much ground they covered: "Building Homeland Security in Our Cities and States," "A Counterterrorism Policy for Our Own Backyard," "Security for a Nation in Motion," "A Healthy Medical Response System," "Emergency Response: Restoring Discarded Strategies that Worked," "Preventing Nuclear Terrorism," and "The Perils of Neglecting America's Waterfront." The authors of this volume present a powerful case that although much has been done it has not always been either the correct or most effective action. The report, however, is considerably more than a critique, for it offers a way to translate the present underlying public concern into an enhanced agenda.

For The Century Foundation, this report is the latest in a series of projects that began before the September 11 terrorist attacks and includes in-depth studies of ideas for reform of America's intelligence operations. After September 11, we launched a major Homeland Security Project cochaired by former Governors Thomas Kean and Richard Celeste, and supported by the John S. and James L. Knight Foundation, the Carnegie Corporation of New York, the Robert Wood Johnson Foundation, and the John D. and Catherine T. MacArthur Foundation. This project is premised on the notion that the United States will be better prepared for the tests ahead if we are a nation armed not just with a powerful military and well-organized intelligence apparatus but also with a deeper public understanding of what we are up against and what we need to do in the face of changing threats.

One of the most important products of our effort was a publication similar to this one in that it was written by a team of experts under the direction of Richard Clarke. Titled *Defeating the Jihadists: A Blueprint for Action,* that book provided comprehensive details about the nature and scope of the terrorist threat as well as a concrete, multifaceted strategy for defeating it. Other Century Foundation publications focusing particularly on strengthening the nation's capacity to prevent and respond to terrorism within our borders include *Breathing Easier? The Report of the Century Foundation Working Group on Bioterrorism Preparedness,* a report card evaluating the Department of Homeland Security's performance, a special issue of *Governing* magazine titled *Securing the Homeland,* and a report by Donald F. Kettl on security challenges facing state and local governments. On the civil liberties challenges posed post–September 11, our publications include a collection of essays titled *The War on Our Freedoms: Civil Liberties in an Age of Terrorism,* Stephen J. Schulhofer's *Rethinking the Patriot Act: Keeping America Safe and Free,* and *The Basics: The USA PATRIOT Act.* More information about these publications, as well as related issue briefs and commentary, are available on our Homeland Security Web site, www.homelandsec.org.

There is little doubt that we shall need a continuing willingness to assess our security efforts in the years ahead. Today, after the frustrations and failures of the governmental response to Hurricane Katrina, and the miscalculations and uncertainties of the Iraq invasion, there is a need for a strong and candid reassessment of our homeland security strategies over the past five years. We clearly have weaknesses that were unexpected. Just to take these two examples: in the aftermath of Katrina, we were incapable of organizing an effective response to help hundreds of thousands of citizens; and in the ongoing conflict in Iraq, we may being sending the wrong message to our enemies. Namely, instead of demonstrating our overwhelming strength, we may well be producing examples that define our limitations.

Future policies, then, must be more rigorously debated or mistakes will be inevitable. And, of course, even if we consider all options, homeland security will never be easy or complete. To the extent we make progress, however, we will be indebted to those like Richard Clarke and Rand Beers and their colleagues in this book who seek the truth and offer wise advice. On behalf of the trustees of The Century Foundation, I thank them for their work on this valuable report.

RICHARD C. LEONE, *PRESIDENT*
The Century Foundation
June 2006

CONTENTS

TASK FORCE MEMBERS

CATHERINE A. ALLEN is CEO of BITS, a nonprofit, CEO-driven financial services industry consortium made up of one hundred of the largest financial institutions in the United States, and chairman and CEO of the Santa Fe Group, a consulting firm serving financial institutions and other critical infrastructure companies and a strategic partner to BITS. She is chair of the Advisory Council for the National Foundation for Credit Counseling and sits on a number of nonprofit and for-profit boards, including those of the Financial Services Technology Consortium, the Financial Services Sector Coordinating Council, the Identity Theft Assistance Center, the Electronification of Authentication Partnership, Giesecke & Devrient, Stewart Title Guaranty Company, NBS Technologies, and Hudson Ventures.

RAND BEERS is president of the Valley Forge Initiative, an organization that develops and disseminates a twenty-first-century-progressive vision of national security. He served as the national security adviser to the Kerry-Edwards 2004 campaign. After serving as a Marine Corps officer and rifle company commander in Vietnam, he entered the Foreign Service in 1971 and the civil service in 1983. From 1988 to 1998, he served on the National Security Council Staff at the White House as director for counterterrorism and counternarcotics, director for peacekeeping, and senior director for intelligence programs. From 1998 to 2003, he was assistant secretary of state for international narcotics and law enforcement affairs. From 2002 to 2003, he was special assistant to the president and senior director for combating terrorism at the National Security Council.

JANE A. BULLOCK is a founding partner of Bullock & Haddow, LLC, a risk mitigation and emergency management consulting firm. She has worked in emergency management for over twenty-five years. Prior to founding Bullock & Haddow, she served as the chief of staff to James Lee Witt, director of the Federal Emergency Management Agency, from 1992 to 2000. She serves on the adjunct faculty at the Institute for Crisis,

Disaster and Risk Management at George Washington University. She is a coauthor of a disaster management textbook titled *Introduction to Emergency Management* (Butterworth-Heinemann, 2003) and of *Introduction to Homeland Security* (Butterworth-Heinemann, 2004).

RICHARD A. CLARKE is the chairman of Good Harbor Consulting, LLC. Clarke served the past three presidents as special assistant to the president for global affairs, national coordinator for security and counterterrorism, and special adviser to the president for cyber security. Prior to his White House years, he served for nineteen years in the Pentagon, the intelligence community, and the Department of State. During the Reagan administration, he was deputy assistant secretary of state for intelligence. During the George H. W. Bush administration, he was assistant secretary of state for political-military affairs and coordinated diplomatic efforts to support the 1990–91 Gulf War and the subsequent security arrangements. He is the author of *Against All Enemies: Inside America's War on Terror* (Free Press, 2004) and is an on-air consultant for ABC News.

R. P. EDDY is senior fellow for counterterrorism at the Manhattan Institute, where he is executive director of the Center for Policing Terrorism, and managing director of Gerson Lehrman Group, where he leads the Geopolitical Risk Division. He has served as a senior adviser to the New York Police Department, the Los Angeles Police Department, and others. He has served variously as director at the White House National Security Council; senior policy officer to UN Secretary-General Kofi Annan; chief of staff to the U.S. ambassador to the UN; and senior adviser for intelligence and counterterrorism to the secretary of energy. He was honored as a World Economic Forum Global Leader for Tomorrow and is a member of the Council on Foreign Relations.

CHARLES D. FERGUSON is a fellow for science and technology at the Council on Foreign Relations, adjunct professor in the security studies program at Georgetown University, and adjunct lecturer in the homeland security certificate program at the Johns Hopkins University. Previously, he was a scientist-in-residence in the Washington, D.C., office of the Monterey Institute's Center for Nonproliferation Studies, where he codirected a project that systemically assessed how to prevent and respond to nuclear and radiological terrorism. The project's major findings were published in *The Four Faces of Nuclear Terrorism* (Routledge, 2005). He has served as a foreign affairs officer in the Bureau of Nonproliferation, Department of State, where he helped develop U.S. government policies on nuclear safety and security issues. After graduating with distinction from the United States Naval Academy, he served as an officer on a fleet ballistic missile submarine and studied nuclear engineering at the Naval Nuclear Power School. He has done scientific research at the Los Alamos National Laboratory, the University of Maryland's Institute for Physical Science and Technology, the Harvard-Smithsonian Center for Astrophysics, and the Space Telescope Science Institute.

STEPHEN E. FLYNN is the inaugural occupant of the Jeane J. Kirkpatrick Senior Fellow in National Security Studies at the Council on Foreign Relations and a commander in the U.S. Coast Guard (retired). He has served as director and principal author for the task force report *America: Still Unprepared—Still in Danger,* cochaired by former Senators Gary Hart and Warren Rudman. He is the author of the critically acclaimed national bestseller *America the Vulnerable: How Our Government Is Failing to Protect Us from Terrorism* (HarperCollins, 2004).

JOHN GANNON is vice president for global analysis at BAE Systems. Previously, he was staff director of the Homeland Security Committee of the U.S. House of Representatives. In 2002–2003, he was a team leader in the White House's Transitional Planning Office for the Department of Homeland Security. He has served as the CIA's director of European analysis, deputy director for intelligence, chairman of the National Intelligence Council, and assistant director of central intelligence for analysis and production. In the private sector, he developed the analytic workforce for Intellibridge Corporation, a Web-based provider of outsourced analysis for government and corporate clients. He is an adjunct professor in the National Security Studies Program at Georgetown University.

JULIETTE N. KAYYEM is a lecturer in public policy at Kennedy School of Government at Harvard University and a faculty affiliate at the Belfer Center for Science and International Affairs. Previously, she was executive director for Research at the Belfer Center and oversaw the terrorism and homeland security research program at Harvard from 2001 to 2003. From 1999 to July 2001, she served as former House Minority Leader Richard Gephardt's appointment to the National Commission on Terrorism. She served in a variety of capacities at the Department of Justice, including as a legal adviser to Attorney General Janet Reno. Her work focuses on counterterrorism, law enforcement, and homeland security and has appeared in numerous academic and popular publications. She is the coauthor of *Protecting Liberty in an Age of Terror* (MIT Press, 2005) and coeditor of *First to Arrive: State and Local Response to Terrorism* (MIT Press, 2003), and is a national security analyst for NBC News.

ROBERT K. KNAKE is a senior associate at Good Harbor Consulting, LLC, where he advises clients on homeland security and counterterrorism issues. He has served as a research associate in national security studies at the Council on Foreign Relations, where he worked with Stephen Flynn and led research for the second part of the report of the Hart-Rudman Commission, and as a research assistant on the Homeland Security Partnerships Initiative at the Belfer Center for Science and International Affairs at the Kennedy School of Government at Harvard University. He authored the Medical Consequence Management Plan for the 2004 Democratic National Conference for Boston Emergency Medical Services.

LAWRENCE J. KORB is a senior fellow at the Center for American Progress and a senior adviser to the Center for Defense Information. Previously, he was a senior fellow and director of national security studies at the Council on Foreign Relations. Prior to joining the council, he served as director of the Center for Public Policy Education and senior fellow in the Foreign Policy Studies Program at the Brookings Institution, dean of the Graduate School of Public and International Affairs at the University of Pittsburgh, and vice president of corporate operations at the Raytheon Company. He served as assistant secretary of defense (manpower, reserve affairs, installations, and logistics) from 1981 through 1985. In that position, he administered about 70 percent of the defense budget. For his service in that position, he was awarded the Department of Defense's medal for Distinguished Public Service. He served on active duty for four years as naval flight officer, and retired from the Naval Reserve with the rank of captain.

PAUL B. KURTZ is executive director of the Cyber Security Industry Alliance (CSIA), an advocacy group dedicated to ensuring the privacy, reliability, and integrity of information systems through public policy, technology, education, and awareness. Prior to joining CSIA, he was most recently special assistant to the president and senior director for critical infrastructure protection on the White House's Homeland Security Council, where he was responsible for both physical and cyber security.

MARTIN O'MALLEY currently serves as the mayor of Baltimore, Maryland, and the cochair of the U.S. Conference of Mayors' Homeland Security Task Force. He has been called America's Best Young Mayor by *Esquire* magazine and one of the country's "top five big-city" mayors by *Time* magazine. He has received national acclaim for his "CitiStat" government performance system. Before being elected mayor in 1999, he served on the City Council and as an assistant state's attorney for the city of Baltimore.

BRIDGER McGAW currently is a homeland security policy and strategic communications consultant for public and private organizations. He has held several governmental positions, including for Chicago's Mayor Richard Daley, U.S. Representative Marty Meehan, and as assistant press secretary to Vice President Al Gore. Appointed by President Bill Clinton, he served on the staff of Secretary of Defense William Cohen as a public affairs officer and defense fellow.

JAMIE F. METZL is executive vice president of the Asia Society. He directed the 2003 Council on Foreign Relations Task Force on Emergency Responders and authored the task force report, *Emergency Responders: Drastically Underfunded, Dangerously Unprepared.* His government appointments have included deputy staff director and senior counselor of the Senate Foreign Relations Committee, senior coordinator for international public information and senior adviser to the under-secretary for public diplomacy and public affairs at the Department of State, and director for multilateral and humanitarian affairs on the National Security Council. He is a member of the Council on Foreign Relations, a cochair of the Board of the Partnership for a Secure America, and a former White House Fellow.

BLAKE W. MOBLEY is a Ph.D. candidate in government at Georgetown University specializing in intelligence and counterterrorism. He has worked as a summer associate at the RAND Corporation and with the Center for Tactical Counter Terrorism on projects for the New York City Police Department. He served as a member of The Century Foundation task force that produced the report, *Defeating the Jihadists: A Blueprint for Action.*

DANIEL B. PRIETO is director and senior fellow of the Homeland Security Center at the Reform Institute. Previously, he was research director of the Homeland Security Partnership Initiative and fellow at the Belfer Center for Science and International Affairs at the Kennedy School of Government at Harvard University. He is an associate member of the Markle Foundation Task Force on National Security in the Information Age and led the management working group of the Center for Strategic and International Studies/Heritage Foundation Task Force on the Roles, Mission, and Organization of the Department of Homeland Security. He has served on the professional staff of the Select Committee on Homeland Security in the U.S. House of Representatives. He is a former technology-industry executive and investment banker. He is a past recipient of the International Affairs Fellowship from the Council on Foreign Relations. He is coauthor, with Stephen E. Flynn, of *Neglected Defense: Mobilizing the Private Sector to Support Homeland Security* (Council on Foreign Relations, 2006).

ALISON SILVERSTEIN is a consultant to the electric industry on electric reliability, infrastructure security, energy efficiency, distributed generation, demand response, and technology adoption issues. She worked as senior energy policy adviser to Chairman Pat Wood, III, at the Federal Energy Regulatory Commission, from July 2001 through July 2004. She advised the chairman on a variety of legal, economic, strategic, and administrative issues and served as the agency's lead on infrastructure security, cyber-security, and energy reliability and worked on most of the agency's major cases and rulemakings. Previously, she worked variously for Pacific Gas & Electric Co., ICF Inc., the Environmental Law Institute, and the U.S. Department of Interior.

STEVEN N. SIMON is the Hasib J. Sabbagh Senior Fellow for Middle Eastern Studies at the Council on Foreign Relations. Prior to joining the

Council, he specialized in Middle Eastern affairs at the RAND Corporation. Previously, he was the deputy director of the International Institute for Strategic Studies and Carol Deane Senior Fellow in U.S. Security Studies. He served at the White House as director for global issues and senior director for transnational threats for five years under President Bill Clinton, during which he was involved in U.S. counterterrorism policy and operations as well as security policy in the Near East and South Asia. Before that, he had a fifteen year career at the U.S. Department of State. Mr. Simon is the coauthor of *The Age of Sacred Terror* (Random House, 2002), which won the Council on Foreign Relations 2004 Arthur Ross Book Award, and coeditor of *Iraq at the Crossroads; State and Society in the Shadow of Regime Change* (Oxford University Press/IISS, 2003). Most recently, he coauthored *The Next Attack* (Henry Holt, 2005), which examines the evolution of the jihad since September 11, 2001, and America's response.

AMY E. SMITHSON is a senior fellow in the international security studies program at the Center for Strategic and International Studies. She specializes in in-depth field research on issues related to chemical and biological weapons proliferation, threat reduction mechanisms, defense, and domestic preparedness. Before joining the Center for Strategic and International Studies, she worked at the Henry L. Stimson Center, where in January 1993 she founded the Chemical and Biological Weapons Nonproliferation Project to serve as an information clearinghouse, watchdog, and problem solver on chemical and biological weapons issues. Previously, she worked at the Pacific-Sierra Research Corporation, where she concentrated on strategies and tactics to monitor nuclear weapons accords, and at the Center for Naval Analyses.

MOIRA WHELAN is the director of communications for the Valley Forge Initiative. She formerly served as director of communications and outreach for the Belfer Center for Science and International Affairs at Harvard's John F. Kennedy School of Government and as communications director for the Democrats on the U.S. House of Representatives Select Committee on Homeland Security.

INTRODUCTION
THE FORGOTTEN HOMELAND

The destruction of New Orleans and subsequent degradation of its population shocked the conscience of America. We saw in it evidence that we cannot count on the national government to perform one of its most basic missions: preventing, mitigating, and responding to disaster. The image of Louisiana National Guardsmen in Iraq as the people of Louisiana went without protection and support seemed incongruous and, at some level, wrong.

Hurricane Katrina seemed to come so soon after our country had suffered from September 11. Yet, despite the vivid images still fresh in our minds, that terrorist attack occurred over four years ago. Much can be done in four years. What has been called the "Greatest Generation" of Americans defeated Nazi Germany and Imperial Japan in four years. The Manhattan Project took a physics concept to a deployed nuclear weapon in four years. The entire presidencies of Jimmy Carter and George H. W. Bush each lasted four years. Four years is the entire length of an undergraduate college experience. Over that time span a baby goes from birth, to walking, then talking, and attending pre-school.

Americans understood that, since the tragedy of September 11, billions of tax dollars had been spent creating a new capability to deal with crises in the United States. A large, new federal department was created. Increased funding was made available to emergency responders. Exercises were held across the country to prepare for mass casualty events. Then, with Katrina, when the nation was tested by tragedy at home again, it seemed that we were less capable than we had been before all of this supposed strengthening of our homeland security capabilities.

The cognitive dissonance between what most Americans thought had been done to address homeland issues and the pathetic performance they witnessed after Katrina caused many in Congress and the media to reassess what actually has been accomplished since September 11 to

1

protect our homeland. The former members of the 9/11 Commission also issued a final, and failing, report card on what had been done to prevent another major terrorist attack and what could be done to respond should one occur. What the evidence reveals is a long list of initiatives and few accomplishments, a full agenda of needs and no apparent plan to address them.

In 2006, emergency responders are still unable to communicate reliably or securely across jurisdictions or in large buildings and tunnels. Chemical plants in major metropolitan areas continue to pose an unmitigated risk. Americans ride commuter rail and subway systems that are vulnerable to the kinds of attack that have already happened in Paris, Moscow, Madrid, Tokyo, and London. Few cities are prepared to deal with the mass casualties that would accompany a pandemic or a biological attack. Radiological materials are poorly accounted for and secured, making a "dirty bomb" that would contaminate large parts of a city a very real possibility. The agency charged with finding terrorists in the United States is unable to deploy a modern information technology system and the intelligence community remains incapable of translating the material it collects. Funds to address homeland security have not been allocated on the basis of security needs or as part of a multi-year plan to achieve a specific level of risk and capability. Block grants for homeland security in many places have been squandered, allocated to regions facing little risk or spent without any goal or overall risk mitigation strategy.

After all of the publicity given homeland security, we in fact have no idea how secure the nation really is, how much more secure those funds have made us, or what it would take to achieve an adequate level of risk management. Nor can the president, Congress, or the voters make informed tradeoffs between risk mitigation at home and alternative spending priorities, such as traditional military defense against attack by foreign powers.

How can we have allowed this level of mismanagement while the crumbling towers of the World Trade Center still burn in our memory? The presence of the Louisiana National Guardsmen in Iraq is a metaphor for the problem. America chose to respond in large part to the terrorist attacks in New York and Washington by waging overseas wars. The president repeatedly recited a policy to "fight them over there, rather than here." That policy, alas, is logically fallacious and misleading in its presumption that we can control the venue of terrorist attacks. While it would be clearly preferable not to engage terrorists in the United States, fighting some terrorists overseas does not in any way preclude others from coming to the United States. Indeed, the analysis of many terrorism experts in and out of government is quite the opposite: By fighting in Iraq, the United States has increased the motivation of many potential terrorists to attack Americans at home. They also note that the Iraq experience has increased the skills of many terrorists, some of whom may use those skills elsewhere, including in the United States.

Nonetheless, our post–September 11 response undeniably has had an overseas emphasis. Of the incremental dollars appropriated to address security after September 11, more have been spent in Iraq than in the United States, despite unmet security and preparedness needs at home. Senior-level government officials in both the executive and legislative branches also seem to have spent more time and attention on Iraq and overseas operations than on domestic security and preparedness. Thus, in some ways, America has become the forgotten homeland.

Refocused on our domestic preparedness by Katrina and the 9/11 Commission's final grades, what should we now do? What should be our priorities? What resources do we need and where will we get them? What are the roles of the federal government, of states and cities, and of corporate America?

The Century Foundation asked us to address those questions. To do so, we have called upon nearly two dozen experts to help us define the problem, identify the priorities, and draft an agenda of recommendations.

THE THREAT

Jihadism—the notion that Muslims and their faith are under assault and that it is the duty of able-bodied Muslims to defend themselves—is now more widespread than ever. The result has been the emergence of self-starter terrorist groups, such as the Madrid and London attackers, clusters of (mostly) young men that form spontaneously and move quickly to fulfill their perceived obligation. These are often individuals with no criminal records or reputations as firebrands. They have had little or no prior contact with individuals known to be connected to terrorist organizations. They are, in a British police phrase, "clean skins." Because these groups coalesce in coffeehouses, on cricket pitches, in paintball games, or in neighborhood mosques, and because they lack criminal records, law enforcement has no reason to observe them.

The Internet has played a dramatic role in enabling and accelerating these self-starters, enabling groups to simultaneously recruit, indoctrinate, train, and link together individuals attracted to jihad. Ironically, the Internet has made the American right-wing fanatics' dream of a sinuous, elusive "leaderless resistance" a reality for aggrieved Muslims. For these individuals, their local environments are rich in potential targets, as the Madrid and London attacks show. Murders, such as the killing of Dutch filmmaker Theo van Gogh by an Islamic militant in Amsterdam, demonstrate that targets include individuals as well as infrastructure. For more adventurous souls, there are the ratlines that will take them to Iraq, where there is an ample range of targets and opportunities for martyrdom.

At the same time, the bureaucratic terrorist infrastructure that spawned the global jihad still exists. For this cadre, striking the United States at home remains the gold standard of jihadist success. The imperative of hitting Americans at home stems from several potent impulses, first and foremost the desire for revenge. From the jihadists' standpoint, the United States and its allies, principally Israel, have been on a rampage in the Muslim world for decades and are responsible in one way or another for millions of Muslim deaths. Religion and honor demand that these deaths be avenged, and, as al Qaeda's spokesman put it, that America drink from the same bitter cup from which the Muslims have drunk. Children are not just legitimate targets in this context, they are desirable ones.

The second impulse derives from the jihadists' interpretation of the wartime law of necessity. Scattered, unable to challenge their adversaries on the battlefield, lacking the protection of a government, and without armor, aircraft, or heavy weapons, jihadists argue that they have no choice but to attack soft targets. Thus, while they may prefer to destroy our armies, they have no choice but to engage in terrorism. Killing civilians is amply justified, in their view, by the fact that we are a democracy. According to this interpretation of our political structure, all Americans are implicated in the crimes of their government, since the administration necessarily reflects the "will of the people."

The third impulse is strategic. The jihadists believe that we are sensitive to costs and that Americans cannot tolerate casualties. Thus, the best way to prod the United States to withdraw its abusive presence from the Muslim and, more specifically, Arab world, while pulling the rug from under the autocratic regimes that suppress Islamists, is to kill Americans on their own soil.

Finally, American foreign policy, especially since September 11, is widely seen in the Muslim world as confirming the al Qaeda narrative. From this perspective, the United States has unleashed a broad and ferocious assault on the Muslim world, with the aim of disarming and dismantling the only Arab country that challenged American power—Iraq—and of stealing Muslim oil resources. Widely distributed photos, both real and fabricated, of American excesses at Abu Ghraib reinforce perceptions of a predatory America.

Against this background, we can expect al Qaeda or its sympathizers to try to draw blood within our borders. Unfortunately, jihadists are rapidly gaining experience in urban warfare, especially in Iraq, but also in Europe. If the cities are to become the battlefields of the new jihad, our defenses must be extremely robust. Urban environments confer important advantages on terrorists. Cities offer anonymity, accessibility, the shelter of immigrant communities, and a huge array of killing opportunities.

The questions are whether jihadists from outside this country can establish cells here, whether Muslim residents will help them, and whether new cells might form spontaneously, as one did in Falls Church, Virginia. In short, will the United States face the serious intercommunal problems that afflict Europe?

At this point, Muslims in the United States bear little resemblance to their coreligionists in Europe. They are, on the whole, more prosperous, better educated, and better integrated. American Muslims experienced the same horror and distress on September 11 as Americans of every other religious or ethnic stripe. Many joined the military. Yet many American Muslims feel that their country's foreign policy is too dismissive of their concerns and think that the War on Terrorism has turned into a war against Islam, despite the administration's careful language on this score. Many have also been adversely affected by the implementation of the Patriot Act and believe that they have been stigmatized. Ill-judged remarks emerging from some evangelical Protestant leaders about Islam have contributed to a sense of being beleaguered.

Thus far, the posture of the American-Muslim community has been notably restrained. Unlike their European counterparts, especially in the

United Kingdom, American Muslims have no overarching, authoritative leadership that can represent their interests to the government or can marshal a single Muslim position on policy issues. Notwithstanding these leadership issues and the provocations many Muslims have perceived since September 11, there is no evidence that American Muslims seek the kind of confrontational relationship that exists between Muslim and non-Muslim European communities. There is also no evidence that Muslim militants from outside the country have found haven with American Muslims.

The same media-borne mix of inflammatory images and language that has radicalized European Muslims, however, is available to anyone in this country capable of surfing the Internet. On campuses, these influences may be having an effect, especially against the background of widespread unhappiness with the war in Iraq. The use of immigration law in lieu of intelligence as a way of disrupting terrorist cells has dragged large numbers of people into a law enforcement net with awful results for the "usual suspects," but no successful prosecutions for terrorist activity. These roundups tend to underscore the belief that Muslims are being singled out for punishment. Adding to a combustible mix is the presence of large numbers of Muslim converts in some American prisons. In the New York State corrections system, as many as one out of five inmates is thought to be Muslim.

It is essential therefore that the process of integration and equal treatment that characterized the situation of Muslims in the United States before September 11 be sustained. American Muslims are not only fellow citizens, but they also are indispensable allies in the war against terrorism and our first line of defense against infiltrators from outside the United States.

The growth of self-starters; the ubiquity of tactical guidance on the Web; the determination of al Qaeda to hit us at home; increasing experience in urban combat; and al Qaeda's desire to recruit aggrieved American Muslims demand that we tend to our defenses.

The task force report proceeds in three parts. Part I, "The Governments Nearest the People," addresses what local governments can do. Most previous analyses have been "top down" and have placed primary responsibility for homeland security at the federal level. The task force believes that, with regard to disaster mitigation and response, the leading level of government is the metropolitan area. Governments at that level can also have a major responsibility for prevention of terrorist attacks. The task force examines what resources metropolitan-area governments need to perform these missions.

Next, in Part II, "The Corporation, Responsibility, and Risk Management," the task force examines what has been done and what is yet to be achieved in securing assets owned and operated by the private sector. What private sector assets really matter and why? What are the roles of public-private partnerships, of regulation, and of insurance?

Only then does the task force examine, in Part III, "What Washington Can Do." The task force sought to avoid "move-the-boxes around" organizational solutions and instead focused on ways to improve the federal government's performance in inherently national missions like intelligence collection and aviation and maritime security. The central issue at the federal level is resources: establishing a system to decide how much is enough and determining relevant tradeoffs within the overall realm of security. Following Katrina, questions arose regarding response to calamities (situations worse than disasters) and the role of the military. The task force analyzes those questions and proposes a framework for future responses.

Many of the recommendations can be carried out by Congress. Homeland security will be an issue in the 2006 congressional elections. In 2003, bipartisan action in Congress forced the administration to create the Department of Homeland Security (DHS). Subsequently, Congress as a whole largely has stepped away from a role in shaping the nation's response to the challenges of security at home. Despite the creation of permanent committees on homeland security in both houses of Congress, leadership stubbornly refuses to consolidate all oversight of the department (six committees claim responsibility for some aspect of oversight of the Department of Homeland Security).

Before the next calamitous hurricane or earthquake, before a deadly pandemic, before the next major terrorist attack at home, America needs to do much more to reduce its domestic risks. We offer this volume and these recommendations to ask questions, stimulate debate, and suggest our idea of possible solutions. We do so cognizant of the belief of the former chairman of the 9/11 Commission "that the next attack is a question of when, not if."

When that next attack comes, America's citizens will not understand why so little was done to reduce our vulnerabilities and risks here at home in the years since September 11. They will want to know who did not rise to the challenge, and they will want to know why there was such mismanagement and nonfeasance. Before that happens, let us start anew to protect the people and the land we love.

We offer this volume as a small contribution to that goal.

I. THE GOVERNMENTS NEAREST THE PEOPLE

1. INTRODUCTION
BUILDING HOMELAND SECURITY IN OUR CITIES AND STATES

While it is traditionally the responsibility of the federal government "to provide for the common defense," when it comes to defending against an enemy that will attack our cities and towns, local governments will be primarily responsible for defense and response. Ultimately, all homeland defense, like politics, is local, and must start with governments nearest to the people. While many past analyses of homeland security have emphasized reordering bureaucratic boxes in Washington, the emphasis in the next five years must be at the metropolitan level.

In this part, the task force examines the role of local governments, and specifically addresses:

- the approach taken in federal funding of state and local homeland security activities both since the effort began in the mid-1990s and since the creation of the Department of Homeland Security (DHS)— and the shortfalls of this approach;
- an alternative approach based on multi-year "Metropolitan Protection and Response Plans" and "Minimum Essential Capability Goals"; and
- specific examples of priorities for metropolitan area governments.

INSUFFICIENT FUNDING AND INADEQUATE GUIDANCE

September 11, 2001, gave many Americans a sudden and terrifying sense of vulnerability. Eager to both address this apparent security shortfall and respond to rising public anxiety, federal government officials made a number of relatively quick decisions to enhance the powers of security and law enforcement agencies, establishing the Department of Homeland Security and providing additional resources to local emergency responders. In doing so, however, they forgot to tell responders what to do with the funding to ensure that what was spent today would be valuable in the future.

At the outset, federal officials realized that state and local governments had to play a significant role in disaster response. Under a "federal" system of government, public safety is largely the responsibility of local leaders. DHS reports that there are over 1 million firefighters, 436,000 sworn officers, 186,000 sworn sheriffs, and 155,000 registered emergency medical technicians (EMTs), as well as thousands of volunteers.[1] The overwhelming number of these emergency responders work for state and local governments or will act under their direction in the event of disaster. In addition, as the officials closest to the community, they are the ones in the best position to determine how to organize local efforts to detect, prevent, mitigate, and respond to crises. Indeed, many of the things that went right on September 11 occurred as a result of strong and decisive leadership by local officials and the bravery and professionalism of emergency responders.

In the wake of September 11, the White House assumed that state and local governments would resist instruction from Washington. Rather than confronting this reality and then exercising the necessary leadership to establish baseline security capabilities, Washington ceded the issue to local leaders. At the same time, the White House could not expect these local officials to know how to deal with catastrophic threats and unfamiliar adversaries, or to voluntarily invest in expensive response capabilities that they might never need.

The White House solution to the problem was straightforward: It would provide an infusion of money to states through homeland security grants, and states would simply know what to do. Congress helped shape the initiative. It added a requirement in the Patriot Act, legislation passed shortly after September 11, stipulating that each state receive 0.75 percent of all funds appropriated. The provision was designed to ensure that every state got some help in building the post–September 11 national response system.

That was the plan. It was a plan made in haste. And it was a bad plan.

Finding a Baseline Homeland Security Capability

The implementation of robust homeland security measures at the local level continues to be stymied by political leaders nationwide because there still seems to be a question of where the responsibility lies. Mayors point to the president, the president points to governors, governors point to Congress, and everyone on the committee breaks for lunch.

To provide some perspective, non-partisan groups offered to help. One such effort, the Council on Foreign Relations (CFR) Independent Task Force on Emergency Responders, asked task force members to address a simple question: "What was needed to ensure that every community in the United States had the capacity to deal with a large-scale terrorist attack?"[2] It was the question that Congress and the White House should have addressed before they started throwing money at the problem.

The CFR task force met with local emergency responders across the country, their professional associations, and two of the leading national budgetary analysis organizations: the Center of Strategic and Budgetary Assessments and the Concord Coalition. The CFR report, released in 2003, concluded that emergency responders across the country had neither the equipment nor the training to respond effectively to a terrorist attack.

Many of the gaps identified in the report three years ago—including the dangerous state of America's public health infrastructure, the lack of interoperable communications systems, and the absence of an integrated strategy for agricultural and veterinary security—remain as unaddressed in 2006 as they were three years before. Furthermore, in hindsight, the task force analysts acknowledge that they underestimated the challenge. There was, for example, no accurate data on the needs of local law enforcement, so their requirements were not included.

The response to Hurricane Katrina showed municipal leaders nationwide how vital the role of local police may be in a major catastrophe, organizing and safeguarding the delivery of emergency response services, and ensuring public order for residents and businesses.

WHERE WE STAND NOW

Four years have passed, and it remains clear that the United States will never close the preparedness gap with a few billion dollars a year of federal grants, regardless of a new "National Preparedness Goal" and capability and task lists. Metropolitan areas and towns have filled the federal leadership void with their own attempts to cobble together interoperable homeland security efforts. To better assist local leaders in making use of the reams of task recommendations from DHS, there must first be a strategic accounting of tools that have been bought and deployed before more federal dollars are doled out.

Sending massive amounts of block grants to all states is not the answer. There remains no guarantee that grants will improve security unless there is a mechanism to ensure that existing metropolitan and private sector partners use the money to build the right integrated capabilities, prioritized on the basis of risk and threats.

There have been mistakes along the way. Despite DHS providing responders "approved equipment lists" of gear for which they can use grant money and "national training scenarios"[3] against which state and local leaders were supposed to plan, train, and exercise, questionable purchases abound: air-conditioned garbage trucks, trailers for moving lawnmowers to local lawnmower races, and bulletproof vests for fire department dogs.[4] Justifying these acquisitions might be possible, but only after the municipality has shown that all higher priority requirements had been met.

If distributing grants in a risk-based manner to Urban Area Security Initiative (UASI) municipal areas is to succeed, then Congress, DHS, and municipal leaders must be more deliberate in working together to prioritize the tools, training, and personnel that need to be funded. A new approach is needed to make this happen.

First, overall spending to fulfill the "national preparedness goal" needs to increase. Second, this additional funding must be distributed based on risk. This spending should be tied to specific capabilities needed in vulnerable regions and to a timeline for implementation. This is not a time for more pork-barrel, laissez-faire suggestions—these actions must be taken deliberately by DHS leaders and backed up by congressional action if necessary.

A METROPOLITAN APPROACH: INTEGRATED OPERATIONS AND PRIORITY CAPABILITY PLANS

The federal government can provide funds, set standards, establish goals, provide intelligence information, and augment local response capabilities when necessary. Local governments, however, must provide for the nearest law enforcement and medical response. Beyond these recognized roles, local governments can also collect threat intelligence under appropriate safeguards, reduce the vulnerabilities in transportation systems and other infrastructure, and conduct meaningful training exercises to discover shortcomings and raise awareness.

Since the initiation of programs to respond to terrorism in the homeland beginning in the mid-1990s, the federal government has failed to be specific about the priorities for creating new capabilities at the state and local level. There has also been a tension between state governments and their subordinate jurisdictions, cities, and counties. Both levels of local government have sought to create and manage new programs and to control the use of new federal assistance funds. While billions of dollars have been spent, the lack of explicit and detailed national goals for local governments to achieve has made it impossible to know how close we have come to the minimum defensive and responsive capabilities we need. Every city and town has wanted to have its own new homeland security assets and to decide what they should be. Every state has also sought to centralize homeland security control in the state capitol. In most states, neither of those two approaches (city-centric or state-centric) is ideal.

While the size and population of states has governed the distribution of resources and shaped notions of what the best approaches to homeland security should be, the lives of most Americans are shaped not by state boundaries, but by the metropolitan area in which they live and work. That metropolitan area may include cities and towns in several counties, often in more than one state. While disasters anywhere in the metropolitan area may not affect citizens throughout the state, they will likely affect citizens throughout the region. So a disaster in Philadelphia may not affect Pittsburgh, but it will immediately affect residents of Camden, New Jersey, New Castle County, Delaware, and Montgomery County, Pennsylvania.

The Homeland Security Department's Urban Area Security Initiative earmarks about 25 percent of block grants for 29 metropolitan areas, based on a risk assessment. Many metropolitan areas, however, have made strong cases that they should not have been excluded. For example, San Diego and Norfolk–Hampton Roads were excluded, despite the presence of large numbers of nuclear-powered and nuclear weapons–capable navy ships. Las Vegas was excluded despite al Qaeda's past presence in the city, its symbolic value, and the devastating effect that terrorism could have on its tourist economy. While risk assessment must be a part of the priority allocation of federal funds, all 150 metropolitan areas need integrated plans regardless of their UASI designation.

In metropolitan area crisis, responders of all kinds, as well as their equipment, must work together seamlessly. The creation of local homeland security capabilities must be coordinated so that there is no unnecessary duplication or unintended gaps. Rivalries among cities and suburbs, states and counties often impede the required level of cooperation. As required by DHS, State Homeland Security Strategies (SHSS) will have established statewide goals and priorities with timelines to be able to qualify for DHS grants. However, pet projects are often funded by state and local officials before more essential capabilities are achieved, regardless of the statewide strategy.

For effective cooperation to be achieved, funding should be linked to a metropolitan protection and response plan and to a minimum essential capabilities plan in each of the nation's approximately 150 metropolitan regions, and then tied back into the SHSS.

METROPOLITAN PROTECTION AND RESPONSE (MPR) PLANS. These plans should delineate the roles and missions of the relevant departments of each city, town, and county in a mutual-aid operation; the command and control arrangements for the emergency response departments and the executive officers (mayors, county executives); and the concepts of operations for several scenarios, drawing on the fifteen national planning scenarios (including attack on transit, chemical attack, radiological attack, attack at major sports venues, and highly contagious disease or biological agent). These plans should take into account state homeland security plans and goals without being beholden to them, should prevent redundancies, should maximize the usefulness of funding, and should create integrated efficiencies. To ensure that these plans are developed and used in training, federal homeland security funds should be made dependent upon the plans meeting basic requirements.

MINIMUM ESSENTIAL CAPABILITIES (MEC) PLANS. Drawing on the expertise of local governments, industry and academic experts, and federal officials, the Department of Homeland Security should specify the baseline capabilities that are required for metropolitan areas of various sizes. This would differ from the current DHS Target Capability List (TCL), which lists thirty-seven broad areas such as "intelligence analysis," "communications," and "volunteer management," but provides only vague guidance. The TCL only suggests that a capability should exist, rather than designating what level must be achieved, by when, and in what order. Using the TCL, a jurisdiction could, for example, decide to buy tow trucks with federal block grants without first having achieved interoperable radio communications for emergency responders.

Our proposed minimum essential capabilities plan would divide metropolitan areas into five categories based on population size and would designate specific, detailed capabilities they must achieve in prioritized order. It would link funding to achieving those capabilities. For example, the plans would specify the percentage of the fire, police, and medical responders that should have personal protective equipment; the number of patients that mass casualty and trauma centers should be able to handle and how many respirators should be available; how many heavy rescue units there should be and what basic equipment they should have; what level of radio interoperability there should be in crises; what chemical, biological, and radiological detection capabilities should be in operation; and what level of evacuation planning and exercising should be achieved. The plans will show how each minimum capability is to be achieved over the next five years. Federal homeland security grants to jurisdictions within a metropolitan area should be spent only on capabilities stipulated by the plan, unless a waiver is granted. Requests for a waiver should demonstrate how unique regional conditions require reprioritization. Waivers should be approved by the secretary of homeland security.

SPECIFIC METROPOLITAN PROGRAMS

To improve our homeland security, we must strengthen the public safety of our metropolitan cores. Public safety pays dividends in our communities whether or not terrorists strike. Programs in community policing, public vigilance, and civic engagement all improve the safety of our neighborhoods, regardless of the size of the city or its risk from terrorist attack. However, city budgets are stretched to the limit in providing for day-to-day public safety even without additional expenses for homeland security. While cities understand that the maintenance, recruitment, training, and coordination of our first responders is a local function—as is coordination with private sector partners, such as private security guards in large buildings and health care providers in hospital emergency rooms—more leadership is required at the federal level to ensure necessary investment in homeland security is made.

So, how do we make our metropolitan areas safer? What are the security capabilities we are actually trying to create? What will "improved security and preparedness" look like when we have achieved it? In short, what effective capacities and protections can we create that do not exist now?

RECOMMENDATIONS

Nine recommendations emerged: Vulnerability assessment, personal protective gear for responders, interoperable communications, surveillance systems, intelligence sharing programs, realistic training exercises, closed-circuit monitoring, better security for public transportation, and evacuation and shelter-in-place plans that are tested.

1.1. EVERY MAJOR METROPOLITAN AREA SHOULD HAVE COMPLETE VULNERABILITY AND MITIGATION ASSESSMENTS. Governments need to conduct thorough assessments of the vulnerabilities in critical infrastructure (such as transportation, water, and communication facilities) and potential targets controlled by the private sector (such as chemical plants, rail lines, and power plants). Some vulnerabilities can be eliminated, others can be reduced by improved security. For example, many cities will find that there are shipments and storage of lethal chlorine gas within their jurisdiction. Substituting liquid bleach for chlorine gas in the water purification process can eliminate the need for the lethal gas. If lethal gas must continue to be stored, highway barricades and checkpoints can make it difficult for a truck bomb to get close to the gas storage tank or railcar. Most cities will also find that cesium and other highly toxic radioactive material is stored at their medical facilities or at the research reactor of the local university. Ensuring that access to the material is limited and that inventories of it are regularly conducted may reduce the possibility that such materials will be used in a "dirty bomb."

1.2. EVERY MAJOR METROPOLITAN AREA SHOULD HAVE PERSONAL PROTECTIVE EQUIPMENT FOR ALL FIRST RESPONDERS. Police officers, firefighters, and emergency medical providers should have ready and immediate access to breathing apparatus, protective suits, and medicines to cope with explosions involving lethal gas, radiological materials, or other toxic material. Specialist units with high-performance equipment are insufficient, because most major events or Incidents of National Significance (as outlined in the National Response Plan) will require all first responders to deploy. First responders should also be trained and equipped so that initial arriving units can diagnose whether an apparently conventional explosion actually contained toxic material. Having ready access to this equipment will also allow local responders to contain an incident while federal assets are deployed in support.

1.3. EVERY MAJOR METROPOLITAN AREA SHOULD HAVE INTEROPERABLE COMMUNICATIONS. We saw so tragically on September 11 how many lives could have been saved if only first responders had been able to communicate with one another once it became known that the towers were going to collapse. The Hurricane Katrina response showed that the situation has not significantly improved in four years. Every metropolitan area should now have reliable and pervasive communications in buildings and tunnels, among departments and across jurisdictions. Baltimore, for $5 million, enabled firefighters and police officers from two cities and five counties to communicate instantly on their existing radios. Despite the low cost of this technology, most metropolitan areas have not deployed it or made interoperable communications a funding priority.[5]

In the long run, more radio spectrum must be allocated for emergency use as outlined in the *9/11 Commission Report* and subsequent Report Cards. Senator John McCain's proposed legislation would wait three years to re-allocate some of the frequencies now reserved for television, despite the fact that few people in metropolitan areas receive television over the air. It should be amended to permit metropolitan areas to petition the Federal Communications Commission (FCC) to allocate parts of the spectrum to emergency communications sooner. Special interests cannot be allowed to block this initiative. Owners and operators of critical infrastructure should support this effort to ensure the effectiveness of responders, who will be needed to protect their facilities in a crisis.

Cities should be able to decide that it is more important to have reliable police/fire radios than to have both digital and analog television signals that provide entertainment to as little as 10 percent of viewers in their market area. Several cities have deployed encrypted wireless broadband signals for emergency responders to receive on their laptops in their vehicles as virtual emergency operation centers. Such laptop systems can provide officers a better understanding of the situation, including detailed maps and schematics, threat information, access to databases, and collaborative crisis management tools. Reliable, interoperable communications are a key component of the National Preparedness Goal and should be an initial priority in federal funding to metropolitan areas.

1.4. EVERY MAJOR METROPOLITAN AREA SHOULD HAVE A PUBLIC HEALTH AND BIOLOGICAL/CHEMICAL/RADIOLOGICAL SURVEILLANCE SYSTEM. An around-the-clock system for monitoring symptoms seen at emergency rooms and by paramedics, as well as in over-the-counter sales of pharmaceuticals, would alert local public health officials to the possible release of biological agents or outbreaks of infectious disease. Such a system could provide a forty-eight-hour edge in responding to an attack and could save tens of thousands of lives. Some cities, such as Baltimore, created such systems at no cost by analyzing data already collected. Technologies for chemical, biological, and radiological air sampling in large venues (sports arenas and train stations) and wide areas should also be deployed and research and development accelerated. (The medical system requirements are further addressed in Chapter 4.)

1.5. EVERY MAJOR METROPOLITAN AREA SHOULD HAVE AN INTELLIGENCE COLLECTION AND SHARING PROGRAM. In addition to their participation in the FBI Joint Terrorism Task Forces (JTTFs), local police departments should have their own system to collect and exchange information. It should be possible for the latest intelligence collection requirement or tip to be imparted to every patrol officer in a metropolitan region at least as often as the next shift change. While DHS has established the Homeland Security Information Network (HSIN) to share real-time threat information, it has yet to be fully integrated into local efforts. Integration of the DHS, JTTF, and local assets in state and local intelligence fusion centers would greatly enhance preventative efforts. Supplementing work by the FBI, local police should increase size and use of intelligence units that use confidential informants and undercover officers to detect terrorist sleeper cells. Because of the potential for domestic intelligence units to abuse civil liberties, they should be subject to oversight by citizens, who should be granted security clearances for this purpose. (The issues of domestic intelligence collection and civil liberties are discussed at greater length in Part III.)

1.6. EVERY MAJOR METROPOLITAN AREA SHOULD CONDUCT REALISTIC TRAINING AND PREPAREDNESS EXERCISES. Since the mid-1990s, under the Nunn-Lugar program, cities have held terrorism exercises for training and awareness purposes. Just as we drill and train our soldiers before sending them off to war, we must train our homeland defenders to work together. Our first responders and their commanders should know each other and how to work together long before a crisis erupts. Clarity of procedure and familiarity with responsibilities and response plans will save time and lives. In addition to training personnel, however, there must be realistic exercises that stress systems in order to identify their weaknesses before those systems are tested by an actual emergency. Many exercises to date have been unrealistic or too limited. As a result, they failed to reveal "real-world" problems, especially those that would be caused by follow-on attacks against responders, or attacks that precipitate cascading effects. Similarly, mass casualty drills typically involve only a small number of "patients" and, therefore, have not introduced such issues as how to set up a mass treatment facility or deal with a shortage of respirators, medical personnel, or special pharmaceuticals.

Too often, drills and exercises have failed to take seriously the role of the media and the need to communicate with the public in crises. The difficulty of controlling the dissemination of key messages and vital directions in the age of "blogs" and twenty-four-hour news necessitates integrating this communications challenge into testing of these plans.

Members of the media and government public relations personnel have essential roles to execute in a developing crisis or implementing an evacuation. By strategically building this training and exercise capability into field and tabletop exercises, agency leaders will have the opportunities to test more accurately the procedures and capabilities the media and Web community will employ when a catastrophe strikes.

Considering the failed federal response to Hurricane Katrina, it would be worth staging a full-scale drill at the next DHS exercise involving top officials (TOPOFF 4) scheduled for May 2007. Most metropolitan areas have not tested evacuation and shelter-in-place plans realistically and would likely suffer the same fate that Houston endured in its attempted evacuation in 2005. Short of large-scale exercises, senior government officials should regularly engage in "tabletop" exercises to prepare themselves and their staff members for the kinds of decisions and obstacles they would face in various crises. In these exercises, there is no substitute for the senior operators and elected officials, who would actually be involved in a contingency. Participation in such exercises should be considered a requirement of their jobs.

1.7. EVERY MAJOR METROPOLITAN AREA SHOULD HAVE CLOSED-CIRCUIT TELEVISION (CCTV) SYSTEMS TO SECURE INFRASTRUCTURE. CCTV cameras, like those used in London to apprehend the July 21 bombers, can serve as a deterrent and can help catch terrorists and their networks before they strike again. They need not be expensive. For $2 million, Baltimore installed an initial system.

In many cities, numerous CCTV networks exist, but are not integrated or monitored by public safety officials. Software can integrate existing networks and handle large numbers of cameras simultaneously by searching for suspicious behavior (such as leaving a package in a train station and walking away). Thus, operators do not need to watch every camera feed, but can be alerted when something specific is happening. In addition to assisting in counterterrorism, camera networks have been proven in several cities to reduce crime in neighborhoods that are monitored. Smart cameras have even been utilized in recovering stolen cars. Because the misuse of surveillance cameras could infringe on privacy rights, citizen oversight should be integrated into the program. As in London and Baltimore, having the camera system managed by a civilian department (rather than the police) may also provide a level of assurance that civil liberties are protected.

1.8. Every metropolitan area should have an enhanced security program for public transportation. Terrorists have struck public transit systems in Tokyo, Moscow, Paris, London, and Madrid. It is likely that an American city will be added to that list. While terrorist attacks against transit systems can best be stopped by intelligence that reveals the plot before the attack is launched, there are additional steps that can be taken to deter, deflect, or mitigate the effects of an attack, such as the random bag searches practiced in New York. Radio repeaters, ventilation upgrades, public address system improvements, and enhanced emergency escapes can mitigate the effects of a blast. (Transportation security is discussed in greater depth in Chapter 3.)

In many American cities, security on public transit systems is carried out by small police forces operated by the transit system, rather than by the city's police force. Metropolitan areas should consider integrating transit police into the larger force, or conducting outside performance audits to identify and rectify problems or capability shortfalls that come from having a separate transit force.

1.9. Metropolitan areas should create and periodically test evacuation and shelter-in-place plans. The few American cities that have attempted evacuations in recent years have experienced significant command and control and public information failures. Decisions to use reverse traffic lanes were delayed. Gasoline and food ran out. Tow trucks were poorly deployed. Citizens without privately owned vehicles, the aged, the hospitalized, and the infirm were overlooked. In other cases (such as September 11 in Washington or New York in the 2003 Northeast power blackout), spontaneous evacuations jammed roads and made it difficult for emergency vehicles.

In certain chemical release or radiological exposure scenarios, shelter-in-place responses may be more appropriate. Because current evacuation and information systems are inadequate, citizens may place themselves at greater risk by evacuating. Thus, metropolitan areas need detailed and tested plans for shelter-in-place procedures. Public awareness programs are needed. Loudspeaker systems and BlackBerry/PDA or SMS text messaging alert systems should be instituted to provide emergency guidance to citizens.

◆ ◆ ◆

Mayors and county executives are not asking for their fire and police departments to be federally funded. They are simply asking for federal help in covering the additional costs brought about by this foreign threat to America's national security. The investments we make to pursue homeland security today could well produce both an elevated standard of public safety and health and standard of living. While these efforts will not happen overnight, none of them will ever happen until we make a conscious decision to invest in America's security.

2. A COUNTERTERRORISM POLICY FOR OUR OWN BACKYARD

While much of the propaganda and leadership for radical Islamist terrorism is overseas, U.S. federal counterterrorism policy should be grounded in the realization that U.S. cities are likely to be a critical battleground. The prospect of homegrown, localized terrorism demands that our local police be not only "first responders" but also "first preventers." Even though the nineteen September 11 hijackers lived in the United States for months or even years prior to the attacks, our federal government focuses relatively little effort on the possibility that terrorists may already have penetrated our borders or live among us. If September 11 taught us anything, it is that prevention cannot be solely a federal responsibility.

There simply are not enough FBI agents working on preventing terror domestically, and those who are often are not attuned to the right things. To find and arrest terrorists already in the United States, the federal government has attempted to canvass the entire nation with a force of fewer than 5,000 FBI counterterrorism agents (by comparison, 7,000 FBI agents were mobilized in the wake of the September 11 attacks and the New York Police Department [NYPD] alone has nearly 38,000 police officers).[1]

There is no other federal force solely directed to apprehending terrorists within our borders. Recent observations from the 9/11 Commission, as well as the FBI leadership's own admissions, reveals that even the few FBI agents who are charged with domestic terrorism prevention are not specifically trained in Islamic radicalism, Arabic, the history of terrorism, and other critical subjects.[2] President Bush's creation of a new FBI National Security Service could be a large step in the right direction, but indications since its launch are that it is unlikely to force real change. (This issue is discussed in greater detail in Chapter 12.) While a great deal of time and effort has been spent by the U.S. government on military operations to defeat al Qaeda and its allies overseas, the effort, dollars, and use of the bully pulpit required to find and defeat terrorists already within our borders has been relatively small. Local law enforcement has been grossly underfunded and largely ignored in the federal government's counterterrorism plans.

This problem is not a new one. Less than one month after the September 11 attacks, U.S. intelligence received word that terrorists were planning to detonate a stolen, 10-kiloton Russian nuclear bomb in the middle of New York City.[3] Although this intelligence ultimately proved to be false, the information was only released to a handful of senior federal officials and was not disseminated to local officials or law enforcement. The 38,000 members of the NYPD—the best hope we would have had to thwart such an attack—were never mobilized to look for this threat, or even put on high alert.

Despite the crucial role that police could and should play, less than 25 percent of the 2005 DHS grant budget will go to empowering local law enforcement to be "first preventers" in stopping terrorists from planning and mounting an attack. These DHS grants do not allow hiring or retention of any personnel, including police officers or terrorism analysts, and include only minimal funding for training and exercises. One pointed example of misunderstanding the counterterrorism value of local police: Shortly after September 11, the Bush administration cut the budget significantly of the highly successful COPS program, which had supported the hiring of 100,000 local officers nationwide since 1994. The president's budget has proposed cuts every year since. New York City has 3,000 fewer officers on the job than it did on September 11.[4] And this is a problem not just for New York City.

A federal government approach that sees local law enforcement solely as a tool to manage the aftereffects of an attack with a weapon of mass destruction (WMD) has yielded a police force that is ill-equipped to prevent more prosaic, but nevertheless dangerous, attacks of the kind staged in London, Madrid, Amman, Istanbul, and Bali. We must certainly continue to ensure that our local police, fire, and emergency medical services receive first responder training and equipment—to mitigate the effects of an attack after it occurs—but we also must empower them to succeed at the very difficult and important task of detecting and disrupting terrorists before they attack us.

Police that Prevent Terrorism

State and local police are well placed to help prevent acts of terrorism. Estimates vary, but there are well over 870,000 sworn state and local law enforcement officers in the United States.[5] Not only does this dwarf the number of federal agents assigned to detect and prevent terrorism at home, but also state and local law enforcement enjoy an advantage as preventers because they are integrated into the communities in which they work. Proximity and familiarity allow local police to spot suspicious behavior that outsiders would miss.

Recall that two of the September 11 hijackers were stopped by state police on routine traffic violations and were released. Imagine if those police officers had been trained and equipped to spot certain clues and to run the individuals' names through federal databases and terrorism watch lists. Regrettably, the federal system had not shared any warning information with the locals and the state police noticed nothing suspicious. We must learn from such mistakes if we are to have any hope of preventing future attacks.

The new paradigm of "first preventers" is relevant to both federal and local law enforcement. Both the FBI and local police departments have traditionally focused less on prevention and more on the investigation and prosecution of crime. Teaching police to be "first preventers" requires specific training and represents—to a degree—a cultural shift in officer thinking. Just as a seasoned drug enforcement officer can see telltale signs of drug dealing or use, these programs seek to train police to identify signs of terrorism: religious radicalism, clues of bomb-making, pre-operational surveillance, and other suspicious activities. Just as most police officers know what marijuana smells like and what paraphernalia is used to smoke it, they should know what sarin or ricin production smells like and the tools used to make these poisons.

Effective prevention programs must also include a commitment to training for intelligence collection and analysis. In the vast majority of police departments across this nation, intelligence collection—if used at all—is directly applied to counter gang or drug activity. Only a handful of police departments have trained counterterrorism intelligence analysts. It is critical that when we train police to notice and report signs of terrorist activity or support, they are reporting into an organized and fluent counterterrorism intelligence center that can put the pieces together.

The NYPD has begun these complex prevention efforts, but without much federal support. Ironically, confirmation of New York City's imposed self-reliance was provided by a recent study funded by the FBI that criticized the NYPD for running an independent terrorism-prevention operation. Using its own budget, supplemented by private donations, the NYPD has built a local and international intelligence capacity. The police leadership has placed officers around the globe to act as liaisons with local law enforcement. These liaisons collect information on the terrorist groups and activities in their host nation and swiftly provide the intelligence to NYPD headquarters. Back in New York, under the leadership of former senior CIA officials, intelligence analysts review data from these liaisons, from news sources in numerous languages, from classified federal intelligence, from tips called in by citizens, and from local police patrols or investigations.

Through another program, Operation Nexus, NYPD has built outreach activities to the private sector to encourage certain businesses to be vigilant in watching for suspicious activities. Under Nexus, specially trained police detectives liaise with and train representatives from specific businesses such as truck rental agencies, chemical manufacturers, and real estate managers. The police offer the private sector training on suspicious activities, and provide a channel for feedback and reporting. The NYPD also moves heavily armored and visually imposing "Hercules" police units throughout the city to deter attack and provide protection to high value targets, should deterrence fail. These teams carry assault rifles, wear body armor, move in armored vehicles, and cost New Yorkers $5 million per week.

At least one attacker is thought to have been deterred by the sight of intensive police activity. Iyman Faris was sent by al Qaeda to attack New York's Brooklyn Bridge. After he cased the target, he reported back that the police presence was too alert and too great for him to expect success with such an attack.[6] While these teams have been repeatedly deployed due to federal warnings of threats to the Wall Street financial district and other high value targets, the federal government is not helping to defray these costs.[7]

The NYPD initiative is a model for first preventer policing. Analysts are trained by counterterrorism teams from around the globe, fed unique and valuable information, and, after they distill its intelligence value, they push it to police officers on the beat to inform further collection or disrupt terrorists' activities. The Los Angeles Police Department's (LAPD) Chief William Bratton is now leading a similar initiative. Under this effort, the Manhattan Institute's Center for Policing Terrorism will be coordinating training throughout the LAPD, and its area partners such as the L.A. Sheriff's Department, and providing analysis from an international network of counterterrorism experts. Training will be conducted by experts from countries more experienced in the War on Terrorism, such as the U.K. and Israel, and will begin at the academy level and move to the top of LAPD leadership. Instilling this capability in the culture of law enforcement agencies early on confers advantages that should register with the FBI and intelligence community educators. DHS should also consider how it might replicate and standardize these practices in new state and local intelligence fusion centers.

This arrangement will not only foster a first-preventer mentality and capacity in Los Angeles, but will also help bolster intelligence capacity and the ease of information sharing with the city's homeland security partners. Los Angeles, like New York City, will have to fund part of these initiatives through donations from private sources. Unfortunately, few other U.S. police departments can draw on the same resource base as the NYPD and must therefore rely on federal funding for intelligence and prevention, with all the limitations this implies.

Police as first preventers foster deterrence. Officers who are taught to identify the support structures of potential terrorists are more able to create an environment in which the terrorist will not feel safe. This sort of environment shaping can be accomplished in unexpected ways. For example, while federal efforts to crack down on crimes that support terrorism—such as money laundering and credit card fraud—have grown, local police are rarely trained to see these crimes as part of the breeding ground for terrorism. How can a city police department determine which, if any, of the dozens of credit card fraud cases they are investigating may move beyond local crime and constitute support for terrorism? Is the local ring of identification forgers in business to profit from underage drinking, or is it providing false IDs to terror cells? Federal support to train police to identify and disrupt the criminal activities of terrorists will help not only to make life difficult for terrorists, but also to reduce crime. Many local police officers have more experience with the key tools to prevent terrorism (for example, creating human intelligence, investigation, and interrogation) than do many federal agents. This is especially true in large cities, where seasoned detectives may have conducted hundreds more investigations than their FBI counterparts.

RECOMMENDATIONS

2.1. CREATE COPS II FIRST PREVENTERS PROGRAM. Congress must address the harsh reality that more personnel are needed in our cities and towns if we are to interdict terrorist cells within our communities and prevent attacks. The Bush administration should reverse its imprudent decision to eliminate the COPS program and initiate a hiring effort for "first preventers" in our highest risk Urban Area Security Initiative cities. With many military veterans returning from overseas and many politically motivated citizens, willing and motivated candidates for public service as police officers, intelligence analysts, and community outreach specialists (such as detectives with Operation Nexus) abound. Congressional funding for this program will help staff state and local intelligence fusion centers while actively supporting high-risk communities with useful tools.

2.2. BUILD AND INSPIRE A CULTURE OF "FIRST PREVENTERS." DHS, with congressional action if needed, should start working with state and local civilian and law enforcement leadership to include terrorism identification and prevention training for all police academy graduates as well as implementing this training as part of the ongoing education of their current force. Federal Law Enforcement Training Centers should follow suit for federal field agents.

2.3. THE DHS SECRETARY SHOULD CREATE A REGIONAL NETWORK INTEGRATED WITH STATE AND LOCAL INTELLIGENCE FUSION CENTERS FOR COORDINATING PREVENTION, PREPAREDNESS, AND RESPONSE ACTIVITIES WITH THE STATES AND MUNICIPAL AREAS. As required in the 2002 law, establishing regional offices would facilitate DHS planning and operations. This network would be managed by the new undersecretary for preparedness, who would be responsible for ensuring a more robust national training, exercises, assessment, and certification program for "first preventers and responders" that tells

Washington how well the nation is doing and ensures that federal money is being spent efficiently and effectively. Failure to develop and train first preventers among local law enforcement leaves our cities and towns defenseless in the face of an increasing threat of homegrown terror. Local prevention is the first—and may also be the last—line of defense before any attack. The new White House deputy national security advisers for preparedness and crisis management recommended in Part III would be well placed to oversee the implementation of this concept.

2.4. DHS SHOULD ESTABLISH STANDARDS FOR COLLECTION, ANALYSIS, AND REPORTING FOR STATE AND LOCAL INTELLIGENCE FUSION CENTERS. Executing a prevention mission requires homeland security stakeholders to collect, analyze, and share intelligence information with state and local law enforcement departments. Using the new intelligence fusion centers, state and local civilian and law enforcement leadership should ensure that where possible they house an internal counterterrorism intelligence collection and analysis capacity. Policymakers should ensure access to intelligence fusion centers for smaller jurisdictions to promote integration, reduce redundancies, and leverage funding appropriately. These standards should include procedures and plans for coordinating the communication of fusion center analysis to state and local emergency operations centers and partner agencies. At the same time, federal, state, and local leaders must ensure intelligence centers understand and follow national guidelines designed to protect civil liberties.

2.5. PROVIDE ADVANCED PREVENTION TRAINING AND PROPER SECURITY CLEARANCES. The DHS secretary should also increase the funding and quality of the Anti-Terrorism Intelligence Awareness Training Program, and waive the fees police must currently pay to attend the few advanced training courses DHS offers on terrorism prevention. DHS should ensure that all major city police chiefs are cleared to the Top Secret level and receive very regular intelligence briefings. Recognizing that local police understand their cities and threats, these briefs should not be distilled by analysts in Washington, D.C., but rather should be as close to the raw intelligence as possible.

2.6. ENSURE PREVENTION TRAINING AND EXERCISES INCLUDE REALISTIC ADVERSARIAL PLAY FOR BOTH CONVENTIONAL AND

WMD SCENARIOS. The Undersecretary of Preparedness at DHS can enhance the value of first-preventer training by establishing an integrated process for using existing adversarial emulation efforts ("red teams"). This process would coordinate "outside-the-box" thinking within DHS component agencies such as Intelligence and Analysis, Infrastructure Protection, and the "Universal Adversary" program to enable a more robust training and exercise experience for first preventers. In addition, the National Planning Scenarios need to be broadened to include conventional attacks such as the oft-postulated simultaneous suicide bomb attacks on a handful of suburban shopping malls. Creating a more integrated adversary emulation exercise effort will enable first preventers and state, local, tribal, and private sector stakeholders to better prepare together to prevent future failures of imagination.[8]

3. SECURITY FOR A NATION IN MOTION

Our mass transit and surface transportation systems play a significant economic role in the daily operations of most cities, and their security falls largely on the shoulders of the state and local community and private sector. Mass transit systems are a favored target of terrorists because they are "open," offer high concentrations of people, and provide the potential to cause large-scale disruption and fear throughout a community. This chapter will explore the challenges in the way we approach making improvements to transit security.[1]

Transit systems are inherently difficult to secure because of the volume of their riders, the high number of access points with few obvious inspection and control areas, the need for convenience, and fares with no advance purchase or identification requirement. These facts lead to two key questions:

- To what extent do these characteristics make it impossible to secure public transportation systems in the same way that we have secured aviation since September 11?
- What key actions can realistically improve efforts to prevent, mitigate, respond to, and recover from attacks on transit networks?

SOFT TARGET BUT STILL ONLY LIMITED ATTENTION

According to the Congressional Research Service, fully one-third of terrorist attacks worldwide have targeted transportation systems, and public transit is the most frequent transportation target.[2] Analysis of more than 22,000 terrorist incidents from 1968 through 2004 indicates that attacks on land-based transportation targets, including mass transit, have the highest casualty rates of any category of terrorist attack.[3] On average, attacks against such systems created more than two-and-a-half times as many casualties per incident as attacks on aviation targets. In terms of fatalities, attacks on surface transportation are among the deadliest, ranking behind attacks on aviation and nearly equaling attacks on religious and tourist targets.

So why are transit networks in America still so vulnerable? There are plenty of examples, including the most recent bombings in London, to remind decisionmakers of the vulnerability of mass transit systems. The most notable attacks over the past decade provide significant insight into threats, tactics, and vulnerabilities that need to be addressed by new security measures.

LONDON, JULY 2005. On July 7, 2005, Islamist terrorists struck the Transport for London system with four bombs during the morning rush hour, targeting subway trains and buses.[4] Fifty-two people were killed and 700 injured. The incident was the deadliest single act of terrorism in the United Kingdom since the 1988 bombing of Pan Am Flight 103, and it is the deadliest bombing in London since World War II. Responsibility for the bombings was claimed separately by the Secret Organization Group of al Qaeda of Jihad Organization in Europe and later by the Abu Hafs al-Masri Brigade, which had claimed responsibility for the Madrid attacks in 2004. The attacks marked the first suicide bombings in western Europe, and were carried out by domestic terrorists affiliated with or inspired by al Qaeda.

On July 21, 2005, a second series of four explosions took place on the London Underground and a London bus. However, this time only the detonators of the bombs exploded, resulting in only one injury and no fatalities. The suspected bombers were apprehended by authorities.

MADRID, SPAIN, MARCH 11, 2004. Ten bombs detonated in four locations on Madrid's train line by jihadist terrorists killed 191 riders and injured 1,460 others. The bombs were left in backpacks and detonated by cell phones. The Abu Hafs al-Masri Brigade claimed responsibility on behalf of al Qaeda. By the end of March 2004, authorities had arrested over twenty people in connection with the attack. The suspects hailed from Morocco, India, Syria, and Spain.

ISRAEL, 2000–PRESENT. In Israel, there have been more than 70 Palestinian bomb attacks since the current conflict erupted in September 2000. Roughly one-third of those attacks have been carried out by suicide bombers targeting buses, bus stops, and railway stations, resulting in hundreds of fatalities.

TOKYO, JAPAN, MARCH 20, 1995. The Japanese extremist sect Aum Shinrikyo attacked the Tokyo subway system using the nerve gas sarin. The gas was released from packages brought on to five subway cars by ten sect members. Twelve people were killed and 6,000 injured. Passengers and personnel in fifteen subway stations were affected by the sarin.

DON'T WAIT FOR THIS U.S. VULNERABILITY TO BECOME REAL

Although attacks similar to those in London, Madrid, Israel, and Japan have yet to occur in the United States, the threat is real and chances of an attack succeeding are high. There are over 140,000 miles of train routes in the United States and more than 500 major urban transit operators. Americans take public transportation 32 million times a day, sixteen times more than they travel on domestic airlines. The U.S. Department of Homeland Security (DHS), Department of Transportation (DOT), and the Federal Bureau of Investigation continue to warn public transportation officials of the possibility of terrorist strikes against their transit networks. Khalid Sheik Muhammed, one of Osama bin Laden's chief lieutenants, told his interrogators that al Qaeda had plans to attack the Metro system in Washington, D.C.,[5] and the release of Osama bin Laden's January 2006 tape showed a similar inclination toward the transportation sector.

Public transportation systems in the United States are vulnerable to attack because of their inherent openness, their number and geographic dispersion, and the volume of passengers that they carry. But not all systems are equally at risk. Major urban systems with higher passenger loads are more likely targets. Of particular concern to homeland security planners should be the dense concentration of high-ridership systems, especially along the northeast corridor between Washington, D.C., and Boston, Massachusetts, as well as the San Francisco, Atlanta, and Chicago public transit networks.

THE CHALLENGES FACING INCREASED SECURITY EFFORTS

More than four years after September 11, there is still no good road map guiding how we spend homeland security dollars in this area. Members of Congress offer new press releases and bills, but build little of the consensus that is so essential to policy success. The 9/11 Public Discourse Project, which sustains the continued efforts of the 9/11 Commission, issued a report card in December 2005 and gave efforts relative to private sector preparedness, critical infrastructure protection, and transportation security strategy grades of C, D, and C– respectively.[6]

The lack of direction and prioritization on homeland security efforts is reflected in the pitifully small sums we spend to improve the security of mass transit.

The federal government now spends roughly $4.5 billion annually on aviation security, and has cumulatively spent nearly $20 billion on protecting air transportation since September 11. By and large, this money has been well spent, even if serious problems still exist in the screening of passengers, luggage, and cargo and even if gaps remain in the security of commercial or unscheduled aviation. Yet at the same time, as of 2005, the Department of Homeland Security has spent, by its own estimate, only $255 million on helping secure ground-based public transportation. That number rises to roughly half a billion dollars if security-related monies from the Transportation Department and for Amtrak since September 11 are counted in the total.

Within a risk management framework, the disparity between the budget allocation for aviation and ground transportation is troubling. The U.S. government maintains the Continuity of Operations Plan (COOP) as a strategy for addressing a certain number of catastrophic risks to our nation and way of life. On a much smaller scale, the private sector calls this "risk management." Risk management generally requires organizations to:

- ◆ analyze their own risks and threats to their operations;
- ◆ prepare mitigation measures;
- ◆ if a crisis arises, keep the event from spreading; and
- ◆ ensure their ability to recover and restart operations quickly.

The problem with the current thinking is that many elected and appointed officials use the excuse of not being 100 percent able to protect against transit attacks as a justification for not aggressively trying to apply a risk management framework to transit security. For example, Senator Judd Gregg (R-NH), chairman of the Senate Appropriations Subcommittee on Homeland Security, invokes "slippery slope" reasoning when he argues that "there isn't enough money in the federal treasury to [secure] the entire transit system in America."[7] Secretary Chertoff reacted to the London transit bombings by making an argument based on prioritizing risk and sharing responsibilities among federal, state, and local authorities: "The truth of the matter is, a fully loaded airplane with jet fuel, a commercial airliner, has the capacity to kill 3,000 people. A bomb in a subway car may kill thirty people. When [the federal government] start[s] to think about [its] priorities, you're going to think about making sure you don't have a catastrophic event first."[8]

While preventing catastrophic attacks is a vital goal of DHS, it reflects a strained notion of federalism implying that securing public transportation is not a top-order federal priority and assigning the responsibility for preventing terrorist attacks on public transportation largely to state and local officials and owners of mass transit systems. While it is true that the September 11 airplane attacks inflicted more casualties than either of the transit attacks in London and Madrid, attacks on ground-based transportation are far easier to plan and much more likely to occur than another September 11–style attack. Together, London and Madrid killed 250 and injured over two thousand. While the Tokyo sarin attack in 1995 killed only twelve people, it injured six thousand. A similar non-conventional attack on transit, done more effectively, could be devastating.

These facts suggest that the gap between investment in aviation security and ground transportation should be closed. State and local transit authorities have made very serious efforts to improve the security of public transportation, spending $1.7 billion from September 11, 2001, through 2003 (and this despite a substantial shift in funding for public transit operations from the federal treasury to state taxpayers and transit riders). But three-quarters of that money went to cover labor-intensive operating expenses, including the sheer manpower cost of extra patrols and overtime. This has left transit authorities with few resources for much needed capital investments in security. The funding needed to protect ground transportation should not come at the expense of aviation security, but from new federal matching appropriations for ground transportation security and from greater creativity in management.

COMPLEX REALITIES OF
MAKING IMPROVEMENTS

At the end of the day, there is no "silver bullet" to improve the security of public transportation. The preparedness, public awareness, and extensive closed-circuit television systems that London put in place in response to a long history of IRA bombings could not prevent the attacks of July 2005. Even Israel, the most security-conscious country in the world, cannot prevent frequent deadly bus bombings. The fact that, with the London bombing, suicide attacks have been introduced into subways suggests that deterrence and prevention may get even more difficult going forward. But doing nothing is not the answer to heightened danger.

A LAYERED DEFENSE IS NEEDED

Successful transit security must have multiple layers that prepare, deter, detect, protect, and respond. While this poses a significant challenge in deciding which measures to prioritize, enhancements at any layer should seek to present obstacles to would-be terrorists, help limit damage and casualties should an attack occur, and mutually reinforce other measures. Furthermore, the more that security enhancements are integrated with other basic objectives—preventing crime, dispatching and tracking vehicles, monitoring the condition of infrastructure, and assuring safe operations[9]—the more transit operators will be able to meet their main objective: getting riders to and from their destinations quickly, cheaply, and safely. For example, the Transportation Security Administration's (TSA) new "Visible Intermodal Protection and Response" (VIPER) teams represent an introduction of randomly deployed units that resemble in form and function the Hercules teams described in the preceding chapter.[10]

The Limits of Intelligence

It is often observed that while we need to be right all the time, the terrorists need to be right only once. This is true on many levels, but most especially with regard to the fallibility of the intelligence process. While a number of the September 11 hijackers were on terrorist watch lists, the information was not effectively put to use to keep the terrorists from entering the country or being discovered once they were here. Unlike the September 11 terrorists, the London bombers were home-grown, British citizens and not perpetrators from overseas. In the future, we may have no prior intelligence on our attackers, and even if we do, the information still might not allow authorities to stop an attack. As proposed in the preceding chapter, ensuring that the new state and local intelligence fusion centers in major cities are plugged into local transit police departments will at least get the right agencies communicating and reacting to threat information.

Funding

Surveys and interviews of transit officials nationwide by the Government Accountability Office (GAO) indicate that "insufficient funding is the most significant challenge in making their transit systems as safe and secure as possible."[11] In fact, survey respondents were more than 2.5 times more likely to cite insufficient funding as the main impediment to security than any other factor.[12] Major transit networks are already hard pressed to make needed operational improvements (or even maintain current service) while keeping transit travel affordable; adding the cost of needed security enhancements only compounds the transit systems' precarious financial situations. After the Madrid bombings in 2004, staff of the House Select Committee on Homeland Security conducted similar interviews and surveys of officials at five large U.S. transit authorities that accounted for up to 20 percent of total annual U.S. passenger trips.[13] Their study confirmed the GAO's findings of deep concerns about funding among transit authorities.

RECOMMENDATIONS

Without greater federal assistance, we will fail to make the investments that the most vulnerable transit systems in our largest cities need now: better communications interoperability; CCTV cameras; detection equipment for and countermeasures against explosives and weapons of mass destruction (WMD); a backup command center for the D.C. Metro; investments to improve survivability in older systems like those in New York, Chicago, and Boston, including better ventilation, fire safety, lighting, and tunnel and stairwell access.

To increase the ability for law enforcement to prevent or interdict terrorists before they can strike our transit systems we recommend:

3.1. INCREASE VISIBILITY AND FREQUENCY OF PERSONNEL AND INCREASE USE OF CCTV SYSTEMS, much as the preceding chapter recommends for cities above ground. The London and Madrid attackers used tactics that are vulnerable to interdiction if vigilant security personnel are in place and there is an atmosphere that leads terrorists to believe they are under surveillance even before they enter a station. Roaming units of heavily armed police officers, combined with increased CCTV systems, can transfer a sense of insecurity to terrorists, thereby deterring them from carrying out their plans or making it harder for their plans to succeed. These programs should be considered for further application nationwide.

3.2. PROMOTE PUBLIC ENGAGEMENT TO FOSTER SECURITY AWARENESS. ABC News producers were able to leave bags unattended for hours on an Amtrak train heading from Washington, D.C., to New York. That fellow passengers failed to do anything about the suspicious backpacks—similar to the ones used in Madrid—demonstrates the challenge officials face in trying to persuade the public to engage in its own security. New York's "If you see something, say something" public awareness campaign to instill a security mindset in staff and enlist public vigilance is a good start; similar efforts are under way in other cities. Elected leaders and the media must play a role in increasing citizen awareness of suspicious activity and readiness to then tell police. These efforts should be followed by market surveys to monitor their effectiveness in heightening transit riders' awareness and vigilance.

3.3. ENSURE THAT INTEROPERABLE COMMUNICATIONS SYSTEMS AND ROBUST COMMAND AND CONTROL SYSTEMS ARE EXTENDED TO GROUND TRANSPORTATION SYSTEMS. Police officers operating below ground in the tunnels of a transit system need to be assured they can get the right message to the right people, at the time when it most matters. Installing repeaters in the tunnels is a first step, but this network must also support those agencies that will react to a crisis from above ground.

3.4. CONDUCT ANNUAL RISK ASSESSMENTS AND REVIEW POTENTIAL THREATS, VULNERABILITIES, AND CONSEQUENCES WITH LOCAL AND FEDERAL OFFICIALS. The Transportation Security Administration should conduct or update these assessments annually to ensure that the threat and risk information has been integrated into the state and local intelligence fusion centers and that funding for closing security gaps is coordinated with metropolitan preparedness efforts.

3.5. ENSURE ADEQUACY OF CRISIS MANAGEMENT AND COMMUNICATIONS PLANS, AWARENESS OF PLANS, READINESS OF EQUIPMENT AND PERSONNEL, AND ACCURACY OF ALL CONTACT INFORMATION. Hold regular training and exercises on the full spectrum of threats. The full range of transit personnel has a role to play in the security and effective operations of a transit network in times of crisis. In Hurricane Katrina, a lack of bus drivers was blamed for inadequate execution of a portion of the city's evacuation plan. As DHS continues to focus on catastrophic attacks using WMD, these exercises should include more robust and realistic training in quarantine and decontamination following an attack on a transit system.

3.6. CONTINUE DEVELOPMENT OF NEW EXPLOSIVE AND WMD DETECTION AND COUNTERMEASURES. Allow the use of DHS grant money for deployment of canine units until effective detection technologies can be brought to bear. Develop countermeasure sensor systems that mesh with biosurveillance and public health networks.

3.7. DIRECT FEDERAL FUNDING TO SUPPORT CAPITAL IMPROVEMENTS THAT WILL HELP PREVENT ATTACKS, MITIGATE THE EFFECTS OF AN ATTACK, AND ALLOW THE TRANSIT SYSTEM TO BE RAPIDLY RECOVERABLE. Transportation earmarks in congressional appropriations need to begin accounting for risk and recoverability, with particular attention to vulnerable basic infrastructure. For example, if the seawall holding back the Hudson River at the World Trade Center site had failed on September 11, there would have been nothing to stop the river from flooding the entire New York City subway system. It would be useful to install gates that can be closed to contain flooding, fire, or chemical releases. Improving ventilation, drainage, emergency lighting, and ingress/egress are smart security and effective operating investments.

◆ ◆ ◆

These recommendations are not a request for unlimited spending. Addressing the most pressing capital needs would require $3 billion to $4 billion in directed federal aid over the next three to five years. Many of these upgrades will bring additional benefits, helping improve the overall safety, operations, and reliability of public transportation systems. To put these sums into perspective, the transportation bill passed by Congress in 2005 allocated $3 billion for bicycle and walking trail projects.

Reacting intelligently to Madrid, London, and decades of deadly terrorist attacks against public transportation in other locations does not mean that we are doomed to spend ourselves into oblivion. Nor does it mean that we are taking our eye off the ball in the current War on Terrorism. Just the opposite: By doing more to secure and protect public transportation, we will be looking terrorism—both its history and current tactics—squarely in the eye.

4. A HEALTHY MEDICAL RESPONSE SYSTEM

S hortfalls are evident in the national capability to deal with stresses that would be placed on the medical system by large-scale terrorist attacks, particularly those involving chemical and biological materials. Even though programs to enhance these capabilities were initiated after September 11, they have yet to solve fundamental weaknesses in the medical response system. There is one respect in which September 11 was a poor teacher. The attacks left few wounded. Doctors and nurses who arrived on scene had few patients to treat; emergency rooms that stood by on full alert had few admissions. This would not be the case for a range of other likely attacks. Timely medical treatment could save thousands of lives in the event of a chemical, biological, radiological, or major conventional attack. Yet in most cities, hospitals and first responders do not have the necessary surge capacity to transport and treat large numbers of victims.

While terrorist groups have traditionally used conventional bombs and guns to achieve their objectives, an attack using chemical or biological weapons should be considered a realistic possibility. Groups including al Qaeda have expressly stated their intention to acquire these weapons. Midhat Mursi al-Sayid Umar, a member of the al Qaeda leadership who may have been killed in the January 13, 2006, missile strike in Pakistan, was a chemical weapons expert. CIA Director George Tenet has testified that documents found in Afghanistan showed that the al Qaeda terrorist network also was pursuing sophisticated biological weapons research. Sub-national actors used chemical and biological substances mostly as tools of assassination or in other small-scale crimes. Chemical or biological hoaxes have also been used to harass local authorities or scare the public. Out of 1,018 worldwide incidents involving chemical and biological substances from 1980 to 2005, only fifty-one incidents involved a chemical or biological substance that was fatal or near fatal.[1]

This all changed in 1995, with Aum Shinrikyo's sarin gas attack on the Tokyo subway. Though casualties were fairly low from the attack, with twelve deaths and fifty-four critically injured, they could have been much higher. Last-minute cold feet by the perpetrators caused the group to dilute the agent and use a fairly primitive dispersal device to allow for a safe getaway. What is most remarkable about this attack is that a sub-state actor was able to manufacture one of the world's most deadly chemical agents with no support from a nation-state. That they did it over ten years ago, before more recent advances in remote laboratory facilities and techniques, is even more alarming.

For biological terrorism, the 2001 anthrax attacks in the United States could be a harbinger of things to come. Though the attacks infected only twenty-two victims and caused five deaths, this death toll also could easily have been much higher. Given the limited number of people exposed, our healthcare system was able to treat all victims and provide life-saving intensive care to the critically ill. As the case remains unsolved, we may never discover the true motivation of the perpetrators. What is clear is that the dispersal device used, letters sent through the U.S. mail, was not chosen to maximize the number of casualties. The highly refined powder sent in the second round of letters to the Senate offices could have been used for aerial dispersal infecting thousands. Such an attack would have severely strained our medical system. As with the sarin attacks, no nation-state support was required. While contested by some experts, FBI analysis concluded that a "lone individual" could have made the highly potent variety in a makeshift laboratory for as little as $2,500.[2]

These two attacks underscored the different challenges that chemical and biological terrorism present for healthcare providers and the public health system as a whole. Unlike conventional attacks, chemical and biological attacks (and pandemic diseases) require specialized protective equipment and treatment capabilities. These can be used effectively only if our public health and hospital systems have an "all hazard" surge capability to treat thousands of victims. At this time, few metropolitan areas have sufficient hospital beds or basic medical equipment for such an influx. According to former Health and Human Services Secretary Tommy Thompson there are just 100,000 ventilators in the country, of which 85 percent are in daily use.[3]

The Trust for America's Health recently issued a report concluding that our public health system and hospitals are unprepared for a major terrorist attack or pandemic disease.[4] Rating each state on ten key indicators of public health and emergency preparedness, the report found that:

- most states are unable to meet basic preparedness goals and are struggling to manage additional health priorities with current levels of resources;
- only seven states and the cities of Chicago and New York have plans in place to distribute vaccines and antidotes from the Strategic National Stockpile;
- only ten report adequate lab capabilities to respond to a chemical attack;
- only nineteen have pre-positioned repositories of nerve agent antidotes;
- nearly one-third of states do not have adequate plans in place to build surge capacity in the event of a catastrophic terrorist attack or pandemic flu; and
- only two states have taken the steps necessary to ensure health care workers will show up to care for the ill in the event of a major disease outbreak.

As with other efforts in homeland security, our public health and hospital preparedness is hampered by an ill-defined strategy, a lack of standards, and too few resources. As the Trust for America's Health report concluded, "Four years after September 11, there are still no official, agreed upon, measurable performance standards of accountability for state bioterrorism and emergency public health preparedness programs and activities."[5] The Department of Health and Human Services and the Centers for Disease Control and Prevention promise that these standards are being developed. They still have not been implemented. Setting standards and developing a strategy would make clear the resource gap between what we are spending and what we need to spend to achieve the goals of the strategy.

In keeping with our other recommendations for preparedness, we recommend that efforts to bolster public health and hospital preparedness focus on metropolitan areas. While additional funding is needed, current funding should be targeted at our largest population centers, which are most likely to be attacked by terrorists and will receive the brunt of any pandemic. Metropolitan public health and hospital plans should be developed based on federally set standards. Spending should be tailored to meet the objectives of these plans. In the following sections, we look at current detection, mitigation, and surge capabilities in detail and make recommendations to bolster them.

DETECTION

CHEMICAL DETECTION

When a chemical agent is dispersed, its presence is likely to be apparent within minutes as its first victims are exposed and then succumb to its effects. The goal of detection for chemical agents is to give people in the vicinity of a release a few additional minutes to flee or shelter-in-place. The technology to detect most chemical weapons is readily available and battle-tested. Because chemical weapons are deadliest in closed environments, detection systems for chemical weapons should be installed in subways and metro stations, convention and athletic centers, and other public areas where large numbers of people congregate. Rapid detection, along with rapid response (discussed in the next section), can greatly reduce mortality from chemical attacks.

BIOSURVEILLANCE

In sharp contrast to a chemical attack and without investment in advanced warning capabilities, authorities may not recognize for several days, or even weeks, that a disease agent has been deliberately released. The first signs will likely be a trickle of victims visiting emergency departments, clinics, and personal physicians to complain of symptoms that are likely to be generic and flu-like. If no dispersal device is found and patients do not have a secondary common link (for example, attendance at the same event, or consumption of the same foodstuffs), doctors may not discern a pattern indicative of a major disease outbreak, much less of a bioterrorist attack, until the symptoms and/or the number of incoming patients become more pronounced. This quandary could be amplified if terrorists released an endemic disease at a time of year when it would ordinarily occur.[6]

Biosurveillance programs are designed to alert public health officials to a bioterror attack or disease outbreak before the onset of widespread illness. The federal government and the public health community are pursuing two types of biosurveillance programs, environmental and syndromic. If fully developed and implemented, such a two-track system could lead to reduced contagion, improved response coordination, and better deployment of federal assets. Unfortunately, as is the case so often in the arena of homeland security, efforts are under way to develop these systems, but they are either not operational or not widely implemented.

ENVIRONMENTAL SURVEILLANCE

BioWatch is designed to provide early warning of biological events by detecting trace amounts of biological materials, such as anthrax and smallpox, in the air. BioWatch is currently operational in thirty cities in the United States. However, in the cities where the system has been deployed, systems analysis suggests there are too few monitoring stations to be effective. The BioWatch filters were retrofitted to existing Environmental Protection Agency (EPA) air quality monitoring stations. There are about ten of these in most major American cities. To be effective for biosurveillance, forty to sixty open-air monitoring stations are needed plus additional monitoring stations in public indoor spaces.[7]

Expanding the system would be cumbersome and costly, however, as the technology employed requires technicians to collect samples and bring them to a lab for testing. A fast-track research effort is desperately needed to develop real-time bioweapon detection. Better technology alone, however, will not make BioWatch an effective program. Local officials suggest that the program is managed from the top down, with little input from those in our cities who will have to respond to any bioterrorism event. The locations of the BioWatch systems are kept secret even from city officials who need to be prepared to conduct plume modeling and quarantine planning for any release detected by the arrays. The program needs to be redesigned with local input and cooperative agreements reached for the maintenance of the systems and the use of the data.

SYNDROMIC SURVEILLANCE

The early signs of a bioterror attack are likely to look a lot like an average case of the flu. Patients will report respiratory trouble, fever, diarrhea, and vomiting. Being able to recognize a spike in reports of these symptoms could provide a valuable jump-start on getting a bioterror or natural disease outbreak under control. Syndromic surveillance systems are designed to do this by gathering data on hospital admissions, emergency room visits, perscriptions filled by pharmacies, and other health information to look for emerging patterns of a disease outbreak. Syndromic surveillance was pioneered by the New York City Department of Public Health in the 1990s.[8] This early warning allows authorities to aggressively pursue a diagnosis while also mobilizing the requisite resources for lifesaving intervention.

Other cities, including Baltimore, Boston, and Washington, D.C., have invested in syndromic surveillance systems. Unfortunately, the capability of federal systems to tie these together does not always match the claims made by federal officials about them.[9] According to a June 2005 Government Accountability Office (GAO) report, there are over half a dozen programs and systems in place attempting to do this, including the National Biosurveillance Integration System, Biosense, and the Biological Warnings and Incident Characterization System. All initiatives are in development and not yet operational.[10] Getting these systems in all major metropolitan areas and tying them together through a federal system should be a top priority of the Department of Homeland Security and the Centers for Disease Control and Prevention.

MITIGATION

THE STRATEGIC NATIONAL STOCKPILE (SNS)

As a cost-saving measure, most hospitals maintain only a few days of supplies. In a major natural outbreak or bioterrorism attack, these local supplies would be quickly depleted and the Strategic National Stockpile would be needed. The SNS program guarantees delivery of its supplies by air to any jurisdiction within six to twelve hours after the order for deployment. The materials are pre-configured in "push-packs," roll-on-roll-off air cargo containers, with the necessary medicines and material to treat or vaccinate against exposure to any number of potential biological outbreaks, including anthrax, smallpox, tularemia, and other viruses or infectious agents. The stockpile also contains quantities of standard medical equipment for an all-hazard response, including ventilators, intravenous fluid, and first aid supplies.[11]

The SNS was conceived in 1999 as the National Pharmaceutical Stockpile (NPS) during the Clinton administration as part of the spate of new initiatives that followed the Oklahoma City bombing. After September 11, officials expanded the program to include medical equipment in addition to pharmaceuticals. The name change to the SNS was made to recognize the evolving nature of the program. With the creation of the Department of Homeland Security, ownership of the SNS was transferred to the new department, with the Centers for Disease Control and Prevention (CDC) maintaining technical control through a working agreement. There are indications that this working agreement is less than optimal.

Planning for SNS delivery is somewhat hampered because the list of what is in the SNS stockpile is kept secret even from local public health officials.[12] As one contributor to the Trust for America's Health report commented, "In concept, the SNS is a critically valuable resource. In operation, the SNS is shrouded in mystery and the worst kind of bureaucracy."[13] We understand the security concerns that prompted such a policy. They are legitimate concerns. A savvy terrorist organization might get hold of the formulary and choose what disease to weaponize based on what medications are not in the SNS. This is, however, an unlikely prospect and protecting against it comes at a cost. Local public health officials must be able to plan for the worst. They can only do that if they know what tools will be at their disposal. The formulary should be released to all local officials with a legitimate need to know, including city medical directors, local emergency management agency officials, and the directors of major hospitals.

City public health officials have also been critical that the program does not have enough basic medical equipment to create surge capacity in the event of catastrophic attack. The program also does not include medications to treat radiation sickness, an oversight that should be corrected in the near term. One of the lessons of Hurricane Katrina is that food, water, and other basic supplies are just as important to emergency relief as pharmaceuticals. The federal government should not rely on Wal-Mart to supply these. The SNS has relationships with a number of pharmaceutical companies to supply material in real time under their Vendor Managed Inventory program. This aspect of the SNS should be expanded for food, water, and other basic supplies.

THE CHEMPACK PROGRAM

The CHEMPACK program is a forward-deployed component of the SNS. In order for chemical agent antidotes to be effective, they must be administered within minutes of exposure. This means that if federal assets are not already close to the release site they are not going to save lives. The CDC developed the CHEMPACK program within the SNS to store containers of nerve agent antidotes in cities around the country. In order to maintain the "economic feasibility"[14] of this program, program designers established the Shelf-Life Extension Program, a rigorous set of storage requirements that allow the antidotes to be maintained well beyond their normal expiration dates. These requirements dictate that the containers be stored at a hospital in a controlled access location with specific ranges for light, humidity, and temperature. If the seal on a CHEMPACK container is broken, the Shelf-Life Extension Program is violated and the original expiration dates take effect. Distribution of the material is mandated to take place post-event and only with the authorization of the hospital pharmacy director.

Unfortunately, given the restrictions placed on the program, the antidotes will still not reach victims in time to save lives. Because these antidotes need to be administered within ten minutes of exposure, there is little chance the supplies in the CHEMPACKs could make their way from hospital basements to the exposure site in that time. While the cost-saving objectives are laudable, their effect is to render the investment useless. The CHEMPACK program should be redesigned to put the antidotes in the only places where they stand a chance of reaching victims in time: ambulances, fire trucks, police cars, and other mobile emergency units. Fixed storage sites should also be considered for stadiums, train stations, and other large public places.

THE CITIES READINESS INITIATIVE (CRI)

Despite the problems that plague the SNS program, the capacity to deliver life-saving pharmaceuticals to any airport within twelve hours is an impressive achievement. Federal efforts rate less well on delivering these antibiotics, vaccine, and other supplies from the airports to sick and exposed citizens. The Cities Readiness Initiative (CRI) was launched as a pilot in 2004 to help cities build the capacity to deliver antibiotics to entire populations within forty-eight hours.[15] While the CDC has "greenlighted" seven states and two cities as being ready to administer and distribute SNS material, one senior official at the Department of Health and Human Services went on the record last summer stating that no city in the nation had the capability.[16]

Again, as with so many other programs, CRI was conceived, piloted, and expanded with little input from practitioners. A plan to use postal workers to distribute antibiotics has gone nowhere due to a lack of interest from their union. The initial development of the program may in part explain why so few cities have gotten a green light from the CDC. The challenge is not small, however, nor is it solely a matter of inadequate funding or federal intransigence. There are indications that the program has been a success in cities with more competent and professional public health departments. To distribute antibiotics to all residents of New York City in a timely manner would require a minimum of 40,000 volunteers trained and equipped to show up under the worst of circumstances.

Public communication and intra-government coordination will be fraught with difficulty. Recognizing these challenges, grants for the CRI should include funding to hire a full-time CRI coordinator with the singular mission of implementing a workable plan within one year. This individual should have ultimate responsibility for the success or failure of the program and should be given sufficient support staff and lines of communication to relevant local, state, and federal officials.

PROJECT BIOSHIELD

Even the best plans for stockpiling and distribution will not help with a bioweapon for which there is no vaccine or treatment. In 2004, Project BioShield was launched to accelerate research to discover, develop, and test new vaccines, next-generation antibiotics, and antiviral medications. BioShield also provides avenues for speedier research and, in the event of an emergency, the use of medications that may not have received final approval from the Food and Drug Administration.[17] Spending was set at $5.6 billion over the next decade. It sounds like a lot of money, but BioShield's incentives are still insufficient to attract serious private interest in developing medical countermeasures given the expense of drug development and the expectation that little or no profits are to be made.[18] Additional policy and fiscal adjustments will probably be needed to cement a robust public-private partnership to field new drugs.

QUARANTINE

Quarantine is an age-old concept that does not easily fit into the rubric of our modern lives. Yet it is an essential capacity for preventing the spread of a disease for which treatment is ineffective or unavailable. Decision makers at local, state, and national levels must enact graduated quarantine measures to interrupt the chain of transmission for a catastrophic outbreak of disease. In the first level, nonessential public gatherings (such as concerts and sporting events) might be cancelled, use of public transportation might be curtailed, and schools could be closed. More drastic measures might include quarantine of possibly exposed individuals at home at predetermined locations. Executing quarantine will pose tremendous challenges for local law enforcement, public health, health care, and emergency management officials. Plans to carry out quarantine must be prepared and drilled. To the extent that a legal framework is necessary for such emergencies, state and local law should be amended. Over thirty states have revised their public laws in recent years for the purpose of clarifying lines of authority for mandatory health screening and quarantine measures.[19] The other twenty states and the District of Columbia should follow suit.

SURGE CAPACITY

As with any other private sector enterprise, market imperatives have forced our hospital systems to cut waste, reduce duplication, and operate on just-in-time delivery systems and razor-thin profit margins. This system provides some of the best medical care in the world, including advanced procedures available nowhere else. As a nation, there are many reasons to be proud of our medical system. However, its capacity to deliver critical care to large numbers of people in a catastrophe is not one of them.

In the Trust for America's Health survey, hospital administrators in all fifty states were asked if their hospitals could provide a minimal surge capacity of being able to handle ten additional patients requiring mechanical ventilation.[20] Aggregated answers showed that, on average, the hospitals in twenty states did not have this capability. Yet there are scenarios in which hospitals could need far more additional capacity.

The interim Public Health and Healthcare Supplement to the National Preparedness Goal sets minimum goals for metropolitan-area hospital systems. These include the capability to expand capacity by five hundred patients per million population for acute infectious diseases; fifty patients per million population for ventilator support; fifty patients per million population for burn and trauma; and fifty cases per million for radiation injuries.[21] The goals are reasonable and should be achievable. The resources dedicated to meeting them are not. As the Trust for

America's Health points out, in a country that spends $515 billion a year on health care, $500 million is not going to expand capacity significantly. We endorse their recommendation to double these funds and further recommend they be targeted at major metropolitan areas.

RECOMMENDATIONS

As with other areas of homeland security, a great deal of activity is occurring in the field of medical preparedness, but not much progress can be identified. The overarching conclusion of this task force is that current programs need to be reengineered based on practitioner feedback, that standards must be set, and that a timeline for meeting these standards be put in place. Appropriate resources must be made available to meet these goals. The task force endorses the following specific recommendations:

4.1. METROPOLITAN HEALTH AND HOSPITAL PLANS SHOULD BE DEVELOPED BASED ON FEDERALLY SET STANDARDS; federal funding initially should be targeted at our largest cities.

4.2. DETECTION SYSTEMS FOR CHEMICAL WEAPONS SHOULD BE INSTALLED in subways and metro stations, convention and athletic centers, and other public areas where large numbers of people congregate.

4.3. BIOWATCH MUST BE REDESIGNED to include developing cooperative agreements for the maintenance of the systems and the use of the data; increasing the number of air monitoring stations in each city to 40 to 60; and the fast-tracking of research for real-time detection.

4.4. BUILDING SYNDROMIC SURVEILLANCE SYSTEMS IN ALL MAJOR METROPOLITAN AREAS AND TYING THEM INTO A FEDERAL BACKBONE SHOULD BE A TOP PRIORITY of the CDC and Department of Homeland Security.

4.5. THE STRATEGIC NATIONAL STOCKPILE SHOULD REVERT TO THE DEPARTMENT OF HEALTH AND HUMAN SERVICES WITH A DHS LIAISON RELATIONSHIP; the SNS formulary should be released to local officials with a legitimate need to know; the program should be expanded to include treatment for radiation sickness and additional all-hazards material; and the Vendor Managed Inventory should be expanded to include food, water, and other basic supplies.

4.6. The CHEMPACK program should be redesigned to put antidotes in mobile emergency units.

4.7. The Cities Readiness Initiative should be redesigned based on input from the public health community; or funding should be provided to hire a full-time CRI coordinator for each metropolitan area with the goal of implementing a plan within one year.

4.8. Additional financial incentives and policy adjustments must be made to bring private sector interest to the BioShield program.

4.9. Decisionmakers at local, state, and national levels must prepare graduated quarantine measures; plans to carry out quarantine must be prepared and drilled; and states that do not have the authority to quarantine should make necessary legal modifications.

4.10. Hospital surge capacity must be built, starting with the nation's largest metropolitan areas. Funding should be increased to meet the goals set by the Department of Health and Human Services in the National Preparedness Goal.

II. The Corporation, Responsibility, and Risk Management

5. INTRODUCTION
A NEW APPROACH TO THE PRIVATE
SECTOR AND HOMELAND SECURITY

Much attention has focused on the prospect of terrorists acquiring weapons of mass destruction, but in the near term they are much more likely to use our own infrastructure against us. On September 11, terrorists wielding knives and boxcutters turned four of our aircraft into guided missiles. Other relatively low-tech attacks could be even more devastating. Most of our infrastructural vulnerabilities are in the private sector. Following September 11, the administration recognized this and issued a National Strategy for the Physical Protection of Critical Infrastructures and Key Assets in February 2003. The strategy set out an approach to protecting these targets that relied largely on letting market forces dictate investment in security. The administration believed that Adam Smith's "invisible hand" would lead executives to reduce vulnerabilities.

It hasn't. In their August 2004 report, the 9/11 Commission concluded, "the private sector remains largely unprepared for a terrorist attack." Despite glaring vulnerabilities in multiple sectors, most estimates place the post–September 11 rate of growth in security spending in the low single digits. In order to close this private sector gap in security, the federal government must act. In this part of the report, we sketch out a new approach to securing the private sector based on the lessons learned over the past four years. The elements of that new approach include:

- developing an approach to security that treats essential systems and high-impact targets as separate problems that require different solutions;
- creating an effective framework for partnering beyond the current arm's-length approach;
- using smart regulation within a partnering framework; and

59

- providing an in-extremis federal backstop for companies that make sound investments to reduce risk and meet federal requirements.

Based on this approach, the Department of Homeland Security (DHS), together with Congress and the White House, could develop a new strategy that would secure the private sector in a way that is now impossible. Unlike previous DHS and White House "strategies," this strategy would set tangible goals and specific timelines for achieving them. For each sector, the strategy would begin by identifying existing vulnerabilities, the measures needed to reach an adequate level of security, and the mechanisms that would best promote that level of security. In this chapter, we expand on the elements of the approach outlined above. In the following chapters, we apply these principles to the financial, chemical, energy, and cyber sectors of the economy.

ESSENTIAL SYSTEMS VS. HIGH-IMPACT TARGETS

In its National Strategy for Homeland Security, released in 2002, the administration identified thirteen sectors of the economy as "critical infrastructure." That number has since expanded to seventeen. Four years later, the Department of Homeland Security has yet to determine what assets and operations within these sectors are, in fact, critical. When DHS compiled a list of critical assets supplied by the fifty states, it ran to several thousand facilities. But if everything is critical, nothing is. Widespread application of this term has made it impossible to focus on the private sector operations that are at greatest risk of being attacked, either because they could generate large numbers of casualties, or because an attack would have a cascading effect on the rest of the economy.

Before we can develop a workable strategy to protect critical infrastructure, we need to more narrowly define what we mean by the term. We propose dividing critical infrastructure into two categories: essential systems and high-impact targets.

ASSURING CONTINUITY OF ESSENTIAL SYSTEMS (ACES)

For an asset to be considered an essential eystem its interruption must have a widespread, cascading effect that would make the sector incapable of providing minimum essential service for a long enough period of time to significantly affect the economy, public health, or national defense. For essential systems, our concern is with key nodes and assets whose failure would prompt this type of outcome.

Revealing the influence of the military on homeland security policy, the administration continues to call upon infrastructure owners and operators to increase their level of protection through the "hardening" of facilities and systems. But other risk management options, such as creating redundancies, relocating assets, and developing rapid response and recovery capabilities, should be seriously considered as alternatives to protective measures. If other nodes or assets have additional capacity to replace what is lost in an attack, additional protective measures may be unnecessary. The ability of the entire system to perform minimum essential functions is the important thing. In some cases, physical protection may be the best, or the only, defense. In others, building resilient systems, focusing on response and recovery, or encouraging the markets to respond quickly may be a better way to manage risk.

SECURING HIGH-IMPACT TARGETS (HITS)

We call private sector entities whose operations can be exploited by terrorists to kill large numbers of people high-impact targets. HITS include chemical plants, natural gas facilities, and nuclear power stations—operations where poor security can endanger thousands of lives. HITS provide terrorists the opportunity to use a conventional attack to generate disproportionately damaging effects. Securing HITS may not be possible through purely voluntary private sector measures. Unlike essential systems, an individual HIT might not be critical to the economy. Owners of HITS are more likely to conclude that terrorism poses little financial risk to their operations and that spending on security is not a necessary investment. This is when partnering between government and the private sector enters the picture. Within the meaning of the term, the government might mandate security measures in coordination with the private sector, provide financial incentives, or do both in order to maximize security.

MAKING PARTNERING WORK

The owners and operators of critical infrastructure are currently without a competent government partner. There is a growing consensus among experts and policymakers that the prevailing partnership model is not only flawed, but is a major factor in the currently poor state of critical infrastructure protection. Traditional government regulation of security is offered as the only alternative to the partnership model now on the table. This is a false choice. We believe that partnering with the private sector instead of establishing an adversarial relationship is in fact the most effective means of securing infrastructure vulnerabilities. We also believe, however, that smart regulation is consistent with effective partnering, and that it may be needed in certain instances and certain sectors to correct the market's failure to deliver appropriate levels of security. The problem of securing our critical infrastructure is not with public-private partnerships, but with the administration's approach to establishing such partnerships.

POOR EXECUTION VS. FLAWED DESIGN

The Bush administration has correctly identified public-private partnering as a cornerstone of U.S. homeland security policy. The administration has repeatedly stated in its national strategies, plans, and presidential directives that partnership between private industry and government is essential to securing the nation's key resources and critical infrastructure. What it has failed to do is create a structure in which partnering can in fact be an effective mechanism for protecting the homeland. There are no joint processes for developing, implementing, or reviewing partnership plans. There is no agreement between the government and private sector on the end-state to be reached, the basis for determining when it is reached, or the requirements to sustain it once it is reached. The National Infrastructure Protection Plan (NIPP) is currently in its third draft. We have yet to agree on the process for cataloging critical infrastructure, let alone securing it. The NIPP remains too cumbersome and centralized, and fails to recognize that the sectors are not single players that can easily interface with one small office in Washington.

The result of the Bush administration's approach to homeland security and the private sector is a relationship characterized by a series of arm's-length transactions rather than by close collaboration. The approach creates a division of labor whereby government provides general guidelines of what it would like the private sector to do, and the private sector is expected to carry out in detail what it thinks the government wishes. But matters of security are rarely self-evident, let alone self-executing, in the marketplace. Unsurprisingly, government is frustrated and unhappy with the lack of industry progress in securing itself, but cannot describe the results it wants. Without establishing conditions for effective partnering, defining appropriate levels of security, and recognizing that partnerships and regulation are not mutually exclusive, partnership will remain an ever-receding goal.

Elements of Partnership

As a first step, the nature of an effective partnership in the context of homeland security must be defined. Partnerships are collaborative enterprises established between parties having defined roles and responsibilities for the purpose of achieving a common goal or outcome. Parties usually enter into such relationships because they cannot achieve their goals through independent efforts, or because independent efforts, even if feasible, would not be cost effective. In the context of critical infrastructure security, public-private partnerships are essential for the purpose of attaining levels of security appropriate to the risks posed by known and evolving threats. These risks must be managed; they cannot be eliminated. Threats must be identified, vulnerabilities assessed, consequences estimated, and resources allocated *in a collaborative process* to reach an optimal, cost-effective security posture.

As with any collaborative enterprise, public-private partnerships can succeed only to the extent there is agreement on:

◆   the outcome to be achieved and the basis for determining when it has been reached;
◆   the respective roles and responsibilities of the parties;
◆   the processes and procedures by which strategies and plans are to be jointly developed and implemented; and
◆   how senior executive participation and commitment will be obtained, and how progress will be assessed, problems identified, course corrections taken, and performance evaluated.

None of these conditions apply in the federal government's current approach to partnering with the private sector on homeland security.

ROLES, RESPONSIBILITIES, AND PROCESSES

To effectively secure critical infrastructure, we must move from the Bush administration's process-driven approach to one geared toward outcomes and results. With no shared strategic vision or end-state, sector partnerships serve today mainly as devices for fostering political inclusion, conduits for exchanging generic information, channels for communicating government policy, and bully pulpits for exhorting industry to make greater strides in security.

As stated above, the desired outcome is to assure the provision of essential services and prevent high-impact targets from being used by terrorists to generate amplified effects. A shared focus on this explicit outcome must be the foundation for effective partnership. A second condition for effective partnering requires agreement on the roles and responsibilities of the parties. In this respect, it is important to remember that government is ultimately responsible for all activities undertaken to secure the homeland, even if it relies on its private sector partners to carry out some of these activities. The government also is responsible for making the case for partnership, establishing the conditions necessary for launching and sustaining such partnerships, and managing public expectations as to what partnerships can and cannot accomplish. These responsibilities ultimately derive from the government's constitutional obligation to defend the nation against enemies at home and abroad.

Private industry is responsible for working with government to manage critical infrastructure risks that exist beyond the scope of normal business operations, support government operations during national crises or recovery efforts, and continue to manage, on its own, security risks that arise in the course of doing business. The responsibilities of private industry derive not from the Constitution, but from the government's ability to impose such responsibilities through laws and regulations to compel compliance.

Private sector participation cannot be relegated to a select few CEOs on advisory committees. These committees tend to stay away from taking any action that would obligate or commit the private sector to act. The administration, for its part, prepares its strategies and plans without meaningful participation from the private sector.

Industry's hands-off attitude is natural enough. The administration's reluctance is more complicated. The White House insists that the Federal Advisory Committee Act (FACA) prevents the government from engaging with industry on joint plans or operations. At first glance, this seems to be the case: FACA provides that all public-private planning sessions be open to the public unless otherwise exempt. However, Section 871 of the Homeland Security Act of 2002 authorizes the secretary of homeland security to exempt public-private planning from the open-meeting requirement under FACA. The secretary has thus far refused to exercise his authority. This is likely due to political considerations stemming from the administration's poor record on information sharing and public disclosure.

Given the strategic stakes, the administration would be wise to put political considerations aside and instruct the Department of Homeland Security to move quickly to establish joint planning committees for each sector. Exercising his authority under Section 871 of the Homeland Security Act of 2002, the secretary should exempt these joint planning committees from FACA. Once established, these committees should develop infrastructure security plans that specify the security end-state to be achieved, the goals and milestones for achieving it, the standards for implementation and compliance, and the timelines for accomplishing intermediate actions. Provisions of relevant anti-trust laws must be amended to exempt explicitly standard-setting discussions and planning sessions that would necessarily be part of this joint process. Congress should establish an oversight subcommittee to ensure that partnering between the government and the private sector does not willy-nilly sanction collusion between or among market players.

Even with an open dialogue, the temptation to refer significant partnership disagreements to working group committees rather than resolve the disagreements will at times be irresistible. One way to minimize this is to ensure that chief executives are involved in planning and implementation. Chief executives bring perspective and authority to problems that mid-level officers find insurmountable. They also bear ultimate responsibility for the security of their company, as well as the role their company plays in securing their sector. Chief executive participation would also ensure that jointly developed strategies and plans are followed through. They should not only review and approve such plans, but also commit to implementing them and allocating the resources necessary for success. At this juncture, corporate chief executives—apart from the select few who are members of presidential advisory committees—do not generally view security as their responsibility, or give it much consideration. Their disregard could and should be countered by integrating chief executive review into the joint planning process and by obtaining CEO approval and commitment to carry out plans according to agreed upon timelines.

For individual infrastructure owners and operators, the partnering process should begin by examining their core business functions and operations, in concert with relevant federal partners, to determine which of their assets and systems, if any, qualify as HITS, essential systems, or both. Plans must then be jointly developed with government to manage the resulting security risks.

The Chemical Facility Anti-Terrorism Act of 2005 offers a framework for this joint planning process. The bill, sponsored by Senator Susan Collins (R-ME), would create infrastructure protection regional security offices in each of the eight Federal Emergency Management Agency (FEMA) regions. The bill would also create area security committees for urban areas within each of the regions to work with local partners, both private and public, to secure chemical facilities, share information, and develop response plans. Though the bill would establish this structure explicitly for the chemical facility, it is clear that the drafters intend the regional approach to be used for other sectors. It is unfortunate that, due to the costs involved, these provisions are likely to be the first on the chopping block when the act is considered this spring. They would represent an immense leap forward in partnering and should be included in the final version of the bill.

SMART REGULATION

Despite appearances, partnership and regulation are not necessarily incompatible approaches to security. Smart regulation can create what the market alone cannot: a set of conditions and incentives that encourage proactive investment and adoption of necessary security measures. Seen in this light, smart regulation could make partnerships more effective. Whether smart regulation is needed, however, depends entirely on the economic and operating conditions that exist within each of the sectors. A one-size-fits-all approach to smart regulation and security will not work.

The development of an appropriate security posture for each of the sectors that need to be defended hinges on a detailed understanding of industry operations and risk management practices. Owners and operators are in a better position than the government to know how to translate homeland security goals and objectives into specific standards and operating procedures for their industries and companies. Close collaboration and coordination between the sectors and government are therefore indispensable.

DHS must be given the authority to regulate industries that could endanger the public if targeted by terrorists. The kind and type of intervention, however, does not necessarily need to follow a traditional regulatory model. To prevent terrorism, security must be dynamic and adaptable. Countermeasures must be designed to thwart adversaries who will engage in reconnaissance and planning. A regulatory model that sets universal standards may be well suited to stopping acid rain, but will do little to prevent a determined terrorist. If regulation requires an eight-foot fence, terrorists will know to bring a ten-foot ladder.

Smart regulation focuses on results or end-states rather than dictating how those results should be achieved. Smart regulation relies on auditors and best practices, rather than government inspectors. In the financial industry, the Securities and Exchange Commission (SEC), with a staff of just 3,100, oversees the $500 billion securities industry. It does this by requiring that certified accounting agencies audit industry reports against Generally Accepted Accounting Practices. A small number of federal auditors then follow up to verify that the self-regulatory regime is in fact working. While the Enron trial may remind readers of the recent failings of this model in the securities industry, those failures are indicative of poor management and execution, not of any flaw in the design itself.

Applying this to the private sector for security, the Department of Homeland Security should be empowered to certify security-auditing firms, which in turn would evaluate the security of private sector operations and judge whether they meet general standards, given potential threats and consequences. DHS needs the resources to train and certify the auditors and to audit the auditors, as in the SEC model. Such an approach will allow dynamic security regimes to be built cooperatively with industry and tailored to individual facilities and operations. The system would focus on results, rather than dictate how to achieve them. Auditors would certify that companies have assessed their vulnerabilities and taken reasonable measures to remedy them.

USING THE FEDERAL BACKSTOP TO PROMOTE SECURITY

In December, Congress passed a two-year extension of the Terrorism Risk Insurance Act (TRIA) with only minor modifications. The act provides a federal backstop for insurance companies in the event of a terrorist attack, while requiring no action on the part of the private sector to reduce vulnerabilities. Passed as a stopgap measure, TRIA was intended to allow the insurance markets to recover following September 11 and adjust policies and pricing for the newly realized risk of terrorism. Under the program, commercial insurers must offer coverage for terrorist incidents and would be responsible for paying an "insurer deductible" before federal assistance begins. The federal government will then pay the remainder of insured losses. In the current revision these provisions remain largely unchanged.

The structure of the program, however, disrupts the normal market incentives that insurance companies need to promote risk reduction. When these incentives are properly aligned, insurance companies can actively promote risk reduction. This is why insurance companies give consumers discounts on auto insurance for safe driving records, anti-lock brakes, and airbags, or give non-smokers discounted rates on health and life insurance. For terrorism, however, TRIA removes the market incentive for the insurance industry to quantify the risk, determine the appropriate price of insurance, and provide incentives to reduce risks. In short, TRIA does not promote a "managed care" approach to the problem of terrorism.

If the federal government continues to subsidize terrorism insurance through TRIA as currently enacted, it will effectively encourage the private sector to continue to defer the costs of adjusting to the threat of terrorism. The likely result of this policy will be that losses from future attacks will be greater than they would have been if no federal program were available at all. An insurance program in which the insurer collects no premiums, where the majority burden falls on the government and the taxpayer, and where premiums do not vary with risk or reduction of risk is not in the best interests of the American people.

To fix TRIA, intervention should be retargeted so that companies in critical sectors and high-risk areas are encouraged to invest in reducing their vulnerabilities in exchange for lower insurance premiums. Companies that buy into this insurance program would receive federally backstopped insurance. That insurance would cover damage to property, business continuity losses, group life insurance, and protection from negligence lawsuits. The program would also cover acts of domestic terrorism, which are currently excluded from TRIA. Premium reductions would be tied to mitigation efforts. Participating companies would be granted access to a victim's compensation fund if an attack succeeds. Insurance companies offering policies under the program would be required to contribute a percentage of the terrorism premium to a federal terror reinsurance pool, with the goal of fully capitalizing the federal government's obligation without the use of general revenues over a ten-year period. Such a program could reinforce partnering and regulatory approaches, raising security to altogether higher standards.

The insurance industry as a whole has resisted steps to make insurance more of a player in reducing the risk of terrorism. Industry associations maintain that without adequate data from the federal government on the threat of terrorism, they cannot appropriately determine the value of policies on their own. This argument is not without merit. The Department of Homeland Security should establish an office for TRIA, staffed with industry veterans, and should work to provide usable threat data to insurance brokers so that they can make informed decisions on issuing terrorism insurance.

RESPONSE AND RECOVERY

Finally, the administration's approach to the private sector fails to provide a system for managing economic reconstitution in the aftermath of catastrophic events. The administration established the National Incident Management System (NIMS) to enable the federal government to manage national crises and their consequences. In its National Response Plan (NRP), DHS recognizes the potential for large-scale incidents of national significance—caused by cyber or physical attack—to overwhelm government and private-sector resources by disrupting and taxing critical infrastructure systems. DHS also acknowledges, especially in the aftermath of the botched response to Hurricane Katrina, continuing challenges to the effective management of nationally significant incidents, including weak government coordination with the private sector and the uneven availability of secure and reliable communications needed to coordinate response and recovery efforts.

While the effects of some terrorist attacks may be felt immediately, potentially larger and more significant impacts could develop over time and across the economy. For example, many manufacturing systems dependent on critical infrastructure could cease operations, creating further cascading effects down the economic food chain; financial transactions might be halted and coordination of the delivery of goods, especially those dependent on just-in-time delivery systems, could be seriously disrupted. In the event of a catastrophic cyber event, software patches and other IT solutions designed to address specific cyber vulnerabilities and security problems might not get to their intended destinations because the normal electronic delivery processes provided by the Internet are degraded or disabled.

Neither the NRP nor the NIMS address the complicated problems arising from the need to maintain an orderly functioning national economy in the event that, at the same time, enormous recovery demands are being made in specific affected areas. Administration planning does not consider the question of how two different economies—one market, the other command—might have to coexist during long periods of recovery and reconstitution.

Given the vast amount of corporate resources involved, chief executive involvement is essential; yet there is no process in place to engage executives in an organized and timely way. Indeed, the very magnitude and complexity of reconstituting economic assets and sustaining macroeconomic functionality under these circumstances appears to have led DHS to deem this sort of contingency unfeasible, and thus ineligible for systematic planning and organization.

RECOMMENDATIONS

The root cause for the lack of progress of public-private partnerships is a failure of administration leadership to create the conditions necessary for establishing and supporting those partnerships. If the administration means what it says—that homeland security is a national priority and public-private partnerships are essential to securing the homeland—then establishing effective partnerships with the private sector must also be afforded the status of a national priority.

Below is an eight-point plan for the administration to promote security in the private sector:

5.1. FOCUS ON SECURING HIGH-IMPACT TARGETS AND ASSURING CONTINUITY OF ESSENTIAL SYSTEMS OVER A BLANKET APPROACH TO CRITICAL INFRASTRUCTURE.

5.2. ESTABLISH JOINT PLANNING COMMITTEES FOR EACH HITS AND ESSENTIAL SYSTEM SECTOR. Exercise authority under Section 871 of the Homeland Security Act of 2002 to exempt joint planning committees from FACA. Amend provisions of relevant anti-trust laws to

exempt explicitly standard-setting discussions and planning sessions. Establish a congressional select committee to oversee joint planning.

5.3. ONCE ESTABLISHED, THESE COMMITTEES SHOULD DEVELOP INFRASTRUCTURE SECURITY PLANS THAT SPECIFY THE SECURITY END-STATE TO BE ACHIEVED, goals and milestones for achieving it, standards for implementation and compliance, and timelines for accomplishing intermediate actions.

5.4. INTEGRATE CHIEF EXECUTIVE REVIEW INTO JOINT PLANNING PROCESS; obtain approval and commitment to carry out plans according to agreed-upon timelines.

5.5. IMPLEMENT THE INFRASTRUCTURE PROTECTION REGIONAL SECURITY AND AREA SECURITY FRAMEWORK as set out in the Chemical Facility Anti-Terrorism Act of 2005.

5.6. ADOPT SMART REGULATION ON A SECTOR-BY-SECTOR BASIS TO ENCOURAGE THE DEVELOPMENT AND IMPLEMENTATION OF APPROPRIATE SECURITY MEASURES.

5.7. REVAMP TRIA TO PROMOTE RISK MITIGATION and create a safe harbor against litigation following a terrorist attack where targeted companies have complied with government-approved security standards.

5.8. DEVELOP A CEO-LEVEL SYSTEM FOR MANAGING RESOURCE ALLOCATIONS during recovery and reconstitution phases following a catastrophic national event to allow a coordinated effort with the federal government.

◆ ◆ ◆

Securing the nation's homeland and critical infrastructure requires a new social contract among government, industry, and the public. All three parties are essential to this contract, because all three have obligations to fulfill. The government must assure the private sector and the public that it recognizes its responsibility to manage all aspects of homeland security competently and effectively. It must create the conditions for the private sector to carry out its security responsibilities. The government and public must assure the private sector that, if it fulfills its responsibilities to secure HITS and assure essential systems, in the event companies are attacked, they will be shielded from liability. The public must recognize that there is no such thing as perfect security in a free society. It must develop reasonable expectations about what the government and the private sector can accomplish through managing risks to high-impact targets and essential systems. It must also develop the resilience and confidence to go on with life in the wake of an attack, knowing that government and industry are working together in partnership to do all they can to secure the homeland.

6. FINANCIAL SERVICES
LEARNING FROM SUCCESS

Since September 11, the cooperation between the financial services sector and government regulators has offered a glimpse of a process that promises to protect America's long-term economic security.

Because the health of the financial services infrastructure is critical to the health of our nation, coordination of crisis management efforts is a top priority among industry leadership. The commitment to financial security is seen in the numerous conferences, meetings, and tabletop exercises held by senior executives, including the recent Department of Homeland Security (DHS) sponsored multinational exercise Cyberstorm,[1] which brought financial services leaders together with top thinkers in other critical infrastructure industries, such as telecommunications, information technology, and energy as well as with legislators, regulators, and security experts, to test and evaluate the processes, procedures, and safeguards in place. The results of these efforts are robust emergency communication tools, strengthened industry resources, and documented lessons learned from disaster situations.

The industry's response to September 11 and subsequent recovery would not have been possible without the lessons learned from previous crises. While no one could claim to have been prepared for September 11, the efforts made to prepare the industry and promote resiliency allowed a coordinated response when disaster struck. Arguably, the quick response and recovery by the financial sector following the attacks gave the American public and the world a clear signal that our economy was stable and the assets of 270 million Americans were secure.

Though a highly competitive industry, financial services firms have been able to work together in noncompetitive forums to address emerging threats. A small pool of key industry associations including the Financial Services Sector Coordinating Council (FSSCC) and the

Financial Services Information Sharing and Analysis Center (FS/ISAC) are especially vital.

The FSSCC's mission is to act as a focal point for private-sector engagement with industry regulators, law enforcement, the Department of the Treasury, the Department of Homeland Security, and the Federal Reserve. The FSSCC then works in concert with the Treasury Department and other government agencies to address critical infra-structure and homeland security issues. It currently has thirty-three members representing 8,000 financial institutions ranging from BITS and the Financial Services Roundtable[2] to the New York Board of Trade and the American Bankers Association. Launched in 1999, FS/ISAC was established by the financial services sector in response to Presidential Directive 63 in 1998. That directive—later updated by Homeland Security Presidential Directive 7 in 2003—mandated that the public and private sectors share information about physical and cyber security threats and vulnerabilities to help protect U.S. critical infrastructure.[3]

Efforts by the financial services sector to improve preparedness highlight the utility of specific measures that are transferable to other sectors:

* improving communications during crises;
* building regional partnerships;
* enhancing the resiliency of telecommunications services;
* increasing the reliability of the electrical grid;
* tightening security of software, hardware, and the Internet; and
* intensifying oversight of third-party providers.

August, 14, 2003, the Northeast was hit with a devastating black-out. That day, BITS held a bimonthly meeting of senior executives of financial institutions in Detroit, at the headquarters of member company Comerica Incorporated. On the agenda was cyber security and critical interdependencies with the nation's telecommunications networks. At about 4:30 in the afternoon, lights in the conference room flickered and extinguished. It quickly became clear that the situation was not a momentary lapse. Through pagers, cell phones, and BlackBerries, the group learned within minutes that power was lost not just in Detroit, but also throughout much of the Northeast.

Executives immediately activated their company business continuity plans, including the BITS Crisis Communicator,[4] a high-speed, automated alert system that allows financial services executives to communicate and coordinate with each other, government agencies, and other industry sectors. Within the hour, it became known that the blackout was not a terrorist act. This information helped executives to understand the scope of the incident and strike the appropriate note in messages to their personnel, customers, and the broader public.

Multiple conference calls throughout the evening had CEOs, CIOs, and crisis management executives from BITS member companies discussing effects to their institutions, the backup systems that had been activated, and the point at which power might be restored. In the absence of landline telephones and waning cell phone batteries, the BITS Crisis Communicator functioned as intended, providing members with a real-time forum to exchange information.

Several weeks later, BITS convened a series of conference calls to discuss lessons learned from the blackout. Backup systems had worked, alternate communication systems were used successfully, and there was no adverse impact on settlements and payments. Moreover, each institution had benefited from the cooperation and communication that took place among the financial services regulators, the Treasury Department, and the private sector via the BITS Crisis Communicator.

Donald Donahue, chairman of the FSSCC, testified to Congress that the post–September 11 environment was a strong impetus for improvements to resiliency and continued vigilance and coordination between financial entities. He stressed that beyond their efforts to share best practices broadly, trade associations have published recovery and resiliency guides such as the "BITS Guide to Business-Critical Telecommunications Services"[5] and the "Report of the Assuring Telecommunications Continuity Task Force."[6] His testimony covered cyber security measures as well as physical security.

"The industry's other 'core clearing and settlement organizations'—handling payment and securities and derivative settlement transactions—have implemented a variety of steps since September 11 to reinforce the resilience of their operations, ranging from the same type of duplicated and regionally dispersed operations my company has implemented to reciprocal backup arrangements between organizations. . . . In addition, key trading markets have thought through reciprocal

arrangements permitting one market to trade another market's financial instruments in an extreme situation where the latter market was completely unable to operate."[7]

Donahue's comments were echoed in congressional testimony by Scott Parsons, the deputy assistant secretary for critical infrastructure protection and compliance policy at the U.S. Treasury Department. Chaired by the assistant secretary of the treasury for financial institutions, the Financial and Banking Information Infrastructure Committee coordinates the twenty agencies with regulatory powers throughout the financial sector. This group works to identify the interdependencies of the financial services, telecommunications, energy, and transportation sectors.[8] Their efforts have also improved information sharing among federal, state, and local partners by publicizing a number of lessons learned through documents and impact studies.[9] Together, these strategic public and private partnerships show how businesses engage in a collaborative effort to improve economic security and preparedness, particularly when backed up by strong federal leadership. Continuation of outreach and coalition building should remain a priority for both the Treasury and Homeland Security secretaries.

The Government Accountability Office (GAO) issued major reports in 2003[10] and 2004[11] about the level of preparedness and potential for disruption of financial sector operations. Significant strides were made after the 2003 GAO assessments, which showed major vulnerabilities in continuity of operations planning. The financial sector began creating backup facilities at diverse locations separate from primary facilities, decentralizing key personnel, and increasing physical and information security measures. In order to improve resiliency, the industry has worked with the telecommunications and power sectors to outline its needs and develop plans for the restoration of critical communication services, including the creation of a private phone network for financial service providers. The importance of the telecommunications infrastructure to the security of the financial services sector has not been ignored by federal regulators and telecommunications providers who are working closely to improve the redundancy of the infrastructure. The 2004 GAO report also stresses the importance of the SEC mandating specific rules for the industry relating to business continuity as well as SEC requests for additional resources and personnel to conduct necessary audits on resiliency issues. Both Donahue and Parsons stress in their comments that

smart regulation, in concert with strategic public-private partnerships, increases the likelihood of effective security implementation.

The entire sector understands it has vulnerable interdependencies and, as a result, the FSSCC and FS/ISAC work closely with other critical infrastructure sectors, key software providers, and government leaders to increase regional coordination efforts. This initiative was prompted by a consensus that, beyond New York City, existing activities at the regional level did not adequately address the critical infrastructure protection concerns of financial institutions. As illustrated in our recommendation for metropolitan-area security coordination, the financial services model is applicable to other regions and other sectors.

Two examples of cooperative efforts to assist in preparing for and successfully addressing risks associated with catastrophic events illustrate this point: One is the industry's development, in conjunction with the Securities Industry Association, of a set of considerations for actions to be taken by individual financial institutions and the sector broadly at each of the DHS homeland security alert levels. The goal is to give institutions a step-by-step plan of action to use in response to change in the homeland security alert levels. The second is the successful work of the Treasury Department and a range of organizations in the Chicago area to establish ChicagoFIRST.[12] Begun in 2003, ChicagoFIRST is a coalition of banks, security exchanges, and clearinghouses that ensures emergency management personnel are available to assist crisis managers in protecting financial interests. ChicagoFIRST was created with the premise that, should a terrorist attack or other crisis occur, it is highly likely that it will be concentrated on one geographic area, rather than on a national level. This coalition secured a seat in Chicago's Joint Operations 911 Center, created secure credentials for personnel, defined evacuation procedures for financial personnel, and participated in tabletop exercises with state and federal agencies. Additionally, ChicagoFIRST produced a handbook, funded by the Treasury Department and coauthored by BITS, and the Boston Consulting Group, for other regions seeking to establish similar coalitions. At this writing, Miami banks have announced plans to create a similar coalition, FloridaFIRST.

When Hurricane Katrina struck, the financial services industry again tested its ability to respond effectively to a devastating situation. Executives had immediate access to coordinated information for making critical decisions as the disaster was occurring and in the hours and days that followed.

That information included communications directly from the Treasury and the Department of Homeland Security, such as impact assessments, updates on critical cash supplies, the status of FEMA's distribution of debit cards, talking points for call center representatives as they assisted customers, guidance from regulatory agencies, and important contacts for additional support. These actions kept confidence in financial markets stable.

REGULATION AND SECURITY

Financial institutions are heavily regulated and actively supervised by state and federal agencies. At the federal level, these include the Federal Reserve, Federal Deposit Insurance Corporation, Office of the Comptroller of Currency, Office of Thrift Supervision, National Credit Union Administration, and the Securities and Exchange Commission. Although the financial services industry might prefer less regulation, it also recognizes that some regulations provide predictability, stability, and a foundation for public trust.

Security requirements that result from regulation may increase the cost of doing business, but the financial services sector remains very profitable nonetheless. The security required by regulation is borne equally by all institutions of a similar type (credit unions, stock brokerage houses, and so forth), eliminating security costs as a liability-affecting competitive advantage. The success of the security regulation also depends on active auditing to ensure compliance. The auditing is conducted by third-party accounting firms and federal agencies. Identified weaknesses must be remediated as part of this process. The regulators are aware that, in addition to the physical security of banks, the sector's security depends upon the reliability of:

- key vendors to the sector (software, communications, and so forth);
- continuity of operations plans and redundant capabilities; and
- continuous vetting of employees with access to sensitive systems.

Federal and state regulators have stepped up their oversight of business continuity, information security, third-party service providers, and critical infrastructure protection. The financial exchanges have also added requirements in these areas. As the industry works with leaders to institute best practices and implement the most effective disaster recovery strategies, we also are working diligently to comply with evolving regulations and ongoing examinations.

The Department of Homeland Security proposed a rule to establish procedures for the receipt, care, and storage of Critical Infrastructure Information voluntarily submitted to the federal government through the Department of Homeland Security. There is widespread concern in the industry with the scope and implementation of the procedures. For the rule to be effective, strong safeguards must be in place. It is imperative that the DHS commit to implementing robust controls to protect the employee and customer information submitted by financial institutions.

RECOMMENDATIONS

We can draw numerous lessons from the work of the financial services sector in response to the attacks of September 11, the August 2003 blackout, and most recently Hurricanes Katrina and Rita. The most important and obvious are that preparedness matters and using established risk management practices now will ensure economic viability in the future. An important part of being prepared is looking strategically and holistically at the nation's critical infrastructure and what can be done to enhance resiliency and reliability. Regardless of how well the financial institutions respond to regulations, they alone simply cannot address these problems. Their partners in other critical industry sectors—particularly the telecommunications, energy, and software industries—must also do their fair share to ensure the soundness of these vital economic contributors. Further, the risks for national security and economic soundness cannot be underestimated, and neither can the importance of our working together to address them.

6.1. DIVERSE AND RESILIENT COMMUNICATION CHANNELS ARE ESSENTIAL. Elements such as cell phones, wireless e-mail devices, landline phones, and the Internet are required. However, both diversity and redundancy are needed within critical infrastructures to assure backup systems are operable and continuity of services is maintained. Closely related to this is the importance of having accurate and timely information about the scope and cause of major events. For example, during the August 2003 blackout, the announcement that the problem was not the result of a terrorist event alleviated public concern and enhanced the orderly execution of business continuity processes. High-impact targets should explore installation of redundant communication networks to key security and response elements.

6.2. THE POWER GRID MUST BE CONSIDERED AMONG THE MOST VITAL OF CRITICAL INFRASTRUCTURES AND NEEDS INVESTMENT TO MAKE SURE IT WORKS ACROSS THE NATION. The cascading impact on the operation of financial services, access to fuel, availability of water, and sources of power for telephone services and Internet communications cannot be overstated.

6.3. RECOGNIZE THE INTERDEPENDENCIES AMONG CRITICAL INFRASTRUCTURE SECTORS. Those of greatest concern to us are the interdependencies among financial services, telecommunications, and energy sectors. The federal government should take action to enhance the diversity and resiliency of the telecommunications infrastructure and the nation's energy grids.

6.4. RECOGNIZE THE DEPENDENCY OF CRITICAL INFRASTRUCTURES ON SOFTWARE OPERATING SYSTEMS AND THE INTERNET. A clear understanding of the role of software operating systems within critical infrastructures needs to be explored, including ways of sharing responsibility and liability more equitably among stakeholders. The financial services sector has endorsed an agenda to improve cyber security, but, in addition to those recommendations, the financial services industry needs to improve the physical security of the cyber network nodes on which it relies to eliminate single points of failure.

6.5. AS HURRICANE KATRINA HAS POIGNANTLY ILLUSTRATED, ESTABLISHING IMPROVED COORDINATION PROCEDURES ACROSS ALL CRITICAL INFRASTRUCTURES AND WITH FEDERAL, STATE, AND LOCAL GOVERNMENT IS ESSENTIAL TO RAPID, COORDINATED, AND EFFECTIVE RESPONSE WHEN EVENTS OCCUR. To minimize the economic and social risks during a crisis, coordination in planning and response between the private sector and public emergency management must improve.

◆ ◆ ◆

While the financial services sector has a long agenda of security improvements yet to be implemented, our national security overall would be greatly enhanced if other key sectors of our economy were as secure as our financial services infrastructure is already.

7. CHEMICAL PLANT SECURITY
PREVENTING A TERRORIST BHOPAL

There may be no better example of a sector encompassing a large number of high-impact targets than the chemical industry. The industry produces, stores, and transports large quantities of highly toxic agents for a wide range of industrial uses. According to DHS planning scenarios released last spring, a truck bomb detonated at a chlorine plant could cause 17,500 deaths and millions of dollars of damage. These figures are probably conservative. With minimal reconnaissance and the technical knowledge to make a fertilizer bomb, terrorists could kill large numbers of people by targeting one of the thousands of facilities that handle large quantities of highly toxic chemicals in close proximity to our nation's cities and towns.

Preventing such an outcome has relied largely on voluntary measures, most notably adherence by the members of the American Chemistry Council (ACC) to its Responsible Care Security Code. In all, the chemical industry has spent $2 billion on security since the attacks on September 11, a not unimpressive figure.[1] Yet, due to the voluntary nature of these measures and a lack of oversight by the federal government, the Government Accountability Office (GAO) and outside experts have concluded that the overall level of security in the industry remains inadequate. The Chemical Facility Anti-Terrorism Act of 2005, a bill introduced to the Senate by Senator Susan Collins (R-ME), would go a long way toward improving security in the chemical industry. It sets the stage for the Department of Homeland Security (DHS) to take the kind of smart approach to regulation we advocate here.

The goal of regulating security in the chemical industry should be to reduce or eliminate vulnerabilities rather than to turn every chemical plant into Fort Knox. The Collins bill provides a "tiered" approach to security, in which companies are placed in tiers according to risk and are encouraged to partner with the federal government in developing strategies for moving from higher tiers with higher security costs to lower tiers with lower costs. Such an approach does not dictate what processes or technologies chemical plants can use but rather provides a strong incentive for investing in so-called inherently safer technologies or moving dangerous operations to more remote locations. Creating this incentive, however, will require that the DHS set standards for the physical protection of the most dangerous facilities that are more than just window dressing.

In this chapter, we provide background on the chemical industry, discuss why the industry's excellent record on safety does not translate into security, discuss previous attempts to legislate security measures, and conclude with a review of the Collins bill. Our ultimate recommendation is that the Collins bill should be modified to make the regulatory action stronger. Doing so would encourage industry members to take real steps toward reducing their vulnerabilities.

BACKGROUND

In the predawn hours of December 3, 1984, a tank holding methyl isocyanate at a Union Carbide plant in Bhopal, India, began to overheat. Water was introduced to the tank, causing a chemical reaction that within minutes raised the tank's internal temperature to over 200 degrees celsius. The heat generated a large volume of highly toxic gas, triggering release valves to prevent an explosion. The heavier-than-air gas rolled along the ground into the communities nearby the plant. In all, some 2,500 people were killed immediately, with ongoing health effects leading to an additional 15,000 deaths. The cause of the incident officially was considered to be a combination of poor maintenance practices, which led to the accidental introduction of water to the tank, and ineffective safety systems. Studies commissioned by Union Carbide, however, contend that the water was introduced through a direct connection to the tank by a malicious employee.[2]

Whether the Bhopal incident was due to poor maintenance or "damage by design," there is little doubt that terrorists could reproduce similar results given the state of security at many chemical plants in this country. A reporter for the *Pittsburgh Tribune Review* has repeatedly infiltrated some of the most potentially dangerous chemical facilities in the nation. These include facilities operated by ACC members that adhere to the Responsible Care program. Security of facilities that store large quantities of chlorine, ammonia, and other hazardous chemicals was found to be lax. Problems included a lack of perimeter control and procedures to maintain entry-exit control at security gates.[3] After the initial story ran, crews from *60 Minutes* were able to infiltrate the very same plants.[4]

The general consensus among the homeland security community is that the chemical industry remains vulnerable to a terrorist attack that could potentially kill thousands of Americans. The Brookings Institution in 2002 reported that an attack on toxic chemical plants ranks third, behind only biological and atomic attacks, in terms of possible fatalities.[5] Much attention has focused on the worst-case scenario projections from facilities regulated by the Environmental Protection Agency (EPA), which predict many millions of fatalities in some instances. These estimates are likely overstated, however, since the EPA based its findings on crude models of chemical releases that do not take into account wind patterns and basic concepts of plume modeling. According to the Department of Homeland Security's revised estimates, there are approximately 4,400 facilities that threaten 1,000 or more people each, with many facilities posing a threat to substantially more than that. In the event of a successful attack on a chemical facility, casualties could easily exceed the mark of just under three thousand who died on September 11. DHS planning scenarios leaked to the *New York Times* revealed that the department estimates that a detonation at a single chlorine plant could kill 17,500 people.[6]

Given the current low level of security and the potentially disastrous consequences of an attack, chemical facilities would be highly appealing targets for terrorists bent on mass slaughter. The DHS planning scenario postulates that a terrorist cell with a minimal technical knowledge of bomb-making, which is still easily found on the Internet, attacking a chemical facility storing toxic substances, could produce effects amplified exponentially beyond more conventional application of a simple bomb.

SAFETY AND SECURITY

Following the Bhopal incident, Congress amended the Clean Air Act Amendments (CAAA) to prevent a similar incident from occurring in the United States. The CAAA mandated that approximately 15,000 facilities develop and submit risk management plans (RMPs) to the EPA. RMPs are now required of any facility handling large quantities of any of 140 hazardous chemicals. Facilities that are required to submit RMPs must identify potential safety hazards and develop plans for reducing the risk of an unintentional release. These requirements have led to a successful partnership between the EPA and the chemical industry, resulting in an excellent record of safety.

Planning for safety, however, does not necessarily mean planning for security. Safety mechanisms are designed to protect against accidents. They may do little or nothing to prevent terrorists from causing an intentional release. The ACC and other industry associations have developed security standards for their respective members.

The ACC Responsible Care program started as a program aimed at improving environmental, health, and safety performance. Following the September 11 attacks, the ACC developed a security component for the program, the Responsible Care Security Code. The code requires ACC members to conduct facility security assessments and implement necessary improvements. One notable component of the code is that it requires the assessments and improvements to be audited by a third-party security firm. As impressive as the code sounds, the ACC consists of only 150 chemical companies and the code covers only a small percentage of chemical facilities. With no current federal mandate to track adoption of voluntary codes or audit adherence to these codes, it is unclear how effective such measures have been at increasing security.

The ACC has voiced support for varying legislative initiatives, while noting that competing companies that do not invest in security undercut ACC members that spend on security measures. Smaller chemical producers, on the other hand, maintain that security costs and compliance with security regulations will put them at a disadvantage against their larger competitors. If there is an attack, however, Congress is likely to quickly institute sweeping and ham-fisted security requirements for all chemical plants regardless of the voluntary measures adopted by some companies. The industry is therefore only as strong as its weakest link.

Such was the case after September 11, when the entire airline industry, not only American and United, was temporarily grounded and fear of flying threatened financial solvency across the industry. Smart security now may avoid the adoption of poorly and hastily thought out regulation following a successful attack.

INITIAL LEGISLATIVE RESPONSES

The National Strategy for the Physical Protection of Critical Infrastructures and Key Assets, signed by President Bush in 2003, charges the EPA and DHS to work with Congress to develop legislation that requires "chemical facilities, particularly those that maintain large quantities of hazardous chemicals in close proximity to population centers, to undertake vulnerability assessments and take reasonable steps to reduce the vulnerabilities identified."[7] Unfortunately, since the adoption of this strategy, no regulation has yet been promulgated.

In March 2003, the GAO recommended that the DHS and the EPA take a series of first steps, including the need to:

◆ identify high-risk facilities based on factors including the level of threat and collect information on industry security preparedness;
◆ specify the roles and responsibilities of each federal agency partnering with the chemical industry; and
◆ develop appropriate information-sharing mechanisms.[8]

Little of this legwork has been completed, mostly because the overall National Infrastructure Protection Plan (NIPP) that is meant to lay the framework for doing this in the chemical and other sectors has not been implemented.

Two relevant bills addressing chemical industry security received substantial consideration in the 108th Congress, but were not passed. The Chemical Facilities Security Act of 2003 (sponsored by Senator James Inhofe, R-OK) would have required chemical facilities to conduct vulnerability assessments, prepare and implement site security plans, and establish a timetable for reducing discovered vulnerabilities. The bill did not require facilities to submit their security plans to the Department of Homeland Security or any other federal agency.[9] A competing bill, the

Chemical Security Act of 2003 (sponsored by Senator Jon Corzine, D-NJ), would have directed the EPA to designate high-priority chemical facilities based on the threat posed by an intentional release and require these facilities to conduct vulnerability assessments, identify hazards that would result from a release, and create a prevention, preparedness, and response plan. The Corzine bill also would have required facilities to share these assessments and plans with the EPA. The DHS and the EPA would jointly review the assessments and plans to determine compliance. The bill included a provision that required facilities to consider inherently safer technologies, for example, using less toxic chemicals.[10] This provision was widely criticized for its vagueness and the potential to open the industry to micromanagement by federal officials.

Both bills focused on the category of facilities currently regulated under EPA's Risk Management Program requirements. However, these regulated facilities are only a portion of those of concern from a security perspective. Under the safety-oriented CAAA, facilities are able to avoid regulation by dividing large storage units of hazardous chemicals into smaller storage containers, thereby mitigating the potential damage caused by an accidental release. However, terrorists could cause a series of storage tanks to rupture and cause the same amount of damage as one large release. Hence, as an unintended consequence of a focus on safety, these facilities are operating under the radar of security efforts.[11]

While a compromise bill made it through the Senate Environment and Public Works (EPW) Committee in October of 2003, action on it stalled on the Senate floor. Both the Inhofe and Corzine bills were pursued through the EPW Committee, but jurisdiction for the issue has since shifted to the Homeland Security and Governmental Affairs Committee, chaired by Senator Susan Collins (R-ME) and with ranking member Senator Joseph Lieberman (D-CT).

THE CHEMICAL FACILITY ANTI-TERRORISM ACT

This past December, Senator Collins introduced the Chemical Facility Anti-Terrorism Act of 2005. The bill addresses the issues that have kept past attempts to legislate from moving forward. It is largely consistent with the general recommendations on how best to promote security in the private sector in Chapter 5. The Collins bill correctly treats most chemical facilities as high-impact targets, creates a regional approach to partnering with the industry, and uses a smart regulatory approach to produce better security. It is loosely modeled on the successful Maritime Transportation Security Act of 2002, which covers some chemical facilities located on or near the waterfront.

The bill would place chemical facilities into tiers grouped by risk, with higher tiers requiring higher levels of security. Within one year of enactment, the bill requires the DHS to set criteria determining which facilities are covered by the act, place facilities within tiers grouped by risk, and establish security standards for each tier. Facilities that are subject to the act would be required to conduct a vulnerability assessment, develop a security plan, and update their emergency response plans to take into account the consequences of intentional acts. The bill would grant the secretary of the DHS the authority to fine or close down facilities that are out of compliance. As discussed in Chapter 5, the bill calls for the creation of regional plans and regional offices to partner with the industry and conduct audits and inspections.

The tiered system does not explicitly require companies to consider so-called inherently safer technologies. It can, however, provide the impetus for companies to make such investments. The bill stipulates that companies can work with DHS to develop a plan for moving from a higher tier to a lower one. If the regulations promulgated for the higher-tiered facilities are appropriate, the costs of physical protection likely will be quite high. Over the long term, moving dangerous operations to more remote locations or investing in inherently safer technologies may be a prudent business decision in order for companies to avoid the costs of a higher-tier status. This is a strong example of how smart regulation can be used to promote security. Instead of Congress dictating the procedures that an industry must use, it can create a legal framework that encourages the industry members to make their own informed decisions on how to proceed. For this process to unfold, the regulations the DHS develops would have to be sufficiently strong.

Given the potential consequences of a successful attack on a high-risk facility, security standards should be similar to those for nuclear plants. Though there are problems that must be corrected in current nuclear facility security practices, as discussed in Chapters 8 and 14, the approach used is certainly applicable to chemical facilities. Security at nuclear plants is developed according to a "design basis threat," a profile of possible attack scenarios that plant security personnel must be able to manage. As at nuclear plants, security personnel guarding facilities in the highest-risk tier must have the legal authority to use deadly force to stop intruders. Without this capability, investments in fences, gates, and intrusion detection devices will prove little more than cosmetic security. For fences to be useful, they must be guarded by security personnel authorized to stop, with deadly force if necessary, anyone who tries to climb over them. This kind of authority is not to be taken lightly, but is ultimately necessary if physical security measures to prevent terrorists from striking these targets are to be effective.

Given the high cost of deploying such a security system, the relocation of plants or switching to safer materials might make sense. Moving from active security (requiring personnel to respond to an attack) to passive security (removing the vulnerabilities that make these facilities targets in the first place), should be the ultimate goal of a serious attempt to regulate security.

The Collins bill, like previous attempts to regulate chemical industry security, would require companies to conduct self-assessments that evaluate the vulnerability of the chemical plant. DHS would be required to develop standards for these assessments, and would have the legal authority to audit and conduct on-site inspections. Yet self-assessments are a weak basis on which to improve security. Reflecting our recommendations in Chapter 5, the bill should be amended to have DHS certify security professionals, and require companies to contract with these professionals to conduct the assessments. Such a model has worked well with the Securities and Exchange Commission in securities regulation, and also could work well with chemical industry security regulation.

Finally, the Collins bill includes a certification provision whereby companies found to be in compliance will be officially recognized by the Department of Homeland Security. This certification should come with a liability shield. Companies that have met their requirements under the law should not be sued if, despite the measures they have taken to improve security, they are successfully targeted by terrorists. In order to create an added financial incentive for investing in security, certification also should result in reduced premiums on terrorism insurance coverage.

RECOMMENDATIONS

The Chemical Facility Anti-Terrorism Act of 2005 has the potential to improve significantly the security of our nation's chemical facilities. Congress should move quickly to fix the problems we have outlined in the bill and then make it into law. These suggested changes include:

7.1. PROVIDING A STRONGER FRAMEWORK FOR DEVELOPING REGULATIONS THAT WILL FOCUS COMPANIES ON INVESTING IN PASSIVE SECURITY OVER ACTIVE SECURITY.

7.2. USING A "DESIGN BASIS THREAT" FOR DEVELOPING SECURITY REQUIREMENTS FOR FACILITIES IN THE HIGHEST-RISK TIER.

7.3. GIVING SECURITY PERSONNEL AT HIGH-RISK FACILITIES THE LEGAL AUTHORITY TO USE DEADLY FORCE AGAINST ATTACKERS.

7.4. ESTABLISHING A TRAINING AND CERTIFICATION PROGRAM UNDER WHICH SECURITY PROFESSIONALS CAN CONDUCT VULNERABILITY ASSESSMENTS AND ESTABLISH SECURITY PLANS.

7.5. PROVIDING LIABILITY PROTECTION AND TERRORISM INSURANCE PREMIUM REDUCTIONS FOR FACILITIES CERTIFIED AS BEING COMPLIANT.

◆ ◆ ◆

In addition to these changes, Congress must provide sufficient funding to enforce the act. The proposed 2007 budget for the Department of Homeland Security includes a paltry $10 million to establish an office to oversee chemical facility security. These funds are entirely insufficient and portend the elimination of the proposal for regional offices that will be crucial in partnering with the industry and in enforcing the provisions of the Collins bill.

8. Protecting Energy Infrastructure

Electricity and transportation fuels are essential to the American way of life. Today, their vulnerability to disruption calls for a better strategy for securing energy infrastructure. Disruptive incidents occur fairly frequently, but rarely cause significant harm because disruptions tend to be localized, whereas infrastructure is redundant, geographically dispersed, and supported by facility owners experienced in repair and service restoration. Nevertheless, America's infrastructure for electricity and transportation fuels is susceptible to damage—natural, accidental, or intentional—that could have devastating consequences.

While the consequences of energy infrastructure failures can be severe, these are low-probability events and there are specific steps that can reduce their likelihood and consequences. Fortunately, most infrastructure is not critical: Of the vast network of pipelines, pumping stations, refineries and other facilities, few would fall into the category of "essential systems," the loss of which would significantly harm large segments of the economy or the population; even fewer would be appropriately classified as "high-impact targets."

These characteristics suggest a three-part risk management strategy for securing energy infrastructure:

- eliminate, or, if that is not feasible, heavily guard energy assets that can be used to injure or kill large numbers of people;
- invest in redundancy to prevent any single failure from bringing down large parts of the national energy system; and
- make systems resilient so that, when they do fail, the system can be restored quickly.

This chapter will survey the security issues and vulnerabilities relevant to the most important categories of the energy infrastructure, review

95

current protective measures, and propose ways to remedy vulnerabilities. It will close with recommendations to reduce the nation's vulnerability to energy infrastructure failure in the future.

INFRASTRUCTURE PROTECTION AS RISK MANAGEMENT

Securing energy infrastructure is fundamentally a risk management exercise, where risk is defined as a function of threat (intent and capabilities of adversaries), vulnerabilities (security and design weaknesses), and consequences (potential adverse effects). Given an understanding of the threats, vulnerabilities, and consequences, security and asset managers can design and implement prevention and remediation programs that make sense.

THREAT ASSESSMENT

The record of the last decade suggests that jihadists possess both the intent and the capability to strike at U.S.-based energy assets and systems. The 2002 attack on the French supertanker *Limburg* showed that al Qaeda is attuned to the energy industry and able to stage attacks of impressive sophistication. In Iraq, insurgents have persistently and successfully attacked energy infrastructure. Jihadists employed these skills, albeit unsuccessfully, in a February 24, 2006, attack against the Abqaiq oil facility in Saudi Arabia. It is clear that jihadist groups have the capability to strike our energy infrastructure and that these attacks against energy assets could fulfill their goal of killing large numbers of Americans and crippling our economy.

Of course, terrorism is not the only threat to the energy sector. Natural disasters, such as earthquakes or hurricanes, can damage or destroy electric transmission lines and transformers, gas pipelines, hydroelectric dams, or coal-carrying trains and tracks. A six-day ice storm that swept Quebec, Ontario, New Brunswick, and Maine in 1998 damaged so much transmission and distribution equipment that over 4.5 million people were left without power. Some of the damage took months to repair. The hurricanes of fall 2005 halted oil and gas flow from the Gulf of Mexico for almost a week, having shut down or damaged refineries, off-shore production platforms, and pipelines across the Gulf.

Human error can be equally damaging. On August 14, 2003, a series of individually small computer software and hardware failures, combined with operator inattention, led to a blackout that cut service to over 50 million people in the United States and Canada. Every major U.S. electrical blackout since 1965 has occurred in part due to human error (misspecification of equipment, faulty maintenance practices, or misjudged tolerances) that led to system failure under stress. The same is true of many accidents at dams and refineries.

VULNERABILITY ASSESSMENT

Energy infrastructure is vulnerable to a range of hazards:

- natural disasters (hurricanes, earthquakes, floods, landslides, ice storms, and forest fires);
- unintentional human-caused damage (construction equipment cutting gas pipelines, vehicles striking distribution poles, bad software, and so forth);
- malicious attacks by individuals (disgruntled employees sabotaging equipment, drunks firing at pipelines);
- coordinated terrorist attacks (armed attack on a nuclear power plant or large dam, use of explosives to damage multiple pipeline facilities, substations, or refineries);
- cyber attack (dissemination of viruses, denial-of-service attacks against control systems, probes that take over or feed false information to a control system); and
- loss of other parallel infrastructures, on which energy operations depend (including telecommunications, the Internet, banking, transportation, fuel deliveries—coal via railroad or gas via pipeline—or water supplies).

CONSEQUENCE ASSESSMENT

Four primary factors determine whether an energy system failure has either localized or major social consequences.

- First, the magnitude and speed of the asset failures. Phenomena such as hurricanes, ice storms, and earthquakes damage multiple facilities across large geographic areas, thereby compromising much of the system simultaneously. Service to millions of customers may be affected and system restoration and recovery can be a slow, asset-by-asset rebuilding process.

- Second, the impact of initial failure on interrelated systems. Electricity systems are particularly vulnerable to cascading failure—that is, where the failure of one element triggers failure in successive elements—because they are heavily computerized, thoroughly interconnected, and react with split-second speed to failures elsewhere in the system. In contrast, infrastructures that move physical commodities such as oil, natural gas, petroleum products, and coal can sustain significant physical damage in a few locations without collapse of the overall system.

- Third, the extent of the damage and the speed with which service can be restored. In most cases, the failure of a single asset will not compromise system performance for long, if at all; the exception is a supervisory control and data acquisition (SCADA) system, a centralized monitoring and control system for transport. However, if multiple assets within a system fail simultaneously, the overall system is much more likely to fail.

- Fourth, the length of time that critical infrastructures are unavailable. In most energy infrastructures, managers can circumvent the loss of a few critical assets and still keep the system working. However, the longer the critical assets are unavailable, the more difficult it becomes to sustain system performance. A metropolitan area can tolerate a blackout for several hours or even a day, but if it lasts much longer, it can trigger failures of telecommunications, traffic, water, sewer, and public safety. An energy system failure caused by the simultaneous destruction of multiple critical assets would cause a lengthy service interruption, and have a traumatic effect on the people and economy of the region.

SECURITY OF ENERGY ASSETS

Each energy asset has a set of unique associated threats, risks, and consequences, which dictate the appropriate set of security measures. Two considerations are central: whether the asset can be protected at all, and the implications of failure for the system as a whole.

Many energy assets can fail without significantly affecting the performance of the larger energy delivery system. The catastrophic failure of an individual asset such as a power plant, dam, pipeline, oil refinery, or liquefied natural gas (LNG) terminal could have disastrous consequences for those who live and work around the facility, but would not necessarily compromise the performance of the entire energy system. The same is true for facility attacks, such as an airplane crashing into a nuclear power plant or a refinery bombing. These attacks could have great symbolic and socially traumatic effects without disrupting system function.

FOSSIL AND NON-NUCLEAR POWER PLANTS

There are approximately 16,770 generators in the United States with a total capacity of 1,049,615 megawatts (one megawatt serves about 800 homes).[1] These generators use diverse fuel sources—32 percent of the capacity is coal-fired, 4 percent oil, 18 percent natural gas, 18 percent dual-fired (oil and gas), 10 percent nuclear, 9 percent hydroelectric, and approximately 2 percent renewable.

Individual plants are commonly taken off-line for maintenance, or because there are times when plant operation is uneconomical. Grid operators are therefore accustomed to juggling planned and unplanned generation outages without compromising system reliability. Thus, in most cases, the sudden loss of the output from one or two power plants due to coordinated attack or a widespread natural disaster would not compromise the ability of the overall electric system to continue producing and delivering electricity.

However, the location of the affected generator matters a great deal. Certain plants, by nature of their place within the grid, provide important reliability services that cannot easily be replaced by a generator located elsewhere. If such a plant were incapacitated at a time of high electric use, the resulting grid imbalance could lead to a wider system imbalance and a local blackout.

A successful attack against a non-nuclear power plant or its on-site fuel supplies is not inconceivable. Although these facilities have large security perimeters, they are accorded only moderate physical protection and limited monitoring. Most of the damage from a major attack on such a plant would be contained within its perimeter, and would be unlikely to cause catastrophic damage beyond the site of the plant itself.

NUCLEAR POWER PLANTS

There are 103 operating commercial nuclear power plants at 65 sites across the United States, providing 10 percent of the nation's electricity production. Although the power plant is the primary focus of concern, security of adjoining spent fuel storage cannot be ignored. Blast and fire damage from a nuclear power plant accident or attack would likely be contained within the plant property.

An incident of this kind could also result in a radioactive release, drifting in an airborne plume from the targeted facility for miles into the surrounding area. Such a release could afflict between 50,000 and 500,000 people in nearby and downwind areas with radiation burns, immediate and long-term cancers, and other health problems. The health effects of a nuclear accident or attack would obviously depend largely on the location of the nuclear source relative to population centers.

The fact is that many nuclear plants are close to major metropolitan areas, including New York City, Boston, Philadelphia, and New Orleans. Consequences of a radioactive release might include the need to permanently relocate entire communities at extraordinary economic, social, and emotional cost. Essential safety measures at nuclear plants include reactor containment buildings designed to protect the reactor against damage from hurricanes, tornadoes, and terrorist attacks (as well as to contain possible radiation releases). Nuclear plants have a variety of automated safety mechanisms that should shut down the plant in the event of an attack or internal failure.

The Nuclear Regulatory Commission (NRC) requires every nuclear licensee to perform a variety of detailed security analyses, implement emergency preparation plans and exercise them in concert with the local community, and provide additional safety and security training for all plant and guard personnel. Since 2001, every nuclear power plant has established concentric security zones around the plant core, and enhanced its physical protection features and defenses with fences, barriers, cameras, and patrols by armed guards. Nuclear plants conduct "force-on-force" exercises and a variety of inspections to test guard and plant readiness. Access to the airspace above nuclear plants and the navigable waters next to them is strictly limited.

There is continuing public debate over whether nuclear power plants are as safe and secure as industry and federal regulators claim. Some of the points of contention revolve around whether the plants, designed and built in the 1970s, can stand up to modern methods of attack—for instance, whether a reactor containment vessel can withstand a direct hit from a large aircraft. The NRC tests plant security and designs against a "design basis threat," which specifies the assumed maximum assault or potential failure mode that the plant could face, and then analyzes the plant's ability to withstand that threat. Organizations such as the Union of Concerned Scientists maintain that the NRC's safety and security requirements are inadequate. A National Academy of Sciences study concluded that cutting the water supply to a nuclear power plant's spent nuclear fuel pool could lead to a high-temperature radiation fire that could release as much radiation and cause as much death and disease as a meltdown within the plant's nuclear core.[2] On the other hand, the Nuclear Education Institute claims that a successful attack on a nuclear power plant would require many experts, and that reactors are so heavily protected that terrorists will probably choose to attack easier targets instead.

HYDROELECTRIC DAMS

Within the United States, there are over 5,500 large dams. Over one-third of them are owned by utilities to produce electricity. These dams are sited and licensed by the Federal Energy Regulatory Commission

(FERC). Most other large dams are owned and operated by federal government agencies, primarily the Bureau of Reclamation and the Army Corps of Engineers, for multiple uses including power production, flood control, transportation, irrigation, and public recreation. Hydroelectricity from private and federal dams contributed 7 percent of the nation's total electricity consumption in 2004.

Some large dams, like the Hoover and Grand Coulee dams, have great symbolic value. A successful attack on such a facility would affect the nation's psyche far more than it would the electric grid. For most dams, the consequence of greatest concern is that a sudden dam rupture could result in an uncontrolled water release that would harm people and property downstream. The Federal Emergency Management Agency (FEMA) has identified more than 10,000 dams as having "high hazard potential," meaning that their failure from any means, including a terrorist attack, could result in significant property damage, environmental damage, and loss of life.

Dam owners and operators have worked with the three federal agencies (FERC, Bureau of Reclamation, and the Army Corps) to develop and implement risk assessment methodology and safety and security practices designed specifically for dams. Since 2001, all dams used for electricity production have made extensive security improvements, such as installing new sensors, barriers, and communications equipment. FERC safety inspectors conduct regular security audits of their jurisdictional dams and require dam owners to develop and practice emergency action plans. Under the Dam Safety and Security Act of 2002, FEMA is the designated federal coordinator for dam safety and security—yet another reason to restore the capacities of FEMA that were undermined through its incorporation into DHS.

ELECTRICITY SYSTEM

The U.S. electric system is a web of power plants linked to customers by 163,000 miles of high-voltage transmission lines, distribution lines, and supporting equipment. U.S. electricity demand for the summer of 2006 is expected to reach 744,000 megawatts, served by almost 890,000 megawatts of generation resources—19.5 percent over demand.[3]

While this surplus capacity suggests that the electrical grid can survive the loss of multiple assets without failing, some assets, as noted above, are more important than others, and the simultaneous loss of too many physical or cyber assets could lead to cascading failure and blackouts over a large part of the grid.

Computer-automated controls and communications manage the entire electric grid, and a failure in one asset-owner's supervisory control and data acquisition (SCADA) system can cascade instantly across the entire grid. This makes cyber security a critical necessity for the electric industry, which has been developing and refining voluntary cyber security standards since 2002.[4] Those standards became mandatory for industry members in 2006, when the Federal Energy Regulatory Commission assumed regulatory responsibility for electric reliability under the Energy Policy Act of 2005.

The Federal Bureau of Investigation recently asserted that terrorist groups such as al Qaeda do not have the ability to disable power plants and other critical infrastructure through the Internet. FBI officials state that they are not aware of any terrorist plans to attack U.S. infrastructure, but that many intrusion cases appear to be sponsored by foreign nations.[5] A survey of utility information technology executives in summer 2005 found that 20 percent reported that their SCADA systems have already been probed by outside threats, and one-third expect that the SCADA or energy distribution systems of at least one utility company will be attacked or compromised during the next two years.[6]

The transmission network faces operational issues, including congestion and steadily rising electricity flows across the grid. For a decade, utilities underinvested in transmission, and are only now building major new facilities to strengthen grid performance, delivery throughput, and reliability. Because the majority of power plants are located far from the large urban areas where most electricity is used, and because many regions of the country import low-cost generation from other regions, an adequate transmission grid is crucial to maintaining service.

Several problems can disrupt transmission system performance: inadequate capacity, as suggested earlier; failure to prevent trees from growing into and shorting out power lines; and the very nature of custom-designed transformers or breakers that are hard to replace when they break. Transmission lines themselves are very long, highly visible, and impossible to hide or protect, and therefore vulnerable to the havoc wrought by nature or terrorist attack.

OIL AND GAS PRODUCTION FACILITIES

Oil and natural gas provide 60 percent of the United States's energy needs and serve as raw materials for the manufacture of plastics, chemicals, fertilizer, medicines, and synthetic fibers. In 2004 the nation consumed 20.7 million barrels of oil per day, and imported 58 percent of that amount from five countries: Canada, Mexico, Saudi Arabia, Venezuela, and Nigeria. Domestic oil production came from over half a million oil wells, with a quarter of production from offshore, primarily deep-water wells in the Gulf of Mexico.[7] The United States also consumed 22,375 billion cubic feet of natural gas in 2003, 82 percent of which came from domestic wells.[8]

Although most domestic oil and gas wells are individually small and dispersed, they are concentrated within particular geographic regions, making it easier and potentially more disruptive should terrorists disable oil and gas gathering systems rather than individual wells or fields. This was illustrated by Hurricanes Katrina and Rita, which together shut down all oil and gas production from the Gulf of Mexico for at least a week. Four months later, only three-fourths of that production had been restored. The hurricanes destroyed many deep-water drilling rigs and damaged others. Although many onshore pipelines were not harmed, over 5.25 billion cubic feet of daily gas processing plant capacity was damaged and took months to rebuild.

Over the short term, the net result of the damage restricted supplies of natural gas to much of the southern United States. Natural gas prices jumped immediately and, combined with curtailed supplies from the Gulf, prices remained at record high levels for months.

OIL REFINERIES

There were 144 refineries operating in the Unites States at the start of 2003, processing over 17 million barrels of oil per day.[9] Most are in the Southeast, along the Gulf Coast. No new oil refinery capacity has been built in the United States since 1976, although refinery owners have steadily worked to improve efficiency and plant reliability. However, with domestic demand for finished petroleum products increasing every year,

United States imports from the Caribbean, Venezuela, and Europe have increased to over 2 million barrels of gasoline per day.

The March 2005 explosion of British Petroleum's Houston refinery was a harsh example of the consequences of an accident, with 15 people dead and over 100 injured. While the physical destruction from a refinery explosion may be contained within the facility perimeter, many refineries use a variety of hazardous chemicals that can threaten adjoining communities. One such chemical is hydrofluoric acid, which as an aerosol will burn human tissue.

The use of these chemicals would be subject to the proposed Chemical Facility Anti-Terrorism Act of 2005, which could increase costs enough to force companies to switch to less dangerous processes. If this act does not pass, other means should be explored to eliminate this danger.

Because of the high level of environmental and physical damage that could result from a refinery explosion and refineries' high capital cost, refineries are closely guarded facilities. Most are closely monitored and have extensive buffer zones and robust physical protection. Refinery owners have worked with the Department of Homeland Security, the Coast Guard, and federal intelligence and law enforcement agencies on security assessments, emergency operation plans, and information sharing about threats and best security practices.

OIL AND GAS PIPELINES

There are over 2 million miles of oil and gas pipelines in the United States. Pipelines transport two-thirds of the oil we consume.[10] Most pipelines are buried at least a meter underground; but some stretches, as well as associated facilities such as pumping stations and tank farms, are above ground.

Almost 190 billion cubic feet per day of natural gas moved through interstate and intrastate gas transmission pipelines in 2004. Much of this gas flows either from Texas and Louisiana (onshore or in the Gulf of Mexico) to the Southeast or Southwest, from the Rockies westward or toward the Midwest, and from Canada southward into the Pacific Northwest and California, into the Midwest, or into New England.

Pipeline investment has grown with natural gas demand, with total mileage increasing by about 1 percent per year and system capacity increasing by 4 percent annually with improved transport and storage practices. Underground natural gas storage facilities supplement the pipeline system by allowing a gas provider to keep a local inventory to help meet demands that exceed pipeline delivery capacity.

Since 1990, there have been nearly 2,300 major natural gas pipeline accidents resulting in over 200 deaths. Most of the accidents were at the local distribution company level (affecting smaller pipelines carrying gas within a metropolitan area), due to "outside forces" such as damage by the pipeline owner, third-party damage (as by contractor dig-ins), and natural disasters such as landslides and fires. There have been very few attacks (crime, vandalism, sabotage, or terrorist attack) upon U.S. oil or gas pipelines. Another principal cause of pipeline failure is pipe corrosion, which leads to a rupture and fuel spill, in the case of oil, or explosion, in the case of gas. However, corrosion protection and leak detection programs have significantly improved pipeline safety.

LIQUEFIED NATURAL GAS TERMINALS

Liquefied natural gas (LNG) is methane that has been cooled to –260° F, which condenses the gas and allows for storage and transportation in tanker trucks or ships. The United States has 108 working LNG facilities including six active LNG terminals (in Louisiana, Georgia, Massachusetts, Maryland, Alaska, and Puerto Rico). At present, LNG deliveries account for only 2–3 percent of U.S. gas imports, but, with high natural gas prices and growing demand, another twelve terminals have been approved for construction (five in Texas, three in Louisiana, two in the Bahamas, and one in Massachusetts), with many more proposed. There are 150 LNG tankers worldwide, with another fifty-five on order or under construction. LNG deliveries into the United States will increase markedly as new LNG receiving terminals go into service.

Since LNG maritime transport began in 1959, there have been only eight significant tanker incidents in over 33,000 tanker voyages, and no hull failures or cargo tank ruptures. The most significant LNG facility accident was in 1944, when a gas tank rupture in Cleveland released gas that ignited in a residential neighborhood, killing 128 people and injuring many more. In 1977, a valve failure in Arzew, Algeria, released gas that froze one worker, although the gas did not ignite. In 1979, a gas leak at the Cove Point, Maryland, LNG terminal ignited within an electrical substation, leading to two deaths and extensive property damage. A fourth gas-related accident occurred in 2004 in Skikda, Algeria, where an explosion killed twenty-seven workers and injured seventy-two others; investigation, however, has not established whether this was caused by an LNG leak.

LNG is a homeland security concern because the potential consequences of an LNG accident or attack could be profound. LNG is not explosive, but when it is released into open air it warms and forms a vapor pool. At the edges of the pool, a 5 to 15 percent mixture of gas to air will ignite if exposed to flame or sparks and will burn at very high temperatures until the supply of gas is exhausted. This floating vapor pool expands as the supply of gas from a leak or tank rupture continues, and can be carried or pushed for up to a mile by the wind. The heat from such a fire is high enough to ignite wood, damage metal, and cause first- or second-degree burns to humans as far as one mile from the initial release site. While there is general agreement on the dangers of LNG, there is some dispute about the details because most LNG damage estimates are based on engineering analyses rather than observation and measurement of actual, large-scale LNG incident results.

The destructive potential of an attack on LNG tankers or onshore facilities makes them potential targets for terrorists. Several methods of attack seem plausible:

- attack a tanker to release and burn its cargo;
- use a tanker to aim a vapor pool fire at an onshore target;
- direct a tanker at an onshore target and then burn its cargo;
- use explosive weapons against a moving or docked tanker;
- run an explosives-laden boat into a tanker;
- sabotage an LNG plant or vessel through a worker or crew member; or
- load a car or truck with explosives and penetrate and damage an LNG facility.

The Department of Homeland Security and others regard LNG facilities as likely targets for terrorist attack for good reasons.

Because of these risks and the very hazardous consequences of a potential LNG incident, LNG terminals and tankers use extensive security measures. The location of LNG terminals is regulated by the Federal Energy Regulatory Commission (FERC). The FERC, the Coast Guard, and the Department of Transportation regulate and inspect facility safety and security. LNG terminal safety features include spill containment; fire-protection systems; gas, flame, smoke, and temperature detection and alarm systems; automatic and manual shut-down controls; and a barrier-enclosed security perimeter.

For LNG tankers, design and construction standards were established by the International Maritime Organization and upgraded by the Maritime Transportation Security Act of 2002. The U.S. Coast Guard requires tankers to follow strict security procedures as they approach and enter a port, including ninety-two-hour advance notification before arrival, harbor escort by marshals, limited port and airspace traffic to prevent collisions, on-board inspections, and verification of crew member identities.

Despite these precautions, LNG tankers and terminals remain a high-impact target, attractive to those intent on killing large numbers of people. The number of import terminals in the United States is set to increase, but government policy can help prevent or limit their development in densely populated areas. Our best defense is to deny our adversaries these deadly opportunities.

RECOMMENDATIONS

The federal government has a critical role in reducing the probability of the catastrophic failure of the nation's energy infrastructure. Policy measures are needed to:

8.1. RELOCATE THE MOST VULNERABLE ASSETS, SUCH AS LNG TERMINALS, AWAY FROM POPULATION CENTERS. Where this is not feasible, mandate increased security measures.

8.2. INCREASE THE REDUNDANCY OF OUR ENERGY INFRASTRUCTURE TO REDUCE VULNERABILITY.
Redundancy entails creating both extra capacity within the network and backup capability to be used if part of the network fails. The latter is expensive but the former can increase system efficiency without significantly increasing the cost of delivered energy.

8.3. INCREASE SYSTEM RESILIENCY AND RECOVERY SPEED.
Federal assistance for nationally critical investments can improve system resiliency and service restoration speed. Measures that improve recovery include careful planning and practice, maintaining inventories of parts that require a long lead time to replace, and effective relationship building and communications before and after the emergency.

8.4. STRENGTHEN OTHER INFRASTRUCTURES AND SYSTEMS, THOSE THAT BOTH SUPPORT AND DEPEND ON ENERGY SYSTEMS.
A region with effective first responders, acute care capabilities, and backup power supplies for telecommunications, sewage, and water will be better prepared for energy system failures. In the long run, it is more cost effective to prepare for worst case outcomes than to respond to failures.

8.5. FOCUS ON ENERGY SECURITY, THAT IS, THE LONG-TERM AVAILABILITY OF RELIABLE, AFFORDABLE ENERGY SUPPLIES TO THE NATION.
Because much of America's critical petroleum infrastructure is overseas, our oil and natural gas imports (with the exception of those from Canada and Mexico) must arrive by tanker, through maritime chokepoints like the Strait of Hormuz (at the entrance to the Persian Gulf), the Panama and Suez canals, and the Strait of Malacca (linking the Indian and Pacific Oceans).

Sudden increases in energy price levels can have dramatic consequences on domestic manufacturing competitiveness and in human social and physical comfort levels, as illustrated by the oil price shock of 1973 and the natural gas and gasoline price shocks of 2005. The United States should take proactive steps to reduce energy imports by making our vehicles, buildings, and business processes more energy-efficient. We must also invest more in wind, solar, and biomass technologies—especially near urban centers and critical security assets that face attacks on conventional energy facilities. The federal government must use grants and tax incentives to expand and diversify our energy portfolio and reduce the need for long-distance fuel transportation.

8.6. INCREASE THE USE OF SMALL-SCALE DISTRIBUTED GENERATION (INCLUDING RENEWABLES AND COMBINED HEAT AND POWER) CLOSE TO ENERGY USERS. This would reduce our dependence on large-scale power plants and long-distance transmission lines, which are more inviting targets for attack and have greater consequences when they fail. Distributed generation is particularly needed to support other critical infrastructures such as telecommunications, sewage, and water, as well as to support natural gas and petroleum pipeline operations, so these infrastructures can continue operating in the event of a power outage.

8.7. INCREASE INVESTMENT IN RESEARCH, DEVELOPMENT, AND DEPLOYMENT OF DESIGNS THAT WILL MAKE ENERGY INFRASTRUCTURES AND NETWORKS MORE RESILIENT AND RESISTANT TO FAILURE.

◆ ◆ ◆

Given the critical role of energy in supporting our economy and our way of life, our nation needs to invest significantly more attention, priority, and money to make our energy infrastructure and sources more reliable and secure. These investments will cause modest increases in the short-term cost of energy, but the long-term benefits of more reliable and secure energy systems are surely worth it.

9. CYBER SECURITY
A SILENT CATASTROPHE

Cyber attacks occur every day and we easily grow inured to them; it is easy to overlook the fact that our digitally driven economy can be paralyzed by a well planned and executed cyber attack. Today cyber security and contingency planning for cyber attacks is overshadowed by a necessary preoccupation with planning for terrorist assaults involving conventional explosives or weapons of mass destruction. It is a grave mistake, however, to ignore the security and reliability of the information infrastructure. The security of cyberspace is essential to national security and to the economy because financial services, communications, transportation, energy, and the military sectors rely entirely upon cyberspace-based systems without which they could not function.

As with physical attacks, protection, prevention, and recovery from a cyber attack requires careful planning and coordination. The major difference between a physical attack and a cyber attack is that in the case of a cyber attack, there are no citizens or first responders to assist with the crisis. Protection, response, and recovery will primarily be in the hands of technical specialists, including security and networking engineers from technology providers and owners and operators of infrastructure. The role of the federal government is to ensure that these private actors have the necessary capabilities and can deliver a coordinated response.

Standards setting, planning, and coordination between sectors must be led by the federal government. Today, however, little federal leadership exists in the area of cyber security and the talk of "partnership" with the private sector is largely rhetoric. While the policies of the Clinton and Bush administrations have explicitly rejected federal regulation to achieve cyber security, Congress has repeatedly enacted laws that resulted in cyber security regulation for specific sectors. Despite this schizophrenic federal attitude toward regulation, or perhaps because of it, there has been no clearly articulated set of cyber security standards.

Cyber vulnerabilities are ubiquitous in both government and the private sector. Cyber security is an instance of both market and regulatory failure.

As the information infrastructure becomes increasingly complex, the path to a more stable, secure, and resilient information infrastructure must be facilitated by the federal government with strong, concise leadership.

The administration must move swiftly to establish a national information assurance policy, with a clear set of priorities:

◆   clarify federal agency roles and responsibilities during a crisis;
◆   clearly differentiate overlapping Department of Homeland Security (DHS) and Department of Defense (DoD) activities;
◆   bring clarity and consistency to federal regulation of cyber security across the different sectors;
◆   build a rapid response and recovery capability; and
◆   initiate a concerted research and development effort to develop and deploy resilient networks.

In this chapter, we will review the threat from cyber attacks, discuss the importance of federal leadership for cyber security, lay out the principles that should guide the development of a National Information Assurance Policy, review existing strategies and directives that can inform such a policy, and offer additional detail on the elements of the policy.

THE THREAT

There are two kinds of threat in cyberspace. First, criminals and espionage organizations routinely exploit vulnerabilities in cyberspace to steal identities, extort money, and collect sensitive information. These attacks cost the economy billons and disrupt the lives of millions of Americans. Second, terrorist groups or state actors have the potential to destroy or disrupt essential components of our economy and national security infrastructure via cyber attack. The fact that these attacks have not yet taken place does not mean that they cannot occur. There is a consensus among academic, industry, and intelligence community experts that such crippling attacks are possible. Indeed, a Chinese military leader openly admitted that China would use such attacks on America in the event of hostilities.[1] The existence of large, new Information Warfare units in the U.S. military suggests that the American government is also readying offensive cyber attack capability. It is not, however, readying commensurate defensive capability to protect the private sector assets upon which the U.S. government and economy rely. We must assume that information systems will be subject to large-scale attack. It is essential that we protect and plan for attacks against information systems alone, and in combination with "traditional" terrorist attacks involving explosives or weapons of mass destruction.

THE IMPORTANCE OF FEDERAL LEADERSHIP

Since the transfer of this issue to the Department of Homeland Security, the importance of cyber security as a federal focus has diminished significantly. Federal research and development (R&D) on cyber security has plummeted. The public-private partnership that had been built to address cyber security challenges has withered. The implementation of the president's own National Strategy to Secure Cyberspace has returned action on only two recommendations. This administration's failure to address cyber security is recognized in the private sector and Congress. It reflects the low priority given to the issue by a department dominated by traditional police agencies and focused solely on the threat of incidents that create "body bags." At the core of this potential disaster exists a lack of understanding of cyberspace at senior levels in the administration, little comprehension of the potential damage from cyber attacks, and an ideological opposition to solutions that involve regulation of cyber security or new federal entities to protect cyberspace. As a result, administration action on cyber security has been limited, slow, and often confined to rhetoric rather than action.

While the private sector has a significant role to play in the protection of critical information infrastructure, DHS is supposed to serve as the nation's point of coordination for all such efforts. Developing a national information assurance policy requires strong leadership from the federal government, in particular the Department of Homeland

Security. Though the responsibilities of DHS can remain narrowly defined, they are nonetheless significant to U.S. economic and national security. DHS is the focal point for the prevention, response, and recovery from cyber security incidents that can have a debilitating impact on our national and economic security. Senior DHS leadership is needed to build an effective public-private relationship, to understand the technical and global complexities of cyber security, and to marshal the resources necessary to provide an effective partnership with private sector organizations and initiatives. In July 2005, Secretary Chertoff announced the creation of an assistant secretary for cyber security and telecommunications, but to date, the post remains unfilled.

FOUR PRINCIPLES OF CYBER SECURITY POLICY

Before a discussion of current policy and the necessary subsequent steps, readers should understand four basic rules about the security and reliability of the global information infrastructure. These rules should also guide the development of our national information assurance policy.

I. CYBERSPACE IS A TOUGH NEIGHBORHOOD

Significant disruptions occur every day. Two separate backbone providers suffered large-scale outages in fall 2005, one due to an error in router configuration and the other because of cuts in fiber connections at two separate locations. While these were not attacks, restoration of the systems required "powering down" routers and bringing them back online slowly. The speed with which attacks spread is accelerating as they become more sophisticated: In 1999 the Melissa virus took three days to cross the Internet; in 2001 Code Red took only minutes; and in 2003 the SQL Slammer worm spread within seconds. Heading from 2005 into 2006 we saw the first significant "zero day" attack. "Zero day" attacks are significant because they give operators little or no time to react. As a reminder, the 2003 Northeast blackout spread within 43 seconds. This brings new meaning to a "bolt from the blue."

II. We Must Expect Some Serious Attacks to Succeed

Despite the best efforts to protect and monitor information networks, ultimately some attacks will disrupt information networks or corrupt data. Cyber attackers face few consequences for their attacks because the probability of being caught or killed is infinitesimal. This presents two important implications. First, we must be prepared to reconstitute networks. Second, we must build networks that can withstand attack or degrade slowly.

III. Cyber Attacks Are Diverse and Evolving

Beyond worms, viruses, and denial-of-service attacks, we must also acknowledge more insidious attacks. For example, the slow, quiet manipulation or corruption of financial or health care data (blood types or medication assignments and distribution), or logistics and shipping data, could have a devastating impact; the results could be catastrophic and difficult to untangle. We must also think about reliability and quality of service. Unexplained spot outages in networks will cause a loss of confidence in the availability of information networks. This issue could be particularly vexing as we transition to Voice over Internet Protocol (VOIP) communications.

IV. Information Technology Will Continue to Evolve Rapidly

The pace of convergence between the public service telephone network and IP networks is accelerating. New technologies such as radio frequency identification tags and nanotechnology are being deployed more widely than ever. In the past year, several cities including Philadelphia, Portland, and New Orleans have announced the deployment of citywide wireless networks to support both citizen and emergency responders.[2] San Francisco is soliciting bids. Increased reliance will lead to increased vulnerability.

THE EXISTING POLICY FRAMEWORK

Though we lack an overall information assurance policy, three documents provide a framework for federal responsibilities to secure cyberspace: the president's National Strategy to Secure Cyberspace (February 14, 2003); Homeland Security Presidential Directive 7 (HSPD-7, December 17, 2003); and the National Response Plan's Cyber Incident Annex (January 6, 2005).

PRESIDENT'S NATIONAL STRATEGY TO SECURE CYBERSPACE

The president's National Strategy is an appropriate place to start. While its recommendations have received substantial attention, the role envisaged for the federal government is equally important. The president's cover letter for the strategy states:

> The policy of the United States is to protect against the debilitating disruption of the operation of information systems for critical infrastructures and thereby help to protect the people, economy, and national security of the United States. . . . We must act to reduce our vulnerabilities to these threats before they can be exploited to damage the cyber systems supporting our nation's critical infrastructure and ensure that such disruptions of cyberspace are infrequent, of minimal duration, manageable and cause the least damage possible.

The strategy adds some additional guidance on the federal role, noting that it is appropriate for the government to assist with forensics, attribute the attack to given perpetrators, protect networks and systems critical to national security, interpret indications and warnings, and protect against organized attacks capable of inflicting debilitating damage to the economy.

Additionally, the strategy holds that the federal government should support research and development that will enable the private sector to secure its critical infrastructure.

The strategy also assigns specific responsibilities to federal agencies, including the Department of Homeland Security. The strategy states that the department should:

- develop a comprehensive plan to secure critical infrastructure;[3]
- provide crisis management and technical assistance to the private sector with respect to recovery plans for failure of critical information systems;
- coordinate with other federal agencies to provide specific warning information and advice about appropriate protective measures and countermeasures to state, local, and non-governmental organizations, including the private sector, academia, and the public; and
- perform and fund research and development along with other agencies that will lead to new scientific understanding and technologies in support of homeland security.

Notably the strategy does not place responsibility for every problem associated with cyber security with DHS, but focuses its role on contingency planning and emergency communications.

HSPD-7

HSPD-7 establishes the U.S. government's policy for the identification and protection of critical infrastructure that, if attacked, would cause catastrophic health effects or mass casualties comparable to a weapon of mass destruction. It advances the president's strategy in a number of areas and helps further refine the federal government's role in securing cyberspace. As discussed previously, HSPD-7 focuses on attacks that would:

- undermine state and local government capacities to maintain order and to deliver minimum essential public services;
- damage the private sector's capability to ensure the orderly functioning of the economy and delivery of essential services;

* have a negative effect on the economy through the cascading disruption of other critical infrastructure and key resources; and
* undermine the public's morale and confidence in our national economic and political institutions.

HSPD-7 designated the Department of Homeland Security as a focal point for information infrastructure protection, including cyber security, stating: "The Secretary will continue to maintain an organization to serve as a focal point for the security of cyberspace. The organization's mission includes analysis, warning, information sharing, vulnerability reduction, mitigation, and aiding national recovery efforts for critical infrastructure information systems."

THE NATIONAL RESPONSE PLAN'S CYBER INCIDENT ANNEX

The National Response Plan (NRP) upholds the president's National Strategy to Secure Cyberspace and HSPD-7. The NRP Cyber Incident Annex states that the federal government plays a significant role in managing intergovernmental (federal, state, local, and tribal) and, where appropriate, public-private coordination in response to cyber incidents of national significance.

EXISTING FEDERAL REGULATION

While the policies outlined above explicitly reject federal regulation to achieve cyber security, Congress has enacted laws that resulted in cyber security regulation. Among those laws are:

* the Federal Information Security Management Act, which regulates security on U.S. government cyber systems;
* the Banking Modernization Act, which directed eight federal regulatory agencies to establish cyber security standards and audit the agencies to ensure their compliance;
* the Health Insurance Portability and Accountability Act, which

authorized the Department of Health and Human Services to audit and enforce cyber security standards, although little has been done to implement the law;

♦   the Energy Act of 2005, which provides the Federal Energy Regulatory Commission with authority to create cyber security standards for the electrical power grid; and

♦   the Sarbanes-Oxley Act of 2002, which resulted in the creation of cyber security standards for publicly traded companies, audited by third-party accounting firms.

BUILDING THE NATIONAL INFORMATION ASSURANCE POLICY

The national information assurance policy would formally establish a framework for protecting the information infrastructure. It would build on the National Strategy to Secure Cyberspace and HSPD-7. The policy would clarify roles and responsibilities and reconcile the number of groups involved in information infrastructure policy setting. It would clearly articulate a set of cyber security standards, developed in conjunction with the nation's experts in the field, and implemented across sectors. It would focus R&D efforts on creating more resilient networks. In support of this directive, an annual report should be prepared for the president's approval, including a requirements-driven multiyear budget, R&D plan, and role and mission statements for all relevant agencies, including the Department of Defense, the FBI, the CIA, the National Security Agency, and the DHS.

DRAWING ON THE EXISTING FRAMEWORK

The president's strategy, HSPD-7, and the National Response Plan yield a possible two-tier framework for federal action.

TIER ONE—FUNCTIONS CRITICAL TO U.S. ECONOMIC AND NATIONAL SECURITY

- Identify and prioritize critical information infrastructure that, if disrupted, would have a debilitating impact on critical infrastructure or systems essential to U.S. economic or national security.
- Prepare for such contingencies by ensuring survivable communication networks among key critical information infrastructure operations in the government and private sector.
- Prepare contingency plans in the event of a disruption that include crisis management and restoration of critical networks, and regularly exercise, test, and refine these plans.
- Provide for situational awareness and possible warning of attack or disruption to critical infrastructure owners and operators from resources or capabilities that are not available to the private sector, through such means as intelligence.

TIER TWO—FUNCTIONS THAT IMPROVE COORDINATION, AWARENESS, EDUCATION, AND PERSONNEL READINESS

- Facilitate coordination between individual sectors of the economy by establishing appropriate government advisory committees.
- Facilitate and support general awareness among all information system users, including home users and small businesses.
- Track trends and costs associated with information infrastructure attacks and disruptions, through such means as the U.S. Computer Emergency Response Team (U.S.-CERT).
- Coordinate and support long-term research and development for cyber security.

CLARIFYING ROLES

At least eight agencies and organizations address pieces of the cyber security puzzle. Several have overlapping responsibilities and membership. In addition, a plethora of committees and commissions are active, including the President's Homeland Security Advisory Council (PHSAC), the President's Council on Science and Technology, the National Security Telecommunications Advisory Council (NSTAC), the National Infrastructure Advisory Council (NIAC), the Federal Communications Commission's (FCC) National Reliability and Interoperability Council (NRIC), the Committee on Foreign Investments in the United States (CFIUS), and the Committee on National Security Systems (CNSS). One committee should be designated for these roles and should reside in the White House.

For operational issues, the directive would seek to clarify DHS and DoD roles in an incident of "national significance." DHS is responsible for coordinating the response to such an event. However, federal civil capabilities could quickly be overwhelmed, and DoD would be called upon to take a leading role. It is imperative that clear lines of authority be drawn to ensure the federal government can effectively respond to such an incident.

The DoD's role with regard to indications and warning (I&W) should also be examined. Currently the DoD's I&W program appears almost exclusively focused on securing its own assets. While this is understandable, it is potentially a crucial mistake, particularly given that privately operated information infrastructure—rather than Defense infrastructure—may be the real target of a terrorist or nation-state attack. The DoD should expand its indications and warning program to include information on potential action against key elements of the private sector, including banking and finance, transportation, energy, and health care. The DoD's efforts must be fully integrated into a national cyber attack sensing, warning, and response capability.

ENHANCING FEDERAL CAPABILITIES

In order to support this policy, the federal government must build two essential capabilities in conjunction with the private sector:

◆ a synoptic, real-time view of the condition of key cyber nodes and systems throughout the United States; and

- a highly developed and regularly exercised plan to restore secure cyber connectivity, on a prioritized basis, after a significant attack on cyber systems.

To achieve these two capabilities, the federal government will need the following:

- presidential leadership on cyber security and a presidentially empowered, high-level coordinator;
- legislative changes concerning pubic-private partnerships and information sharing and protection;
- legislative changes to the Wartime Production Act to bring those emergency powers into the information age;
- increased sentencing guidelines that treat cyber crimes as real crimes and deter would-be hackers; and
- joint exercises involving the DHS and the DoD, as well as key players in the private sector, should be held to test capabilities and coordination. The DoD should be requested to develop contingency plans for all critical assets, not just those that are critical to the DoD.

BUILDING AND SUPPORTING RESILIENT NETWORKS

The U.S. government, in coordination with the private sector, must accelerate the development of more resilient information networks and systems. Critical elements of the information infrastructure must be resilient and have the ability to degrade gracefully. Ultimately, the United States should strive for self-healing information networks. Of most critical concern are the basic protocols that support the Internet. These include the Domain Name System (DNS), the routing infrastructure, and the current Internet Protocol (IPv4). These protocols are vital to the operation of the Internet, but suffer the "tragedy of the commons" because no entity is responsible for them. An attack against an obscure but important protocol could cause widespread disruption.

A "secure and reliable" DoD network sitting on top of an inherently vulnerable infrastructure will do little good. DoD should invest money in partnership with DHS and the National Science Foundation to develop new secure networks that will replace today's Internet. The President's Information Technology Advisory Committee (PITAC) report, released in 2005, calls for urgent attention to cyber security R&D. The PITAC report lists ten areas requiring additional research, including authentication, monitoring, securing fundamental protocols, holistic system security, mitigation and recovery, and cyber forensics. Unfortunately, the PITAC was allowed to lapse and its work will now be assumed by the President's Council on Science and Technology. The directive called for above should include R&D and set forth a ten-year plan for developing and deploying secure and reliable information systems.

The vast majority of work in this area rests on research and development. Unfortunately, cyber security has been left by the wayside in terms of federal funding for research and development, and much of DoD's work in information security remains classified. For example:

- Defense Advanced Research Projects Agency. The FY 2005 budget for cyber security R&D is $50 million to $100 million and is mostly spent on classified projects for DoD.
- Advanced Research and Development Agency. The FY 2005 budget of $17 million for cyber security R&D focuses entirely on the intelligence community.
- Department of Homeland Security. The FY 2005 budget was $16 million. The budget will likely be cut again and could drop below $15 million, limiting the capability to continue existing activities. This R&D activity is focused on key aspects of the cyber infrastructure, including DNS, routing, process control systems/SCADA, and national test-beds and test data.
- National Science Foundation. This agency has the largest piece of the budget for cyber security R&D, at over $70 million, largely supporting basic research and other grant projects within the higher academic system.

RECOMMENDATIONS

The federal government and the private sector may mistakenly choose to tolerate the rampant criminal activity in cyberspace, but the nation cannot allow a successful terrorist or nation-state cyber attack on essential national capabilities. Nor can the federal government assume that it is necessary to protect only the systems of the Department of Defense. The task force, therefore, highlights the following recommendations:

9.1. A NEW NATIONAL INFORMATION ASSURANCE POLICY SHOULD FORMALLY ESTABLISH A FRAMEWORK FOR PROTECTING CRITICAL CYBER SYSTEMS.

9.2. THE DIRECTIVE SHOULD CLARIFY ROLES AND RESPONSIBILITIES, ELIMINATING OVERLAPPING RESPONSIBILITIES.

9.3. A SINGLE COMMITTEE SHOULD REPLACE THE SIX THAT CURRENTLY ADVISE THE FEDERAL GOVERNMENT ON CYBER SECURITY AND SHOULD RESIDE IN THE WHITE HOUSE.

9.4. THE POSITION OF CYBER CZAR SHOULD BE REINSTATED AND, AMONG OTHER DUTIES, SHOULD HEAD THE COMMITTEE.

9.5. JOINT EXERCISES INVOLVING DHS AND DoD, AS WELL AS KEY PLAYERS IN THE PRIVATE SECTOR, SHOULD BE HELD TO TEST CAPABILITIES AND COORDINATION.

9.6. DoD INDICATIONS AND WARNING EFFORTS MUST BE EXPANDED AND FULLY INTEGRATED INTO A NATIONAL CYBER ATTACK SENSING, WARNING, AND RESPONSE CAPABILITY.

9.7. THE POSITION OF ASSISTANT SECRETARY FOR CYBER SECURITY AND TELECOMMUNICATIONS MUST BE FILLED IMMEDIATELY.

9.8. A CONCERTED EFFORT MUST BE MADE TO DEVELOP AND DEPLOY RESILIENT NETWORKS.

9.9. A synoptic, real-time view of the condition of key cyber nodes and systems throughout the United States must be developed.

9.10. Legislative changes concerning pubic-private partnerships and information sharing and protection should be made.

9.11. Legislative changes to the Wartime Production Act to bring those emergency powers into the information age should be made.

9.12. Increased sentencing guidelines that treat cyber crimes as real crimes and deter would-be hackers should be put in place.

9.13. In support of this directive, an annual report should be prepared for the President for his approval, including a requirements-driven multiyear budget, research and development plan, and roles and missions statements for all relevant agencies, including the Department of Defense, the FBI, the CIA, the National Security Agency, and the DHS.

III. WHAT WASHINGTON CAN DO

10. Introduction
Federal Roles and Responsibilities

While the frontline of homeland security is at the city and state levels, the federal government remains an indispensable participant in sewing together the patchwork of vulnerable and very different localities and regions of the country. Guidelines, standards, funding, and coordination are among the federal functions that contribute to building a better deterrent and defense. And in the end, the federal government is the provider of last resort, in capabilities, financing, and leadership at the national level. This part of the report will cover the most important of those federal functions.

Following the September 11 disaster, Americans looked to the federal government to understand why and how the attacks occurred and how to protect against their recurrence. After much back and forth between the executive branch, Congress, and the public (especially the families of victims), the 9/11 Commission was established to examine the "why and how." After a veto-proof congressional majority made clear that there would be a major governmental reorganization, the administration put forward its plan for a new Department of Homeland Security (DHS).

Neither the commission's "lessons to be learned" nor the new department have fared well on the rocky ground of partisan and bureaucratic politics in Washington.

Meanwhile, the president and his team have done little more than frame the general shape and direction of where we should head—an approach that predictably has not worked within Washington's overloaded agenda. The president and his staff have devoted little time to leadership and dialogue on homeland security. Only the *9/11 Commission Report,* the Anti-Terrorism and Intelligence Reform Act, and Hurricane Katrina have broken through the barrier of White House inattention—and in each instance only briefly. At the same time, the administration's focus on fighting terrorists "over there so we don't have to fight them here" has relegated homeland security efforts to the back burner.

To reverse this trend requires leadership from the president himself. The bureaucratic and congressional logjams will not be broken, the media will not provide more coverage, and the public will not begin to feel more secure until the president publicly articulates that reform is a top priority. Presidential leadership will need to extend further in the form of regular and public acts by the president and the White House, as well as by cabinet members and other officials, to ensure that programs that are announced are actually implemented and that government officials are held accountable for failure.

In addition to greater presidential commitment, the White House needs an organizational revamping to deal with homeland security. The initial response to September 11 was to establish a homeland security advisor and a homeland security council to parallel the national security structure in the White House. While the expectation was that such a structure would accord the function the high-profile attention that national security issues receive, it quickly became a way to push homeland security issues to the back burner while still claiming that they were important. This became all too clear when the Department of Homeland Security was established and the White House staff was immediately reduced. The rationale was that the new department was to take over much of the White House function. But when Katrina arrived, it became clear that the White House had little ability to effect an adequate response.

While no organizational arrangement can ensure proper attention without presidential leadership, the Homeland Security Council would benefit greatly from integration into the National Security Council (NSC) staff structure. Most homeland security problems are international in scope because they involve the movement of people, technology, finance, services, and goods across our borders. The borderless technological revolution, which involves rapid advances in information technology, biotechnology, nanotechnology, and materials science (along with the synergistic intersection of these advances), provides U.S. adversaries with unprecedented opportunities to kill Americans wherever they reside in the world. Homeland security is national security and merits the same priority. White House oversight should reside in the NSC.

The NSC has the history and the credibility to provide the homeland security issue with enhanced status within the executive branch. Such integration would also demonstrate that homeland security is an inseparable component of national security, and one that must be coordinated with other national security elements.

Integrating Homeland Security with National Security

To accommodate homeland security within the NSC structure, there would need to be a deputy national security advisor (DAPNSA) for homeland security and a deputy for crisis management. The former would look primarily at intelligence, law enforcement, and other prevention and standard-setting issues; the latter would manage the full range of national security crises for the National Security Advisor and run the situation room and a national exercise program as well.

These two officials would be responsible for coordination of policy and operations in their respective domains, regardless of whether the jurisdiction was domestic or foreign. These functions had been carried out by the Counterterrorism and Security Group in the Clinton administration, but should be institutionalized in the White House and staffed by individuals with direct access to the president as soon as possible. These deputy national security advisors would also serve as essential links between the federal government and state and local authorities. Both deputies would require support staff.

Under the DAPNSA for homeland security, the president should appoint a special advisor for cyber security, as recommended in Chapter 9, and a special advisor for emergency preparedness. The roles of the special adviser for emergency preparedness are described more fully in Chapter 11 on fixing the Federal Emergency Management Agency (FEMA).

In Chapter 5, we endorsed the strategy of creating infrastructure protection regional security offices as proposed in the Chemical Facility Anti-Terrorism Act of 2005. These regional offices would be established in each of the eight FEMA regions. Such a regional approach should be taken for intelligence and other homeland security functions. The resources and authority of the existing FEMA regions should also be strengthened. Tremendous synergies could be achieved by developing a strategic plan for the diffusion of federal homeland security staff, resources, and authorities to these regions.

We make these recommendations reluctantly, realizing that the parade of reorganizations imposed on federal agencies has weakened the nation's ability to respond. Reorganization is not a substitute for implementation, adequate resources, or capable management. Fixing homeland security policy and management, removing FEMA from the morass of DHS, and pushing authority down to the regional level are all necessary but are not sufficient steps toward securing our homeland.

The administration and Congress need to restrain their longstanding tendency to adopt structural solutions to functional problems. Although the political costs of fixing or streamlining existing organizations are high, the cost of massive reorganization is higher. We therefore recommend a halt in further homeland reorganization for at least five years in order to digest the structures that currently exist. While the organization is not perfect, further tinkering will create only organizational and personnel turbulence without a corresponding enhancement of organizational capabilities.

The homeland security budget, across all of the departments and agencies that receive homeland security funding, must be treated as an integrated budget rather than simply the sum of departmental requests. The budget must support a strategy with clear goals, objectives, and requirements, and the existence and size of programs must depend on their relative priority in the strategy and not *ex post facto* rationalizations. We need to address issues such as the balance between funding at the local, state, and federal levels, the ways in which information is shared within and between levels of government—given that the federal government controls the classified information system, the setting of standards, and the writing of regulations—and the balance between civil liberties and security.

Finally, the executive branch should continue to press for the reform of congressional jurisdiction. The 9/11 Commission, the White House, the Robb-Silberman Commission, former House leaders Newt Gingrich and Tom Foley, and others have strongly recommended that the two houses of Congress be reorganized to consolidate homeland security oversight in one policy authorization committee and one appropriations subcommittee in each chamber. Instead of that four-committee structure, Congress has continued a fractionated approach. Despite the creation of the House Committee on Homeland Security and the Homeland Security and Governmental Affairs Committee in the Senate, as the Committee for Public Discourse noted, the Transportation Security Administration (TSA), the Coast Guard, Bureau of Customs and Border Patrol, and other agencies continue to report to other committees.[1] Balkanized in this way, Congress cannot fulfill its oversight responsibility for this important national priority. The refusal to yield turf by committee chairs and by the party leaders in both houses reflects an unwillingness to place national over personal interest. It is Congress at its worst. Until Congress consolidates oversight and empowers a few committee chairs to address homeland security, the legislative branch must share responsibility for the failure of the federal government to prepare the nation to disrupt, or recover from, the next attack.

RECOMMENDATIONS

10.1. ABOLISH THE HOMELAND SECURITY COUNCIL AND STRENGTHEN HOMELAND SECURITY POLICY AND FUNCTIONALITY WITHIN THE NATIONAL SECURITY COUNCIL.

10.2. ESTABLISH DHS DOMESTIC REGIONS TO PUSH DISASTER MANAGEMENT, INFRASTRUCTURE PROTECTION, AND INTELLIGENCE OUT TO STATES AND LOCALITIES. These should be based on the eight existing FEMA regions.

10.3. REESTABLISH FEMA AS AN INDEPENDENT CABINET-LEVEL AGENCY.

10.4. RESIST STRUCTURAL SOLUTIONS TO FUNCTIONAL PROBLEMS.

10.5. PROVIDE ADEQUATE FUNDING FOR HOMELAND SECURITY MISSIONS UNDER AN INTEGRATED HOMELAND SECURITY BUDGET STRATEGY.

10.6. PUSH FOR CONGRESSIONAL REFORM TO LIMIT THE NUMBER OF COMMITTEES WITH JURISDICTION OVER HOMELAND SECURITY OPERATIONS.

11. EMERGENCY RESPONSE
RESTORING DISCARDED STRATEGIES THAT WORKED

Americans who witnessed the ineffectiveness of the government's response to Hurricane Katrina can reach no other conclusion than that the nation is ill-prepared to manage a disaster—whether natural or man-made. The Bush administration's recently released *Report on Lessons Learned from Hurricane Katrina* includes 125 recommendations and eleven critical actions to be completed by June 1, 2006, which is the start of hurricane season. Unfortunately, even if those changes were to be implemented in full, they would not significantly improve the government's capability to respond to a comparable catastrophe. The report's recommendations would actually worsen the situation by further fragmenting responsibility for disaster response: the Department of Transportation will now become responsible for evacuation planning, the Department of Housing and Development will be responsible for temporary housing, and the Department of Health and Human Services (HHS) will be responsible for providing human services. The report also discusses at length the need to improve the National Response Plan and all other relevant federal bureaucratic procedures. But many of its recommendations require legislative action by Congress and therefore could take years to accomplish; since the report is silent on sources of funding for its recommendations, many are not even feasible without significant increases in funding.

A much more promising approach would be to emulate past experience in the 1990s, when the Federal Emergency Management Agency (FEMA) became widely recognized as effective after a variety of reforms were instituted. Many of the reasons why it failed in the aftermath of Katrina were an outgrowth of actions taken by the Bush administration. Rather than compound those mistakes by further diluting responsibilities and capabilities for emergency response, it would be much wiser to reconstruct the system that previously worked well.

A BRIEF EMERGENCY RESPONSE HISTORY

The emergency management system in the United States is built on a partnership of federal, state, and local emergency operations that practice comprehensive emergency management in four basic areas—preparedness, mitigation, response, and recovery. Those governmental partnerships are augmented by nonprofit groups such as the American Red Cross, the Salvation Army, and the members of the National Voluntary Organizations Active in Disasters. In recent years, there has been an effort at all levels of government to include participation by the private sector in the system.

FEMA leads all emergency management efforts at the federal level. It was established by President Jimmy Carter in 1979, in response to several disasters, including the incident at the Three Mile Island nuclear power plant. Under pressure from state and local officials and the National Governors Association, Carter combined programs, people, and resources from other federal agencies to create FEMA as an agency focused on building and coordinating a national emergency management capability. Throughout the 1980s, the agency was hampered by poor leadership and a Cold War emphasis on planning for a nuclear attack. In the late 1980s, the inability of FEMA to effectively respond to Hurricane Hugo, the Loma Prieta earthquake, and Hurricane Andrew led members of Congress to call for eliminating the agency.

FEMA's turnaround was engineered when President Bill Clinton elevated it to cabinet-level status and appointed as its leader James Lee Witt, who had been Arkansas' director of emergency management and gained valuable experience managing the consequences of major flooding there. Throughout the 1990s, Witt, with Clinton's strong support, carried out sweeping reforms inside and outside the agency. He supported using new technologies to expedite the delivery of disaster services and focused on preparedness and mitigation of risks. Outside the agency, he strengthened relationships with state and local emergency managers and built new relationships with Congress, within the administration, and with the media.

FEMA is the lead coordinator for the National Response Plan (NRP), which is an agreement with thirty-two other federal agencies and the American Red Cross designed to bring their full resources to bear on catastrophic events. Each signatory to the NRP agrees to make targeted assets rapidly available in a contingency, and to accept the direction of FEMA in deploying these assets. FEMA manages the collection and analysis of information that serves as the basis for "mission assignments" for the federal departments and agencies that participate in the NRP and reimburses these departments and agencies for all of their expenses.

The NRP is activated by a presidential disaster declaration. When a disaster—natural or man-made—occurs, local government and its cadre of firefighters, police, emergency medical technicians, and other emergency personnel are the first to respond. If the event overwhelms local resources and capabilities, the mayor or county executive appeals for assistance from the state government. The governor then dispatches state resources to assist in the response. When state resources are overwhelmed, the governor makes a direct appeal to the president for federal assistance. FEMA evaluates the governor's appeal and makes a recommendation to the president. The decision to make a disaster declaration is the president's alone. When such a declaration is made, FEMA activates the NRP and coordinates and directs all federal response efforts in support of state and local officials. For natural disasters that can be anticipated, such as hurricanes, presidential declarations are often made in advance of the event to allow for pre-deployment of assets to assist in evacuations and to hasten the response.

FEMA's coordinating role in response to national disasters was conducted successfully during such major events as the 1993 Midwest floods, the Northridge earthquake, the Oklahoma City bombing, and Hurricane Floyd. Its effectiveness helped to build the trust of the American people that the government could be relied upon in a crisis.

THE KATRINA MELTDOWN

In many respects, FEMA's Katrina failures were a predictable outgrowth of steps that were taken over the course of the Bush administration. First, in the aftermath of September 11, FEMA lost its status as an independent agency—and its direct access to the president—when it was absorbed into the newly created Department of Homeland Security (DHS). The director of FEMA was no longer on a par with the cabinet secretaries FEMA had to task and direct during disasters. At the state level, many states created their own offices of homeland security that subsumed emergency management or were competitive structures, further complicating emergency response organization.

Second, FEMA personnel and funds, including money for preparedness and mitigation intended for state and local agencies, were redistributed to support other higher priorities within DHS. The agency was even further hollowed out.

Third, the federal response plan was restructured into the National Response Plan to accommodate the new DHS arrangements and the operational oversight role of the department's secretary. A new level of bureaucracy was added with the creation of the principal federal officer (PFO) as the new coordinator in a disaster. Where previously the director of FEMA had had a clear line of authority and accountability, the existence of a new PFO created confusion over who would be in charge in a disaster. As a result, the necessary civilian and military assets were not deployed to facilitate the evacuations and provide supplies to the evacuation shelters before Katrina hit. FEMA also failed to work with the governors on how to use the National Guard. These problems were exacerbated by the inexperience of both brand-new DHS secretary Chertoff and the relatively new FEMA director, Michael Brown.

A fourth factor was the dramatic post–September 11 change from a focus on "all-hazards" management—in which responders prepare for calamities according to plans that apply regardless of their precise nature—to a focus on terrorism that led to significantly weakened national capabilities. At all levels of government, approximately 75 percent of available resources for emergency management activities was applied to terrorism. Preparing, mitigating, or responding to natural disasters like floods, tornadoes, or hurricanes was subordinated to a narrow, if understandable, focus on terrorism. That re-prioritization depleted capabilities to respond to disasters at all levels of government.

WHAT NOW?

The resignation of Michael Brown as FEMA director will not solve the problem. The system is broken and, until it is fixed, state and local governments and the American people cannot count on the federal government to support them in disasters. Fortunately, repairing the system is well within our means. The model that should guide federal reform is the FEMA that worked so well throughout the 1990s. Maintaining and enhancing the nation's emergency management system, especially the role of the federal government in this system, does not inherently conflict with the primary mission of DHS. In fact, it is a critical element in the overall homeland security strategy. However, there are several steps that should be taken to ensure the health and vitality of the nation's emergency management system and return the federal government to a leadership role in this area.

First and foremost, FEMA should be reestablished as an executive branch agency. In March 2004, former FEMA Director Witt, in testimony before a joint hearing of two House government reform subcommittees, strongly recommended that FEMA be removed from the Department of Homeland Security and be reestablished as an executive branch agency that reports directly to the president. Mr. Witt stated, "FEMA, having lost its status as an independent agency, is being buried beneath a massive bureaucracy whose main and seemingly only focus is fighting terrorism while an all-hazards mission is getting lost in the shuffle."[1]

Moving FEMA out of DHS and consolidating the traditional mitigation, preparedness, response, and recovery programs in FEMA would help to restore the previously effective all-hazards approach and encourage FEMA and its state and local partners to restore their focus on preparing for disasters, including terrorist attacks, as a generic challenge in many respects. Experienced emergency management professionals would resume the work of preparing the public for disasters, developing new approaches to hazard mitigation, enhancing past practices that have been shown to work, managing the resources of the federal government in support of state and local efforts, and implementing speedy and effective recovery systems.

Currently, some key federal emergency management and disaster assistance capabilities that once resided in FEMA are scattered throughout DHS and cannot be effectively managed or coordinated. Consolidating these functions in a reestablished FEMA outside of DHS would not conflict with the department's mission of preventing terrorist attacks on American soil and would enhance those critical elements in the homeland security system that would be called on when the next event occurs.

While there are costs associated with yet another reshuffling of the Department of Homeland Security, moving FEMA out of DHS will make the department's management challenges smaller, not larger. At the same time, the focus of a newly invigorated FEMA must be implementation—not reorganization. As we saw in 2005, the decision to focus on terrorism planning left the DHS ill-prepared to respond to Hurricane Katrina. By removing FEMA and adopting a true all-hazards approach, emergency management professionals will once again be in charge of preparing the public, reducing future impacts through hazard mitigation, and managing the resources of the federal government in support of state and local governments in responding to major disasters.

The legislation that authorizes FEMA to administer the federal disaster programs, the Robert T. Stafford Act, states that those programs are "supplemental to" the resources of state and local governments. But the act also recognizes that there may be unique circumstances in which it is in the best interest of the federal government to simply take over the response or management of an incident by declaring a national emergency. This authority was exercised in the aftermath of the Oklahoma City bombing. Under separate authorities, the president can federalize—or take control over—state resources such as the National Guard, as was done during the desegregation of schools in the 1960s. There has been significant discussion about the need to provide more authority to the federal government post-Katrina, particularly in light of potential quarantines from pandemic smallpox or flu. But before any additional authorities are provided to the federal government, to an independent FEMA, or to DHS, a thorough review of existing authorities and analysis of the pros and cons should be undertaken.

By reestablishing FEMA as an independent agency, the United States can rebuild its image as a world leader in disaster management. Consideration should be given to expanding FEMA's legislative authorities to operate outside the continental United States, not to usurp the authorities or programs of the Department of State, Office of Foreign Disaster Assistance (OFDA), but to complement these authorities, particularly in the areas of hazard mitigation and preparedness.

Fixing FEMA alone will not be sufficient to elevate emergency management and crisis management to the level of attention in the White House that it deserves. The president should also establish a new deputy assistant position on the National Security Council staff: the deputy national security advisor for crisis management. Until the early stages of the first Bush term, the crisis management function at the White House was carried out informally by the so-called Coordinating Sub-Group.[2] A deputy national security advisor with ready access to the president, clearly established responsibility for crisis management, and the ability to convene the National Security Council Deputies Committee to plan and manage the national response to foreign and domestic crises would fill the critical gap demonstrated by Hurricane Katrina.

Under that office, the president should establish a special assistant for emergency preparedness. The special assistant for emergency preparedness would work with the head of FEMA, and would have the clout to bring relevant government agencies and departments into a detailed process of planning, budgeting, programming, and exercising to improve our national capacity to manage the consequences of disasters—natural or manmade. Sharing both status and access to the president with their colleagues responsible for crisis management and counterterrorism would enable the team to mesh preparedness initiatives with crisis response activities.

In this system, FEMA would be the principal executive agent for federal disaster planning and liaison/coordination with state and local governments, with the White House protecting its autonomy and budget. It would also be the lead agency for federal disaster crisis management in the field, whether in support of state and local efforts or as the overall controlling organization.

Much more also needs to be done to educate and involve the public in disaster preparedness. Since September 11, the federal government has done relatively little along these lines with the exception of the Citizen Corps program and Web-based awareness campaigns, such as Ready.gov. The "Redefining Readiness" study conducted by the New York Academy of Medicine identified numerous problems with the development of federal plans to manage the effects of smallpox attacks and strikes involving dirty bombs—without input from local communities. Involving the public in developing community-based homeland security plans is critical to the successful implementation of these plans. That study made clear that citizens are ready and willing to participate in emergency planning efforts and to participate in community-based programs to cope with the new homeland security threats. Mechanisms are needed to facilitate such activities.

One good model is Project Impact, the former FEMA initiative to develop disaster-resistant communities. At its height, over 225 Project Impact communities were active across the country with support from FEMA. Each locality had created a partnership involving the many stakeholders in the community, including the business sector, to identify risks, determine how best to mitigate them, and develop and implement an action plan. The Project Impact model is based on an all-hazards approach; including new terrorism risks would be relatively straightforward. The city of Tulsa has done just this, successfully incorporating homeland security efforts into Project Impact programs that were originally developed to address flood and tornado risks. The bottom line is that the general public must be involved in the development and implementation of community homeland security plans, and DHS and its partners in state and local government should invest more resources in creating and sustaining the planning processes needed to involve the public in the nation's homeland security system.

In conjunction with those efforts, Washington needs to communicate far more effectively with the public. Thus far, DHS has shown little interest in sharing information with the public, and when it has, the results have not always been positive, as the notorious duct tape episode illustrated.[3] DHS, and its state and local partners, need to address three considerations to improve its communications with the American people.

First, there must be a commitment from the leadership, not only at DHS and its state and local partners but also at all levels of government, including the executive level, to communicate timely and accurate information to the public. This is especially important in the response and recovery phases of a terrorist incident. In a disaster scenario, the conventional wisdom that withholding information enhances one's power does not apply. In fact, in a disaster scenario—whether natural or terrorist—the sharing of information does more to help authorities stay in control of events. Two preeminent examples are former FEMA Director Witt and former New York City Mayor Rudy Giuliani. Both leaders went to great lengths to get accurate and timely information to the public during crises. Their efforts inspired the public and greatly enhanced the effectiveness of the response and recovery efforts. The DHS leadership, perhaps a bit scarred by experience, has been reluctant to make the same kind of commitment to share information with the public. This must change if they expect the American people to fully comprehend the homeland security threat and engage actively in homeland security efforts.

Second, homeland security officials at all levels must resolve the dilemmas surrounding the need to publicize information that might have value for intelligence or prosecutorial purposes, either before or after a terrorist incident. This is an issue that rarely, if ever, confronts emergency management officials dealing with natural and unintended man-made disasters. Thus, there is little precedent for current homeland security officials to apply in developing a communications strategy that balances the public's need for timely and accurate information against law enforcement or intelligence officials' need to protect intelligence sources and criminal investigations. As might be expected, the requirements of the intelligence and justice communities have outweighed the demand for public information. The temptation to ignore, or paper over, these dilemmas is therefore strong. Nevertheless, the continued frustration expressed by the public and state and local officials with the Homeland Security Advisory System (HSAS) is but one sign that this issue will not resolve itself, or simply disappear. Members of Congress and DHS Secretary Chertoff have spoken recently about reworking the HSAS. This would be a critical first step in reestablishing public trust in the warning system. From this starting point and given the commitment of the homeland security leadership, additional communication mechanisms can be developed to ensure that the public gets timely and accurate information both in advance of any terrorist incident and also during the response and recovery phases of the next terrorist attack.

Third, more effort must be invested by federal departments and agencies to better understand the principal terrorist threats that our nation faces (that is, biological, chemical, radiological, nuclear, and conventional) and develop communications strategies that educate and inform the public. The 2001 Washington, D.C., anthrax incident is a perfect example of uninformed or misinformed public officials sharing oftentime conflicting and, in too many instances, incorrect information with the public. Government officials must be better informed and ready to and capable of communicating complicated information to the public. As the anthrax incident made clear, this is not a luxury but a necessity if the response to similar incidents in the future is to be successful. Decades of research and a new generation of technologies now inform emergency managers as they provide information about hurricanes, tornadoes, earthquakes, and hazardous materials incidents to the public. Emerging, multidisciplinary work on terrorist attacks and their consequences must be made equally available to emergency managers to ensure that homeland security officials at all levels are capable of clearly explaining to the public the hazards posed by conventional and non-conventional assaults.

At the same time, emergency managers must develop communication strategies that would allow them to deploy detailed, technical information in an accessible way. Such strategies must also consider how to communicate to the public in a manner that inspires confidence, when only incomplete information is available to homeland security officials. A public health crisis will not wait for all the data to be collected and analyzed, nor will the public. This is far from an easy task but it must be done. These communication strategies must be in place prior to the next incident.

DHS SHOULD WORK WITH POLICE CHIEFS, OFFICERS, AND POLICE ASSOCIATIONS TO ESTABLISH AND EQUIP LAW ENFORCEMENT RESPONSE TEAMS (LERTs) TO REINFORCE OFFICERS IN A CATASTROPHIC ENVIRONMENT SIMILAR TO THE DISASTER MEDICAL ASSISTANTS TEAMS. While New Orleans officers did everything they could to maintain order in the wake of Hurricane Katrina, they were overwhelmed by the size of the task they faced and the loss of command and control when their radio networks failed. While mutual-aid agreements between jurisdictions are in place, they will not be of use when a catastrophic event, such as Katrina, affects all departments simultaneously. Training and equipping LERTs around the country with prepackaged standard equipment, radios, ammunition, tires, water, and food rations to self-sustain operations in an emergency can provide officials and law enforcement with the surge support they will need to maintain public safety and delivery of vital services.

Finally, DHS as well as numerous business groups, such as the Business Roundtable, acknowledge that an effective partnership between government and business must be established as part of the nation's homeland security efforts. This makes sense, since almost 85 percent of the infrastructure in this country is privately held. But in the almost five years since the September 11 attacks, the relationship between government and the private sector, as in other areas, has been arm's-length at best. There has been some progress and cooperation, but there is no overall strategy in place to incorporate the business sector into the government's emergency management planning for homeland security. There are numerous issues that must be resolved before such a strategy can be designed and implemented. One significant issue is how the government will use and protect the confidential information it is asking the business community to provide. The business community must be included in the planning process, not only for critical infrastructure protection purposes, as discussed in Part II of this report, but also for natural disaster management.

One possible avenue for establishing and nurturing an effective partnership with the business sector is to start at the community level. There is a history of public-private partnerships in emergency management at the community level that started with FEMA's Project Impact. A "bottom-up" approach to developing public-private partnerships may be the best avenue for homeland security officials at all levels to pursue.

RECOMMENDATIONS

FEMA must be reestablished as the leader of the nation's emergency management system. In that role, it must support community-based mitigation, preparedness, response, and recovery efforts; engage the general public as much as possible in that process; communicate timely and accurate information; and establish a strong and vital partnership with the business sector. Such a truly comprehensive national system of disaster management could meet the challenge of another catastrophe on the scale of Hurricane Katrina. In practical terms, this goal requires several concrete steps:

11.1. REESTABLISH FEMA AS AN INDEPENDENT CABINET-LEVEL AGENCY.

11.2. REVIEW EXISTING AUTHORITIES FOR FEDERAL MANAGEMENT OF DISASTERS WHEN LOCAL AUTHORITIES ARE OVERWHELMED.

11.3. MAKE FEMA ONCE AGAIN AN INTERNATIONAL LEADER IN EMERGENCY MANAGEMENT AND USE THE AGENCY AS A TOOL OF PUBLIC DIPLOMACY.

11.4. ESTABLISH TWO NEW WHITE HOUSE POSITIONS: deputy assistant to the president for crisis management, and special assistant to the president for emergency preparedness.

11.5. DESIGNATE FEMA AS THE EXECUTIVE AGENT FOR FEDERAL DISASTER PLANNING AND LIAISON AND COORDINATION WITH STATE AND LOCAL GOVERNMENTS and the lead agency for federal disaster crisis management in the field, whether in support of state and local efforts or as the overall controlling organization.

11.6. INVIGORATE PROJECT IMPACT and ensure that local authorities have the medical and interoperable mobile communications capabilities to spur development of "disaster-resistant" cities.

11.7. DEVELOP COMMUNICATION STRATEGIES FOR INFORMING THE PUBLIC AND INSPIRING CONFIDENCE IN CRISES, while avoiding undue risk to law enforcement or intelligence collection efforts.

11.8. FOCUS ON MAKING THE HOMELAND SECURITY ADVISORY SYSTEM USEFUL.

11.9. CREATE LAW ENFORCEMENT RESPONSE TEAMS (LERTs) TO HELP REESTABLISH ORDER FOLLOWING CATASTROPHIC INCIDENTS.

11.10. INVOLVE THE PRIVATE SECTOR IN PLANNING AND PREPARATION FOR CATASTROPHIC TERRORIST ATTACKS.

12. An Intelligence Approach to Domestic Security

In the fifth year since September 11, the nation's approach to gathering and analyzing intelligence that could prevent future terrorist attacks remains highly fragmented and susceptible to the same failures to "connect the dots."[1] The responsibility for more effectively coordinating and integrating intelligence should be assigned to the Department of Homeland Security (DHS), because its mission is to share information that could protect the public against terrorism throughout the federal government as well as in relevant state, local, and private entities. That synthesizing, coordinating, and communicating role is not appropriate for the FBI, which remains the dominant domestic intelligence-gathering institution despite its pre–September 11 failures.

The FBI was criticized extensively by the 9/11 Commission and other critics for its failure to track foreign terrorists operating within our borders and to share critical information with the CIA, State Department, National Security Council, and even within the Bureau itself. In the July 2001 "Phoenix memo," a field officer warned that certain Arab males who might be linked to Osama bin Laden were training at an Arizona flight school. FBI headquarters did not follow up. A senior agent in Minneapolis complained that headquarters repeatedly rejected her pre–September 11 requests for a warrant to wiretap and search the computer of Zaccarias Moussaoui, the alleged "twentieth hijacker."[2]

Unfortunately, there is little indication that the FBI has undertaken the kinds of fundamental reform that would prevent a recurrence of similar failures. In early February 2005, Director Robert Mueller told Congress that the $170 million Virtual Case File—a software program intended to give field agents a new capability to organize, analyze, and share data on criminal and terrorism cases—was unsalvageable. In late

March, the Commission on the Intelligence Capabilities of the United States Regarding Weapons of Mass Destruction, in a blistering review, charged that the FBI had done little since September 11 to structure, staff, and fund its new intelligence mission of preventing future terrorist attacks.

State and local governments complain that the FBI, even with its nationwide network of Joint Terrorism Task Forces (JTTFs), still tends to "serve up" to the federal bureaucracy much better than it works "down" into vulnerable localities where vital intelligence needs to be collected.[3]

The White House, surprisingly, accepted the commission's sweeping—and arguably excessive—recommendation that the FBI establish a new national security service to include the FBI's counterterrorism and counterintelligence divisions and its new Directorate of Intelligence under a single executive assistant director, all subject to "the coordination and budget authorities" of the Director of National Intelligence (the DNI, who reports directly to the president).[4] This approach is problematic because it could not be clearer from the intelligence community's experience over the past twenty-five years that it is extraordinarily difficult to blend intelligence and law enforcement, and that the FBI's long-standing orientation of investigating criminal activities is simply unsuited for a national intelligence mission. Gathering evidence to prosecute crimes, which is the FBI's historic mission, entails a fundamentally different orientation and set of practices than gathering and analyzing intelligence in order to prevent terrorism.

This chapter will argue that the problems posed by the need to collect, interpret, and use domestic intelligence are much bigger than the FBI's organization or habits. The challenge is government-wide, has roots that long precede September 11, and involves a range of deadly threats to our national security that are not restricted to international terrorism. This chapter will attempt to define the problem and assess what we have done since September 11, including mistakes made and lessons learned. And it will recommend steps we should take now—especially in terms of White House action—to transform the intelligence community, end bureaucratic turf battles, and build a more constructive relationship with Congress. Improving our intelligence capabilities is imperative if we are to confront the complicated, globally distributed, and increasingly lethal national security threats of the twenty-first century.

WHAT IS DOMESTIC INTELLIGENCE?

Domestic intelligence entails the range of activities focused on protecting the United States from threats mostly of foreign origin. Focused narrowly, it includes the FBI's counterterrorism work with local law enforcement. On a much broader scale, however, it also involves the broader set of intelligence activities overseen by the director of national intelligence (DNI), the secretary of defense, the attorney general, and the secretary of homeland security. The goal is to integrate federal, state, and local governments, and, when appropriate, the private sector in a secure collaborative network to stop our enemies before they act. Those enemies include individuals and groups attempting to transport weapons of mass destruction, international terrorists, organized criminals, narcotics traffickers, and countries that are working alone or in combination against U.S. interests. Our networks must also be prepared to manage the domestic impact of potentially catastrophic events such as global pandemics and financial crises.

Al Qaeda's attacks in New York City and Washington on September 11 revealed that Osama bin Laden had developed—below the radar of U.S. intelligence—a human and electronic network spanning some sixty countries, from pre-modern Afghanistan to post-modern Europe and the United States. Al Qaeda's flat network defeated a vast U.S. government hierarchy, including both our foreign and domestic intelligence agencies, that was not networked. The terrorists knew more about our world, and how to train and operate in it, than we did about theirs—the classic recipe for an intelligence failure. By any reckoning, the U.S. government was not prepared to protect its people, not only against international terrorism but also against the exploitation, by any of our adversaries, of global, IT-driven networks.

Domestic intelligence collectors must be networked to assemble the most reliable information, best expertise, and advanced capabilities—in real time—to deal with today's dynamic threats. It must have state-of-the-art, multilevel, and secure communications to support a broad range of activities—from assisting a big-city police officer pursue sketchy intelligence leads in a subway to helping computer experts track cyber attacks.

Of course, the domestic intelligence challenge predates September 11. It derives from three distinct but intersecting revolutions faced by the intelligence community over the past twenty years, which have encouraged trends—including greater Department of Defense influence over intelligence—that continue today. The 9/11 Commission pointed to the failure of the intelligence community, the White House, and Congress to align their priorities in addressing the need to reform prior to September 11.[5] This three-way alignment will be just as critical in implementing the intelligence community reforms legislated since the al Qaeda attacks.

The first revolution was geopolitical. It swept away the Soviet Union, transformed the face of Europe, and forced the intelligence community to confront new, dispersed global threats in which non-state actors—including conventional and cyber terrorists, narcotics traffickers, and organized criminals—operated against U.S. interests across national borders, including our own. The second revolution involved technological advances, primarily in information technology, but also the rapidly advancing biological sciences, nanotechnology, and the material sciences, all of which unleashed significant progress but also new risks. The third revolution related to homeland security in the sense that the evolving nature of threats requires new stakeholders to become involved in preventing and responding to them—yielding a legitimate need and demand for intelligence support.

The intelligence community, policymakers, and Congress actually began to respond to these changes in the mid-1980s, with the pace picking up dramatically in the ensuing decade. The director of central intelligence (DCI) established the Counterterrorism Center at the CIA in 1986, followed later by the Counternarcotics Center and several iterations of a counter-proliferation center—all mandated to focus on collecting intelligence, integrating analysis, and promoting information sharing. Both the CIA and the Defense Intelligence Agency (DIA) reorganized their intelligence units to meet new threats and upgrade their technological capabilities accordingly in the mid-1990s. In 1998, the White House established the position of national coordinator for security, infrastructure protection, and counterterrorism and appointed Richard Clarke to head it. Just prior to retiring, Clarke launched the first national strategy for cyber security, which DHS has been alarmingly slow to develop.

Advancing technology drove the controversial creation of the National Imagery and Mapping Agency (NIMA) in 1996. NIMA (later named National Geospatial-Intelligence Agency) launched a major push to get ahead of the geospatial technology curve, while the National Security Agency (NSA) began a fundamental transformation to adapt to the global revolution in communications technology. In 1998, the Ballistic Missile Commission, headed by Donald Rumsfeld, included with its report a "side letter" criticizing the intelligence community's analytic performance. Over that same period, the FBI significantly increased its overseas presence and, prodded by the Webster Commission, developed a five-year strategic plan in the late 1990s that included goals to develop a comprehensive intelligence collection and analytic capability. Late in the decade, it established separate counterterrorism and counterintelligence centers.

The FBI also participated in the work of the National Intelligence Producers Board, which did a baseline assessment of intelligence community analytic capabilities and followed up early in 2001 with a strategic investment plan for analysis. The investment plan flagged to Congress the alarming decline in investment in analysis across the community and the urgent need to build or strengthen interagency training, database interoperability, collaborative networks, a system for issue prioritization, links to outside experts, and an effective open-source strategy.[6] The consensus was strong that the intelligence community needed to transform—and it was transforming—but neither fast enough nor in alignment with the unfocused and fast-changing priorities of the White House and Congress.

Five trends were clear as the intelligence community entered the twenty-first century, and they all appear irreversible today. In one way or the other, they relate to America's current efforts to reform its intelligence services and to the particular challenge of domestic intelligence.

First, agencies were beginning seriously to respond to the growing impact of globalization. Globalization—the interconnectedness of networks moving information, culture, technology, capital, goods, and services with unprecedented speed and efficiency across the nation and around the world—came to be seen not as a passing phenomenon but as the defining reality of our age. In that context, the rationales for previous borders between foreign and domestic intelligence have dissipated.

Second, pressures within the community increasingly were toward *decentralization,* not "one-stop shopping" models—including some ambitious interpretations of the National Counterterrorism Center (NCTC)—generally favored by Washington.

Third, the Defense Department gained increasing influence in intelligence community forums and debates, including those setting budget priorities. In the late 1990s, Congress created the positions of deputy director of central intelligence for community management and assistant directors of collection, analysis, and production, all of which were resisted by CIA and inexplicably underutilized by the DCI to run an increasingly complex intelligence community. By sharp contrast, the secretary of defense successfully lobbied, against surprisingly little intelligence community resistance, for the creation of an undersecretary of defense for intelligence position, which was approved in 2002, adding more heft to what already was the community's thousand-pound gorilla. Significantly, the defense community took the lead in calling for—and developing—both centralized and decentralized networks that would bring analysis and collection capabilities closer to military personnel on the frontlines. The defense turf grab further wounded a weakened CIA and eventually raised concerns about military involvement in domestic intelligence, but it also responded to real, unmet defense community requirements for improved analysis and collection management.[7]

Fourth, blue-ribbon commissions in the late 1990s, as well as the intelligence community's own strategic work, recognized the growing need for a homeland security strategy that would address catastrophic threats from terrorism, proliferation of weapons of mass destruction (WMD), and cyberspace attacks. It also stressed the vital role of the private sector as a source of critical information and solutions to hard security problems.

Fifth, FBI leadership saw the dramatic change in the global threat environment, but its commitment to transformation flagged. Its early postwar determination to share information and push the "wall" between intelligence and law enforcement was set back by the sensational Ames, Nicholson, and Hanson espionage cases. In the larger culture war within the FBI, moreover, agents who pushed for change lost out to establishment figures who successfully resisted reforming policies and practices. Instead of building a distinct intelligence career service for intelligence analysts and collectors, with separate budgets and chains of command, the FBI has continued to subordinate both analysts and collectors to agent managers. Accordingly, the analysts the Bureau hired and trained have left in droves, while failing to reform its law-enforcement structure.

LESSONS LEARNED

THE DEPARTMENT OF HOMELAND SECURITY. The core mission of the Department of Homeland Security is to develop new capabilities to prevent another catastrophic attack on the homeland, to prioritize the protection of our critical infrastructure, and to improve our national— federal, state, and local—response if an attack should occur. Making America safer through new capabilities took precedence over the merger-and-acquisition questions related to standing up a 180,000-member department, which was the largest U.S. government restructuring in half a century. The FBI would collect intelligence within the homeland while DHS would be the primary integrator of intelligence from all sources and the primary analyzer of the terrorist threat to the homeland. It would also serve as an indispensable evaluator—an upscale "team B"—of all intelligence inputs into its terrorism threat analysis. The DHS intelligence organization would compete with other agencies in senior expertise, not in numbers. With a broad information-sharing mission beyond intelligence, it would be uniquely positioned to collaborate with non-government experts anywhere in the world.

While the design may have been imperfect, the execution was surely flawed. DHS stumbled from the start and, after three years of trying, has not achieved compliance with the Homeland Security Act. Congressional oversight has been uneven and largely unfocused. Both House and Senate committees, including the intelligence overseers, generally have fought harder to strengthen their own fractured jurisdictions than to coordinate a constructive approach to DHS and its vital national security mission. But the leading cause of DHS's failure has been the steely ambivalence and occasional obstructionism of the White House, which never seemed to resolve its ambivalence about the establishment of the department or to lessen its favoritism toward the legacy intelligence agencies, especially CIA and FBI.[8] The White House believed—incorrectly as it turned out— that the legacy agencies should be allowed to correct their problems without the intrusion of a new department with real clout.

THE INTELLIGENCE COMMUNITY. President Bush's surprising announcement in his January 2003 State of the Union address of the creation of the Terrorism Threat Integration Center (TTIC) was a body blow to the not-yet-functioning DHS, which Congress had just given analogous responsibilities for fusing intelligence and integrating foreign and domestic analysis under the freshly minted Homeland Security Act. Agencies that had committed to provide temporary staff to the fledgling department backed off to husband scarce resources. Congress was surprised and confused and found many other reasons to be disappointed by White House restraints on the department, especially its reluctance to provide DHS's intelligence component with the facilities, infrastructure, connectivity, and personnel it needed to do its job.[9] But congressional oversight rarely approached rigorous standards and ultimately enabled the executive branch to hamstring the DHS.

Since September 11, Congress has consistently favored creating new "boxes" rather than fixing or eliminating the old ones—without seriously assessing the cost to existing critical programs. In the effort to build new structures, Congress and the administration have never taken into account limits to existing resources. Instead, they have stretched analytic resources to the breaking point, dispersed valuable expertise, and come to rely excessively on the contracting community for analytic staffing, workforce management, and training.[10] They have increased production while reducing authoritative analysis—or quality control—and produced the first generation of analysts without experienced managers to train them.

Post–September 11 restructuring has divided—not concentrated—accountability for threat assessments across a larger number of analytic units at the CIA, FBI, DHS, and NCTC.[11] It has confused civilian and military roles and raised alarms about military involvement in domestic intelligence with the emergence of the powerful Northern Command, the expansion of the Defense Department's Counterintelligence Field Activity (CIFA) that protects U.S. military facilities, and in NSA's "warrantless" surveillance of U.S. citizens' communications.[12] All this as the FBI has fallen short in developing analytic and collection capabilities.

Our record since September 11, then, is a mixture of small successes, commendable but stalled efforts, and significant failures. Much of what we have done has been understandably reactive and uncoordinated—often resulting from conflicting priorities and unfocused interplay of the executive and legislative branches in an atmosphere of crisis. Current approaches, as a whole, are not cost effective as a blueprint for the future. America needs a comprehensive strategy for national—including homeland—security and bold leadership to implement it.

WHAT WE NEED TO DO

The FBI cannot effectively lead the domestic intelligence effort, but a resurrected DHS could.[13] Our federal power centers—Defense, Justice, the Directorate of National Intelligence, and the DHS—must be made to collaborate. This simply will not happen without strong and sustained White House leadership—which is the core message of this chapter. Absent that leadership, we will continue to see wasteful bureaucratic infighting, worrisome confusion over roles and responsibilities, and minimal reforms that fall short of transformation goals.

There is now a weighty ball in the administration's court. The crisis-driven policies of the past five years will not be adequate to protect us against the diverse and constantly changing threats we face—including an enduring threat from international terrorism. And now, more than ever, we will need transparency in the reform process, which has not been a strong suit of either the administration or Congress since September 11. The chronic lack of transparency over intelligence community management practices has long been a detriment to congressional oversight, to the public's right to know, and to interagency collaboration.

The hastily drafted Intelligence Reform and Terrorism Prevention Act of 2004 created opportunities to enhance our national security, but left many gaps that only smart leaders can fill. In moving forward, the executive branch, in close collaboration with congressional committees of jurisdiction, needs to develop a strategic reform agenda with clear reform goals and metrics. We should see this as a way to seize opportunities we have missed and correct mistakes—and there is nothing self-correcting about many of the alarming trends we observe today.

RECOMMENDATIONS

12.1. RESTORE ACCOUNTABILITY. The president should establish by executive order an intelligence transformation group (ITG)—or its functional equivalent—of the National Security Council, chaired by the president with delegation to the national security advisor, to include the secretary of defense, the secretary of homeland security, the attorney general, and the DNI. The mandate should be to develop and implement a strategic plan for intelligence community reform, based on agreed-upon priorities consistent with the Intelligence Reform and Terrorism Prevention Act of 2004, led by the president in close collaboration with the major agencies affected. The organization need not be formal, if the president so chooses, but his strong hand must be evident in making relevant agency heads responsible and accountable for implementation of his agenda and for presenting a unified front in dealing with Congress.

12.2. RESIST STRUCTURAL BUILDUP. The hasty establishment of the TTIC and NCTC taught us that the resistance encountered to these centralized models was in part the result of legitimate leadership concern about degrading critical capabilities needed in an increasingly decentralized intelligence community. Whatever the merits of a new, stand-alone domestic intelligence service (including one based on the U.K. or Canadian models)—they shrink when tested against America's commitment to civil liberties. If adopted, the original vision of its proponents would likely be significantly altered in the usual counterproductive interplay between the administration and Congress. The journey would be painful and protracted, and the destination would not be what its proponents planned. Witness the unhappy experience of DHS.

12.3. STRENGTHEN THE DHS'S INTELLIGENCE ROLE. The president should publicly, as well as in his leadership of the ITG, make clear his support for DHS as an intelligence assessment and sharing center. Under this arrangement, the FBI must share information with DHS and, through DHS, state and local authorities. A joint DHS-FBI committee on intelligence chaired by the White House would ensure that sharing of information became a reality.

12.4. USE REGIONAL OFFICES FOR INFORMATION SHARING. The DHS second-stage review should be revised to give the secretary responsibility for assuring a two-way intelligence exchange with state and local governments—as well as with the twenty-two agencies incorporated into DHS. While the federal government in recent years has fallen short in delivering threat-based information to enable state and local governments and the private sector to prioritize critical infrastructure protection, regions around the country have taken impressive steps largely on their own to improve their counterterrorism capabilities across jurisdictions. Obvious examples are New York City (with northern New Jersey), the District of Columbia (with Baltimore and Richmond), Miami, Houston, Los Angeles-Long Beach, Seattle-Tacoma, Chicago, and Detroit. These regions should have unfettered access to all federal intelligence agencies, not just the FBI or the NCTC. The federal government has protested that it cannot grant security clearances to 13,000 police departments across the country. But it can clear selected officials in these eight regions as a start toward a reliable and sustainable national intelligence system.

12.5. Clarify the FBI's particular role in domestic intelligence. The FBI, its fifty-six field stations, and its growing network of Joint Terrorism Task Forces (JTTFs) have a part to play in the development of a national intelligence capability, which in an ideal world would be a collaborative and not a leading role. We should, once and for all, lower expectations of the Bureau's intelligence role. The FBI should not be expected to produce at a local level either the authoritative analysis or the integrated collection assessments that it cannot provide nationally. The WMD Commission excoriated the FBI for its failure to structure and provide adequate resources for these functions, but it settled for a puzzling bureaucratic recommendation to consolidate FBI's counterterrorism division, counterintelligence division, and the new Directorate of Intelligence in a national security service. This does not assure that new functions will be developed, especially under the FBI's agent-dominated leadership. The president and the ITG should make the FBI accountable only for developing an intelligence collection cadre to support law enforcement and a limited analytic capability in collaboration with state and local governments.

12.6. Clarify departmental roles and responsibilities. The president and the ITG should work urgently to clarify roles and responsibilities of key agencies with responsibilities for intelligence and homeland security missions. The NCTC, DHS, the Department of Defense (especially Northern Command), CIA, and FBI, while understandably enlarging their missions, are bumping into each other in the integration of foreign and domestic intelligence, and colliding in establishing working relationships with state and local governments. This is a manageable problem if caught early, but a serious issue with implications for preparedness, response, and civil liberties if ignored. Recent press reports of military involvement in domestic intelligence collection may or may not turn out to be of serious concern for the protection of civil liberties. They are, however, clear indications that the federal government and Congress have failed to clarify roles and responsibilities in a new threat environment.

12.7. PROMOTE GOVERNMENT-WIDE INFORMATION SHARING. The program manager for information sharing, a position given government-wide authorities by statute, should be placed in the National Security Council (NSC), not under the DNI, where it recently has been placed by the White House at least partly on the misguided recommendation of the WMD Commission. The effect of that action is to foster the backward-looking impression that information sharing is just an intelligence issue. Moving the program manager into the NSC will keep the pressure on agencies—including the Department of Justice—to play seriously in this top-priority effort, and it will guarantee the perpetuation of "legacy" behavior over the long term. Without this change, the probability is low that an effective, government-wide information-sharing network, such as the Markle Trusted Network, will be implemented.

12.8. MAKE THE NATIONAL COUNTERTERRORISM CENTER (NCTC) WORK. The NCTC, now a key institution, will continue to struggle to establish itself as the dominant provider of terrorism analysis because of the long-standing and growing pressures for decentralization of analytic production in the intelligence, defense, and law enforcement communities. But the center is making impressive progress as the principal intelligence community venue for sharing sensitive intelligence on terrorism. That progress should be applauded and nurtured. We need to succeed in this difficult enterprise because it will provide a model to be replicated at other secure sites and on other high-stakes national security issues.

12.9. SUPPORT THE DNI, BUT HOLD HIM ACCOUNTABLE. The president and the ITG should actively support and carefully monitor the implementation of the director of national intelligence's agenda to reform management, to professionalize the intelligence service, and to improve intelligence collection and analysis. The DNI's agenda should include priorities of common concern to Defense, DHS, and the attorney general: improving human intelligence (HUMINT) capabilities to steal secrets (with less public exposure); enhancing technical collection and open-source capabilities; upgrading analysis (with greater outside exposure to cultural and topic experts); integrating the use of alternative analysis throughout the intelligence community; establishing a cross-agency program evaluation capability; developing interagency professional and technical training programs in a national intelligence university; building a user-friendly collection management system capable of responding to real-time requirements in the field as well as in Washington; and forging enduring relationships with outside experts, especially with the global scientific community. The high expectations for the DNI, of course, will be realized only if he has the support of the White House.

12.10. Clarify the CIA's role under the Director of National Intelligence (DNI). The advent of the Directorate for National Intelligence has ruptured the CIA's fifty-seven-year special relationship with the president. CIA analysts and HUMINT officers were directly responsible, through their director, to the president rather than to a cabinet-level policymaker. The recent placement in CIA of the new National HUMINT Service, with systemwide coordinating responsibilities, is a good step. The agency's unique analytic capabilities need to be recognized and fostered in a similar fashion. They are an invaluable asset to the DNI and the president that should not be squandered.

12.11. Push congressional reform. On domestic intelligence, it appears that some overseers are more protective of the FBI than they are disappointed with its post–September 11 performance.[14] None of this has changed the inadequate oversight of the intelligence committees or otherwise gone far enough to align, in any lasting way, executive and legislative branch priorities for intelligence community reform.[15]

◆ ◆ ◆

The U.S. intelligence community today is much more than technical collection agencies in league with an espionage service. It is one of the world's largest information companies, which is directly challenged by the IT revolution to exploit the glut of open-source information; to access the best sources of expertise on national security issues, wherever they may reside; and to make the operational focus global—including for domestic intelligence. The IT revolution has fundamentally transformed the intelligence community, significantly raised its customers' expectations in Washington and in the field, and fast-forwarded the movement of the complicated and dangerous world it covers.

Transformation affects all players in the community, who must see intelligence more as a collaborative effort and less as a competitive business. Technical collectors, primarily the National Security Agency and the National Geospatial-Intelligence Agency, are challenged as never before to combine resources, to exploit together technologies of common application, and to integrate their collection strategies. And the espionage service, in its mission to "steal secrets," is impelled to blend foreign and domestic perspectives, to fuse classified and unclassified information, and to collaborate with other collection disciplines in the difficult effort to penetrate evasive, fast-moving targets.

On domestic intelligence, we are challenged to build a national collaborative network—including federal, state, and local governments and the private sector—that can bring together in real time the best information, the foremost experts, and well-trained first responders to meet any threat. This is the goal. Achieving it is a long-term proposition in which we must confront the twin obstacles of smarter, more capable adversaries and of persistently change-resistant U.S. bureaucracies. We know there will be no easy fixes. The core challenge for the executive branch and Congress is to set the right direction and stick with it.

13. LOSING FOCUS ON AVIATION SECURITY

Aviation security has improved dramatically since September 11, yet critical gaps remain. This chapter highlights the current state of aviation security and the most pressing deficits in the existing system and recommends a course of action for correcting those deficits. Six areas of aviation security are particularly important: passenger screening, checked baggage security, air cargo security, the shoulder-fired missile threat, in-flight and crew member security, and aviation worker screening.

WHERE WE ARE TODAY: THE CURRENT STATE OF AVIATION SECURITY

The events of September 11 demonstrated not only how vulnerable our air carriers were to a terrorist hijacking but also how vulnerable our economy is to shocks in the commercial airline industry. Commercial air carriers generate more than $100 billion per year and support approximately 720,000 jobs.[1] The air traffic these carriers generate is even more impressive: Every day in the United States, 30,000 flights carrying 1.8 million passengers take off from more than 450 domestic commercial airports.[2]

In response to September 11, President Bush signed the Aviation and Transportation Security Act (ATSA) into law on November 19, 2001. ATSA endowed the newly created Transportation Security Administration (TSA) with responsibility for securing the commercial aviation system—previously the domain of the Federal Aviation Administration. TSA's mandate included overseeing security operations at over 450 commercial airports, which included passenger screening, checked baggage screening, and the procurement and installation of explosive detection systems.[3] By December 2002, the TSA was screening about 90 percent of checked baggage for explosives and had deployed a workforce of 65,000 screeners and federal air marshals.[4]

Since its inception, the TSA has received direction from congressional acts and commissions. In July 2004, the 9/11 Commission recommended the United States adopt a more robust "layered defense" strategy to address gaps in existing defenses.[5] The Vision 100 Century of Aviation Reauthorization Act, enacted on December 12, 2003, addressed several aviation security concerns raised by the 9/11 Commission, and soon thereafter the National Intelligence Reform Act of 2004 built on the provisions of the Vision 100 legislation.

PASSENGER SCREENING

Effective passenger screening requires thorough prescreening operations. Since the Federal Aviation Reauthorization Act of 1996, the U.S. government has relied on the Computer-Assisted Passenger Prescreening System (CAPPS), or some version of it, to prescreen passengers.[6] CAPPS was designed to distinguish low-threat passengers from high-threat passengers so that the luggage of high-threat passengers could receive more scrutiny for explosives. The events of September 11 revealed both the strengths and weaknesses of the CAPPS system. On the positive side, half of the September 11 hijackers were successfully selected by the CAPPS system for additional security screening, and, had the situation been handled properly from that point, the September 11 plot may have been severely disrupted. However, while additional screening procedures meant that the hijackers' checked baggage was not loaded onto the airplane until the hijackers had boarded, it did not include increased scrutiny of the hijackers or their carry-on items.

When the TSA assumed the responsibility for aviation security it also assumed authority for managing and regulating CAPPS.[7] In March 2003, the TSA began development of CAPPS II, which would have performed two functions. First, the passenger's identity would have been authenticated using commercial databases and then the passenger's name would be checked against terrorist watch lists maintained by the U.S. government. Once flagged, the passenger would be unable to board the flight or would be subjected to secondary screening.[8] Due to privacy concerns raised by the Government Accountability Office (GAO) and an internal review by the Department of Homeland Security (DHS), the CAPPS II program was cancelled in August 2004.[9]

As soon as CAPPS II was shot down, TSA announced the development of a prescreening system called Secure Flight. Secure Flight, now the most likely successor to CAPPS, has four main elements. First, the identity authentication process is scaled back. Second, the passenger names will be checked against a wider set of government-maintained watch lists, which are consolidated in the Terrorist Screening Database (TSDB). Third, passengers that are "selected" will be subjected to a more intensive screening and, fourth, passengers who have been misidentified may initiate an appeals process.[10] Pursuant to the recommendations of the 9/11 Commission, the TSDB is a consolidation of "No Fly" and "Automatic Selectee" lists and is maintained by the FBI-administered Terrorist Screening Center. Additionally, TSA is responsible only for prescreening domestic flights under Secure Flight, with prescreening for international flights handled by Customs and Border Protection (CBP) personnel.[11]

Once prescreening is completed, passengers along with their carry-on baggage are individually screened. This process constitutes the critical second screening function. TSA manages a workforce of approximately 60,000 people, most of whom work as explosives and weapons screeners at airports. Training and developing this workforce has presented a considerable challenge. TSA uses the Online Learning Center to train and retrain its screeners through self-guided courses on the Internet.[12] TSA also conducts unannounced, covert tests at airports to estimate screener performance and uses Threat Image Projection (TIP) software to keep screeners alert by periodically superimposing images of threat objects on X-ray scans.[13] TSA has also pilot tested a biometric-based screening program called Registered Traveler, which would analyze physical characteristics of frequent passengers to expedite their screening.[14]

CHECKED BAGGAGE SECURITY

Prior to the passage of the November 2001 Aviation and Transportation Security Act (ATSA), commercial air carriers were responsible for screening checked baggage for explosives. The passage of ATSA gave TSA the mandate to screen 100 percent of checked baggage by December 2002 using explosive detection machines (prior to ATSA, only a fraction of baggage was screened for explosives).[15] As it became clear in 2002 that many airports would not meet this target, the Homeland Security Act of 2002 extended the deadline to December 2003 for noncompliant airports.[16]

Since November 2001, TSA has procured and deployed approximately 1,200 explosive detection system (EDS) machines and 6,000 explosives trace detection (ETD) machines at over 400 airports.[17] The EDS uses computed tomography (CT scan) technology to generate a three-dimensional image of the contents of a bag in order to recognize the characteristic signatures of explosives.[18] EDS machines cost about $1 million each and are very large.[19] ETD machines, which require a human operator to manually collect a sample from each bag with a swab, work by detecting the residues and vapors of explosives. Relative to EDS machines, ETD machines are $40,000 less expensive per unit, but much more labor intensive, more vulnerable to human error, and less accurate in detecting explosives.[20] Currently, many of the EDS and ETD machines that the TSA has deployed have been placed in airport lobbies, in a "stand-alone" mode, rather than being integrated with baggage conveyor systems.[21]

The 9/11 Commission recommended in July 2004 that the integration of EDS machines "in-line" with baggage conveyor systems be expedited, and that the aviation industry pay some of the cost of installation.[22] On October 18, 2005, Congress approved the DHS fiscal year 2006 budget, which allocates $175 million for the procurement of EDS and ETD systems, as well as $45 million to install this equipment in-line with baggage conveyors.

To supplement these systems, TSA has also deployed 345 explosives detection canine teams at 66 of the United States's busiest airports. TSA plans to expand the program to 420 dog teams at 82 airports.[23]

AIR CARGO SECURITY

The air cargo system consists of all the freight, express packages, and mail carried aboard cargo and passenger aircraft. These goods move from manufacturers to shippers to freight forwarders and finally to airport cargo handling facilities where they are loaded onto aircraft.[24] With the increasing demand for air shipments over the past twenty-five years, the system is vast, complex, and growing.

In 2004, approximately 23 billion pounds of air cargo were shipped within the United States. Three-fourths of that was shipped on all-cargo aircraft and one-fourth was shipped on passenger aircraft. Typically about 50 percent of a passenger aircraft's capacity is taken up by air cargo, which remains a significant source of income for passenger air carriers.[25] It is estimated that by FY2015, domestic air cargo shipments will increase by 50 percent and international shipments by over 85 percent.[26]

TSA has argued that air cargo is the primary aviation target for terrorists in the short term, and therefore one of the most vulnerable links in the aviation security chain.[27] As a result, TSA developed the Air Cargo Strategic Plan in November 2003 focusing on two threats to air cargo security: (1) preventing the introduction of explosives onto passenger aircraft via an air cargo package, and (2) preventing the hijacking of an all-cargo aircraft.[28] TSA hoped to address these threats by enhancing air cargo supply chain security, identifying elevated risk through prescreening, developing technology for screening risky cargo, and enhancing security for all-cargo operations. To some extent, TSA still relies on random inspections to evaluate cargo threats, though more comprehensive non-intrusive methods, such as X-ray scans, are being developed.[29]

TSA is also using the Known Shipper Program to distinguish risky from non-risky cargo. Under the Known Shipper Program, individuals and businesses with an established history are not subject to the same degree of scrutiny as unknown shippers. In addition, unknown shippers are not allowed to ship their freight on passenger aircraft. TSA is in the process of expanding this program—currently only about one-third of air carriers utilize the voluntary central database of known shippers to vet their cargo.[30] Non-participating air carriers are using internal databases and security protocols approved by the TSA.

The DHS fiscal year 2006 allocation provides $55 million for air cargo security. This includes funds to support air cargo inspectors, development and improvement of the Known Shipper Program, and expansion of the canine explosives detection program, among other measures.[31]

SHOULDER-FIRED MISSILE THREAT

Shoulder-fired missile systems, also referred to as man-portable air defense systems (MANPADS), may pose a serious risk to aviation security. These weapons are lethal against aircraft without counter-measures, relatively cheap (only $5,000 in some markets), and read-ily available in the international arms bazaar—an estimated 700,000 MANPADS have been produced worldwide since the 1970s.[32] In addition, such weapons are lightweight, small, and could be smug-gled into the United States with relative ease. Most importantly, al Qaeda and other hostile groups possess and know how to operate MANPADS. In fact, during the recent operations in Afghanistan, numerous MANPADS were recovered from Taliban weapons caches.[33]

The RAND Corporation has estimated that the direct cost of hav-ing an aircraft shot down would be about $1 billion, which includes con-ventional economic valuations of the loss of life.[34] If air travel were shut down for one week following an incident, the economic cost would be about $3 billion, and losses over the following month might bring the total cost to around $15 billion.[35] The National Intelligence Reform Act of 2004 advised the president to vigorously pursue programs that limit the availability and proliferation of MANPADS worldwide. The act also requires that DHS report on the vulnerability of aircraft to MANPADS attacks and devise a plan for securing aircraft from this threat.[36] The DHS fiscal year 2006 allocation provides $110 million for MANPADS countermeasures.

IN-FLIGHT AND CREW MEMBER SECURITY

In-flight security was a clear weakness prior to September 11. Since September 11, a number of security measures, such as harden-ing cockpit doors, have vastly improved crew member security. The Vision 100 Act required that air carriers provide security training for crew members and recommended arming all-cargo pilots in addition to passenger aircraft pilots.[37] The National Intelligence Reform Act of 2004 called for strengthening initiatives that protect the anonymity of federal air marshals and providing counterterrorism and weapons training for law enforcement officials authorized to carry firearms on passenger aircraft.[38]

The federal air marshals program is an important component of in-flight security. Originally called the "sky marshals program," federal air marshals were given an expanded mandate following September 11, including a dramatic increase in the size of the workforce and mandatory deployment on all high-security-risk flights.[39] The DHS fiscal year 2006 budget allocation includes $686 million for the federal air marshals program.

TSA has strengthened its review of crew member security training, including developing a standard form for TSA inspectors to use to document their review of crew member security training.[40]

The recent rash of incidents involving lasers aimed at aircraft cockpits has raised concerns about terrorist use of commercially available lasers to disrupt aircraft operations. None of the 400 recorded incidents involving flight crew exposure to lasers over the past fifteen years were linked to terrorism, though terrorists could plausibly acquire higher powered lasers to incapacitate pilots. Indeed, DHS and the FBI issued a memo in December 2004 stating that terrorists had explored using lasers as weapons.[41]

Aviation Worker Screening

Currently, background checks and displayed identification serve as the primary means for screening aviation workers.[42] This includes air cargo handlers and any other individuals with access to a passenger aircraft or airfields. The provisions of ATSA provide TSA with the authority to use biometric technology to enhance aviation worker screening procedures, though very few airports currently employ such technology.[43] TSA is developing a nationwide transportation workers identification card program, which would provide every aviation worker with a biometric ID card once his or her background check had been completed.

WHERE WE FALL SHORT
SECURITY DEFICITS IN THE CURRENT SYSTEM

PASSENGER SCREENING

There are a number of critical deficits in the current passenger pre-screening process. In December 2005, the 9/11 Public Discourse Project gave passenger prescreening an "F" grade, citing delays in implementing the Secure Flight System's consolidated "No Fly" lists.

The current system both misidentifies low-risk passengers (false positives) and fails to identify high-risk passengers (false negatives). According to one account, TSA was contacted by air carriers as many as 30 times per day with potential name matches. Assuming that a very small fraction of these passengers were actually on the terrorist watch list, false positives are clearly a problem—high-profile misidentifications included Senator Edward Kennedy and Representatives John Lewis and Don Young.[44] Should they persist, misidentification problems could continue to slow down operations and even undermine public confidence in aviation security measures.[45] Though cutting down on false positives may prove to be challenging, TSA is hoping that Secure Flight will at a minimum cut down on false negatives by using an expanded terrorist watch list.[46]

The TSA anticipates that Secure Flight will significantly increase the prescreening workload, requiring increases in staff, space, and funding for support operations at the TSA. The TSA remains uncertain, however, about how much of a funding increase will be required to add Secure Flight to TSA regular operations.[47]

Unfortunately, Secure Flight seems to have foundered on problems related to transparency and privacy, the same concerns that unraveled CAPPS II.[48] Specifically, private organizations and government auditors have raised concerns over widespread collection of passengers' personal information without procedures for preventing misuse of, and unauthorized access to, that information. Until such issues are resolved, Secure Flight is unlikely to move forward.

The quality of passenger screeners is also a lingering deficiency in the current system. A DHS inspector general's audit in March 2005 revealed poor screener performance among both federal and contract screeners during covert testing at screening checkpoints.[49] Part of the problem stems from TSA training policy. The TSA has no formal policies for monitoring the completion of screener training nor has it ensured that all Online Training Centers have the reliable high-speed Internet connections required for online training. As a result, many airports are finding it difficult to keep accurate and up-to-date training records.[50] Security auditors have also noted that due to insufficient staffing, screeners are not always able to meet the training needs within regular work hours.[51]

In addition, most passengers are screened by a metal detector but are not subjected to more thorough explosives detection methods. Only a fraction of passengers have their carry-on items and shoes screened for chemical traces.[52] The 9/11 Public Discourse Project gave explosives screening at checkpoints a "C" grade, citing the lack of ETD systems at security checkpoints.

CHECKED BAGGAGE SECURITY

The key to improved checked baggage security is rapid deployment of explosive detection systems (EDS) and explosives trace detection (ETD) systems. Several barriers remain in the way of accomplishing this objective. First, given the increase in demand for air travel in the coming decade, the size of EDS acquisitions will need to double from the original estimate following September 11.[53]

Second, how EDS and ETD equipment should be deployed continues to be debated. The 9/11 Public Discourse Project gave the effort to improve checked baggage screening a "D" grade as a result of delays in the in-line system installation. As of March 2005, TSA had not yet completed a systematic assessment of how to optimally deploy EDS and ETD equipment at over 400 U.S. airports.[54] Most agree that in-line EDS screening systems are necessary because the current practice of placing stand-alone EDS and ETD equipment in airport lobbies has resulted in crowding, which increases risks for passengers and airport workers.[55] The estimated cost of integrating EDS systems at all passenger airports is greater than $4 billion, and installation would take several years to complete at current funding levels.[56] Numerous problems exist for ETD systems as well. Relative to EDS machines, ETD machines are less reliable in detecting bombs, are more labor intensive, and have longer processing times per bag.[57]

AIR CARGO SECURITY

As of October 2005, TSA had not yet completed a comprehensive assessment of the vulnerabilities of air cargo and other critical assets, including cargo facilities and cargo aircraft.[58] TSA has not adapted its vulnerability assessment tools for air cargo assessments nor has it declared when such tools would be ready.[59] Finally, TSA does not systematically collect information on air cargo security breaches, data that would help assess the system's most vulnerable points.

The Known Shipper Program has its fair share of challenges as well. The information in the known shipper database is submitted voluntarily and, as a result, is incomplete and potentially unreliable. TSA estimates that the database has information about 400,000 known shippers, or less than 30 percent of the estimated 1.5 million shippers.[60] Though TSA has declared that it plans to make the database mandatory, it has not yet done so. Furthermore, verification of data submitted by shippers has been inadequate. Currently, there is very little investigation of a shipper's credibility, and to what extent that shipper is using approved security measures to ensure the integrity of its freight.[61]

TSA is also struggling with the challenge of screening cargo containers and cargo unit loading devices (ULDs) reliably and rapidly. Under current technological constraints, it is not feasible to scan every container and ULD and retain the speed of shipment to which most commercial carriers are accustomed.[62]

Hardened unit loading devices (HULDs) are also being considered as a means of mitigating the threat of a cargo-borne bomb. These containers must withstand an explosive blast without rupturing and must also self-extinguish any post-blast fire.[63] The drawbacks of using HULDs are numerous: increased weight affecting aircraft range and payload capacity, high procurement costs, and incompatibilities with current airframes, to name a few.[64] The 9/11 Commission recommended the deployment of at least one hardened container on every passenger air-craft—on the Boeing 747, however, this accounts for less than 10 per-cent of available cargo storage area.[65]

SHOULDER-FIRED MISSILE THREAT

Though every passenger aircraft in the United States is vulnerable to shoulder-fired missiles, we are still relatively far from installing counter-measures on aircraft. As with other areas of aviation security, a layered defense is required because no countermeasure will be 100 percent effec-tive against MANPADS. A layered defense should include securing a perimeter around airports and improving an aircraft's ability to survive missile-induced fire damage.[66]

IN-FLIGHT AND CREW MEMBER SECURITY

As of September 2005, the TSA had not yet established goals and performance measures for crew member security training, arguing that individual air carriers are responsible for setting their own goals and measuring performance.[67] The TSA is indisputably responsible for monitoring air carrier compliance with TSA-established training stan-dards, but lacks the internal controls for regulating and reviewing air carrier compliance.[68] Observers of the current training system com-plain about the lack of recurrent, realistic training, and the instruc-tors' lack of knowledge about the actual in-flight operating environment.[69]

All-cargo aircraft also face important security challenges. Unlike pas-senger aircraft, all-cargo airplanes do not have hardened cockpit doors or federal marshals to thwart a hijacking attempt. Physical security and access control to cargo operations is also less strict than passenger air-craft security, making all-cargo aircraft an especially inviting target to terrorists.[70]

Finally, the federal air marshals program has successfully expanded its mandate and operations, though it has failed to create a mechanism for marshals to systematically document security incidents that occur during their missions.[71] If federal air marshals do not adequately use, manage, and analyze mission reports, we may miss a valuable opportunity to detect terrorist mission planning and reconnaissance activity.

AVIATION WORKER SCREENING

A major concern for aviation worker screening is the possibility that unauthorized individuals could gain access to secure facilities with stolen or fraudulent identification. In addition, air cargo workers and cargo handlers do not receive formal security training for identification of suspicious activity or training in procedures to reduce physical security breaches.[72]

RECOMMENDATIONS

The following section outlines how we can begin to address many of these security challenges.

13.1. PASSENGER SCREENING. The TSA needs to bring Secure Flight online as rapidly as possible. This will require addressing the privacy concerns raised over the government's collection of personal information. Most importantly, TSA must assure passengers that their personal information will be strictly safeguarded from unauthorized use, and will be used only for the purposes of distinguishing high-risk from low-risk passengers. In other words, for the limited personal information a passenger gives up, he or she gains volumes in aircraft security. The TSA may also consider segmenting the passenger population into travelers who are willing to give extra personal information for Secure Flight and those who are not willing to provide information. Those who are not willing may be subjected to extra prescreening and checkpoint screening as a result. It is plausible that many passengers will decide that their desire to save time outweighs their desire to remain anonymous.

Several technologies may potentially help to improve passenger screening at security checkpoints. One option is the multiview X-ray, which provides screeners with much higher resolution images that can be rotated on the screening monitor in order to improve detection rates.[73] A second and more traditional option is to expand the canine explosive detection teams to operate at security checkpoints.

To keep screeners sharp and alert, the TSA should expand the use of the Threat Image Projection (TIP) program, wherein fictitious threat objects are superimposed on actual images of passenger bags. TIP is doubly effective as it can be used both to train and to evaluate screeners.[74] Airports should also be allowed to opt out of using federal screeners by hiring private contractor screeners if the airport determines that screening operations could be carried out more efficiently and effectively with private contractors.

Biometric identity verification is the obvious next step to enhancing screening effectiveness. The TSA's Registered Traveler pilot program, which uses iris and fingerprint verification, was completed on September 30, 2005, and seems to have been a widespread success. The TSA should aim for a quick review and expansion of this program to all major airports.

On a positive note, the TSA has indicated that it will soon vary its security checkpoint procedures on a regular basis in order to prevent terrorists from studying and exploiting weaknesses in the security protocols.[75] TSA should be sure, however, that variation in screening procedures doesn't result in a loss in screener capability.

13.2. CHECKED BAGGAGE SECURITY. TSA should develop a plan to rapidly deploy in-line EDS systems at the busiest passenger airports, and ultimately at all passenger airports. The current DHS fiscal year appropriation of $175 million for acquiring EDS systems will provide for only a fraction of the systems that are required.

Screener training also needs improvement. Screeners should have access to ongoing training and every Online Training Center should be available by high-speed Internet so that trainers can access and complete training courses more rapidly. TSA should also systematically monitor and document the completion of required screener training.

13.3. AIR CARGO SECURITY. First and foremost, TSA should screen all of the cargo that travels by passenger aircraft with canine explosives detection teams and machines. Backscatter X-ray machines that emit low-dose X-rays are compact, lightweight, and reduce the need for shielding of screeners.[76] Such devices can be mounted on moving platforms and used to scan over containers.

Cargo containers should also be sealed with tamper-evident tape, which offers a visual indication of tampering at a very low cost.[77] Such a measure would be easy to implement during packaging as well.

The use of HULDs should also be explored more vigorously. The National Intelligence Reform Act of 2004 required that the TSA test the use of HULDs for the purpose of determining the feasibility, cost, and logistical difficulties associated with an HULD system. The TSA has not yet released a final ruling on whether this option is feasible.

The TSA should make the Known Shipper Program mandatory for air carriers and known shippers—the current practice of voluntary participation has captured a meager one third of all known shippers. Importantly, the TSA must develop strict monitoring procedures to verify that shippers in the database are actually securing their cargo according to TSA standards. Without verifying shipper compliance, the Known Shipper Program could turn into a worthless investment.

13.4. SHOULDER-FIRED MISSILE THREAT. If a shoulder-fired missile system were used against a commercial aircraft the result would be catastrophic. The TSA should vigorously explore and test countermeasures for airlines against these weapons. Countermeasures should contribute to a layered defense, including securing a perimeter around airports that would prevent an attacker from firing within range of the missile system.[78]

There are several countermeasure options available. Pyrophoric flares are relatively inexpensive, though their effectiveness during a MANPADS attack is not well established. Ground-based high-energy lasers (HELs) would be effective against MANPADS of any sophistication, but will not be available to deploy for several years. Laser jammers, which would be installed directly onto each aircraft, would be capable of defeating all MANPADS currently held by terrorists and are commercial available. RAND estimated that it would cost about $11 billion to equip every aircraft in the U.S. fleet with a laser jammer. RAND further estimated that the full ten-year life-cycle costs of developing, installing, and maintaining laser jammers would be between $20 billion and $40 billion.[79]

Unfortunately, time is not on our side with this problem. The TSA should settle on the superior alternative and accelerate development beyond the current pace.

13.5. IN-FLIGHT AND CREW MEMBER SECURITY. The first step toward improving in-flight security is for the TSA to fund and monitor mandatory self-defense and security training for flight crews rather than relying on air carriers to train their own flight crews according to varying standards.

Though the risk of high-powered lasers disrupting flight operations is relatively remote, the TSA should explore the development and installation of special visors on cockpit windows whose light-blocking properties would be activated only when a laser threat is detected—technology already in development by the Department of Defense.[80]

The TSA should mandate that federal air marshals establish a standard procedure for compiling, analyzing, and responding to mission reports of security incidents.

13.6. AVIATION WORKER SCREENING. The key to protecting the air cargo system from attack is to develop higher standards of identity verification for security workers and higher standards of physical security at facilities in the cargo supply chain.

This begins with training air cargo workers to spot suspicious behavior and by screening them and their personal belongings when they enter secured airfield facilities—particularly when they have access to passenger aircraft. TSA should aggressively pursue development of biometric verification for all aviation workers. The Transportation Workers Identification Card is a good start and should be expanded to include all passenger airports and major air cargo shipping ports.

14. Preventing Nuclear Terrorism

The most chilling scenario for the U.S. government involves terrorists acquiring and exploding a nuclear weapon in the heart of an American city. Security experts agree that this event is unlikely, but low-probability events happen all the time: Witness the September 11 attacks or the devastation wrought by Hurricane Katrina.

A nuclear detonation in a U.S. city would have profound and severe consequences for national security. The ripple effects would quickly extend beyond the destroyed city and could topple the government as Americans could lose confidence in their government's ability to protect them against a horrific weapon of mass destruction.

During the 2004 presidential campaign, President George W. Bush and the Democratic challenger, Senator John F. Kerry, agreed that their greatest concern was terrorists obtaining nuclear weapons. Still, the U.S. government has yet to make preventing nuclear terrorism a top priority. A number of factors have acted against mobilizing more government resources in this fight.

The first impediment is psychological: the human tendency is to fight the last war and to react to the type of terrorism manifested by the September 11 attacks. And though no one doubts al Qaeda's motivations to obtain nuclear weapons, a second impediment is the belief among some current and former senior government officials that terrorists would not be capable of making nuclear weapons even if they acquired weapons-usable materials.

We will first examine the nature of the nuclear threat, then provide several recommendations. Most attention has focused on the international dimensions of preventing nuclear terrorism, and we will address these components first. The second section will focus on domestic steps the United States can take to get its own nuclear house in order.

UNDERSTANDING THE NUCLEAR TERROR THREAT

While building a nuclear bomb is not easy, skilled terrorists could probably construct a "gun-type" device, the simplest and best known nuclear bomb design. This device uses a gun barrel to fire a subcritical mass of highly enriched uranium (HEU) into a second subcritical mass. Combined, the masses form a supercritical mass that results in a chain-reacting nuclear explosion. The first nuclear weapons program, the Manhattan Project, produced a gun-type bomb. Tellingly, the bomb was not tested before it was used against Hiroshima on August 6, 1945.

Making the highly enriched uranium for the bomb was the most difficult step. The industrial-scale effort to enrich uranium required the resources of a nation-state. Consequently, terrorists would have to acquire existing caches of HEU to make even the simplest type of nuclear bomb.

Existing stockpiles of HEU could power tens of thousands of crude nuclear bombs. Russia and the United States possess most of this HEU (an estimated 1,720 metric tons), mainly dedicated for weapons purposes or naval propulsion. Britain, China, France, and Pakistan also have sizable stockpiles in their arsenals. About 50 metric tons of HEU are contained in the civilian sector, with more than forty countries using HEU in research or isotope production reactors. At least 120 of these facilities contain enough HEU in one place to make a nuclear bomb.

Large stockpiles of plutonium, another weapons-usable nuclear material, also exist, but it would be more difficult for terrorists to use this material to make a nuclear weapon. However, since nation-states seeking nuclear weapons could produce plutonium-fueled weapons with relative ease, the United States and other countries with plutonium stockpiles must take stronger steps to secure and reduce this material.

A major misconception is that terrorists can acquire a nuclear weapon only if they receive assistance from a nation-state. According to the U.S. National Research Council, a part of the U.S. National Academy of Sciences that advises the federal government, "Crude HEU weapons could be fabricated without state assistance."[1] While nuclear-armed "rogue" states, such as North Korea, might give nuclear weapons to terrorists, this is unlikely. Even leaders of rogue states value national survival, and recognize that if they are caught transferring nuclear weapons or materials to terrorists, their states would probably experience devastating retaliation. On the other hand, once terrorists acquire nuclear weapons, deterrence would most likely fail.

Terrorists are more likely to obtain nuclear weapons or weapons-usable materials by targeting facilities where security is relatively lax, extorting security guards, enlisting corrupt nuclear custodians, or taking advantage of a coup that brings sympathetic officials to power. The United States has supported programs to reduce the likelihood of these routes to terrorists. However, current nonproliferation and counter-proliferation programs have not significantly reduced the threat of terrorists getting their hands on nuclear weapons or weapons-usable materials. A number of reports have detailed where progress is still needed on the international front to prevent nuclear terrorism.[2]

URGENT INTERNATIONAL EFFORTS TO PREVENT NUCLEAR TERRORISM

In sum, accelerated international efforts are still required in the following areas:

◆ Prevent extremists who are sympathetic to terrorists from seizing control of Pakistan and its nuclear arsenal. This is a priority for U.S. leadership, at least on par with Iran gaining nuclear weapons.

◆ Complete security upgrades of Russian nuclear facilities. While 80 percent of the sites containing nuclear materials have received security upgrades, about 50 percent of the materials have yet to receive such upgrades.

◆ Expand efforts to purchase Russian weapons-usable highly enriched uranium and convert it to non-weapons-usable form. As of September 2005, this program has reached its halfway point by successfully converting 250 metric tons of Russian HEU. However, at the current pace, another ten years will be needed to complete the conversion of the initial 500 metric tons. An acceleration and expansion of this program would quicken this pace and include several hundred additional tons of HEU.

- ◆ Speed up the Global Threat Reduction Initiative (GTRI) in its work to convert civilian reactors from HEU to non-weapons-usable uranium. Expand GTRI to include all civilian reactors that use HEU.
- ◆ Secure and reduce tactical nuclear weapons, especially those that may not be protected by integral security codes, are portable, or outside of central storage. Russian tactical nuclear weapons are particularly of concern.

PUTTING THE U.S. NUCLEAR HOUSE IN ORDER

While much attention has focused on the international dimensions of preventing nuclear terrorism, the remainder of this chapter will examine what is being done and what should be done domestically to secure U.S. nuclear weapons and weapons-usable materials.

NUCLEAR WARHEADS. The United States has a vast nuclear weapons complex and annually spends billions of dollars to maintain and improve its nuclear forces. According to the latest unofficial estimates, the United States possesses almost 10,000 nuclear warheads, including 5,735 active or operational warheads (of these, 5,235 are strategic warheads and the other 500 are tactical warheads). About 4,225 warheads make up the reserve or inactive stockpiles. Some of these warheads are slated for dismantlement. In 2012, when the Strategic Offensive Reductions Treaty will go fully into effect, the United States will have an estimated 5,945 warheads in the operational and reserve stockpiles.[3]

In contrast to all other nuclear-armed countries, the United States continues to base nuclear weapons outside its territory. According to unofficial estimates, the United States has a few hundred tactical nuclear weapons at eight bases in six European countries.[4]

In May 2001, President Bush said, "I am committed to achieving a credible deterrent with the lowest possible number of nuclear weapons consistent with our national security needs, including our obligations to our allies." Later that year, the Bush administration completed its nuclear posture review, which called for research into conventional and nuclear weapons that could destroy or disable deeply buried, hardened bunkers. In addition, this nuclear posture review stated the administration's intention to investigate low-yield nuclear weapons, so-called mini-nukes. So far, Congress has resisted forging ahead with development of nuclear bunker busters and mini-nukes.

In parallel to these programs, the administration is seeking to develop the reliable replacement warhead (RRW), which would be designed without a requirement for full-scale nuclear testing and could replace existing warheads that develop safety or reliability problems. Potential production of the RRW could lead to deeper reductions in the U.S. nuclear arsenal because it could reduce the need to maintain thousands of spare warheads in the reserve stockpile. According to the National Nuclear Security Administration (NNSA), the Department of Energy's semi-autonomous agency in charge of nuclear security, "In the post–September 11 security environment, the nuclear weapon security posture requires improvement. Early integration of use control and security systems within the weapon design could reduce operational security risks and associated costs."[5]

As the United States revises its nuclear posture, it will need to manage carefully the perception problem that it intends never to relinquish its nuclear arms. Prolonged foot-dragging on nuclear disarmament could indirectly fuel further proliferation and increase the risk that terrorists could acquire nuclear weapons.

HIGHLY ENRICHED URANIUM. In addition to having a large number of nuclear warheads, the United States maintains a large stockpile of weapons-usable HEU. According to the latest unofficial estimate, the United States has about 480 metric tons of highly enriched uranium for military purposes.[6] This amount includes material in existing warheads. In addition, during the Clinton administration, the United States had declared about 174 metric tons as excess to defense needs; about 50 metric tons of that have been converted to non-weapons-usable form.

On November 7, 2005, Secretary of Energy Samuel Bodman announced that the United States has declared 200 metric tons of HEU as excess to weapons needs. Of this amount, 160 metric tons are devoted to the U.S. Navy and would postpone the need for a new naval HEU production facility for fifty years. The Navy currently has eighty-two nuclear-powered submarines and surface ships. Another 20 metric tons are mainly devoted to meeting the needs of HEU-powered research reactors until 2014, when the United States plans to complete conversion of these reactors to non-HEU use. A small but unspecified portion of these 20 tons has been set aside for the space program. The remaining 20 tons would be converted to low-enriched uranium (LEU) for both domestic and foreign purchase. This amount is separate from the 17 metric tons that are slated for an emergency low-enriched uranium fuel reserve.

The complete implementation of this plan could take about fifty years. Meanwhile, for most of that time, much of this 200 metric tons would be in weapons-usable form. And even after completion of this decades-long plan, the United States would still have an estimated 280 metric tons of weapons-grade HEU, enough for approximately 11,200 nuclear warheads.[7]

In the civilian sector, NNSA has set a policy goal to "minimize and eventually eliminate any reliance on HEU in the civilian fuel cycle." Despite this policy, it is uncertain whether the United States will convert all of its HEU-fueled non-naval reactors from HEU to LEU, which is not weapons-usable. While most of those reactors are considered civilian facilities, some are at national weapons laboratories and thus may not be considered civilian reactors. The Reduced Enrichment for Research and Test Reactors (RERTR) program has converted eleven U.S. reactors from HEU to LEU. The United States has fourteen reactors in the RERTR program that continue to use HEU. The RERTR program is converting a half-dozen of these reactors from HEU to LEU. However, it is not yet possible to convert some U.S. reactors because the type of LEU needed for these reactors has not been developed.

Elimination of civilian HEU suffered a setback in July 2005 when Congress passed the Energy Policy Act of 2005. This act contained an amendment that weakens export controls on HEU used for producing medical isotopes. Under the previous law, the 1992 Schumer amendment, reactor operators could receive HEU only if they agreed to convert to LEU. The new law permits the export of U.S. HEU even if the operators refuse to convert to LEU.[8]

PLUTONIUM. Although the U.S. plutonium stockpile is not as large as the HEU stockpile, the United States is second only to Russia in the amount of plutonium possessed. The United States has about 100 metric tons of weapons-grade plutonium and has declared about half of that as excess to defense needs.

In spite of the 2000 Plutonium Disposition Agreement with Russia, the United States has yet to dispose of any of this excess material and is still in the process of testing its disposition process. On the positive side, the United States indicated during the summer of 2005 that it was willing to compromise on its desire for ironclad liability protection, opening a path to resolve the problems of liability protection and funding that have bogged down the Russian part of the disposition program.

Since the Ford administration, the United States has maintained a policy of not reprocessing, or separating, plutonium from spent nuclear fuel, and of discouraging other countries from doing so. Spent fuel usually contains large amounts of highly radioactive material and thus provides a lethal barrier to theft. Most reprocessing methods remove plutonium from this protective barrier.

Recent interest of the executive and legislative branches of the U.S. government in restarting reprocessing in the United States, if acted on, could further increase the dangers of terrorists seizing plutonium. The impact of such a decision would depend on the reprocessing method selected; certain methods would not need to separate plutonium entirely from highly radioactive material, but a rush to make a decision in the near term could force the United States to choose a method that makes separated plutonium vulnerable to theft because other less risky methods are still under development. The United States should strengthen its long-standing policy of discouraging the accumulation of separated plutonium, both domestically and internationally.

Department of Energy's Nuclear Security

On May 7, 2004, at the Savannah River Site, then-Secretary of Energy Spencer Abraham presented a set of four initiatives aimed at improving security at Department of Energy (DOE) and NNSA nuclear facilities. Today, two years later, the DOE and the NNSA may have considerable management reform work remaining. An April 2005 independent review, led by retired Admiral Richard W. Mies (former commander of Strategic Command), concluded that "NNSA is plagued by a number of cultural problems," such as "lack of a team approach to security," and that "security is not fully embraced as integral to mission."

Moreover, the independent assessment found an "absence of account-ability" and "lack of trust in the security organization."[9]

Abraham first urged a change of "management culture" at the DOE and the NNSA to encourage constructive criticism, pointing out that "people should never have to be worried about the perils of doing their jobs honestly, safely, and correctly."

Second, Abraham proposed enhancing Internet, cyber, and information-related security. Part of this effort involves moving DOE to a "media-less" computing system in which computers containing sensitive information, such as nuclear weapon designs, would not use removable hard drives, floppy disks, or compact disks. This effort would help prevent theft of sensitive electronic information. Admiral Mies's independent review, however, found that "insufficient resources have been devoted to address many of [DOE's] cyber security issues, particularly the insider threat."[10]

Third, Abraham called for upgrading the physical security infrastructure at facilities. Over a five-year period, the DOE will replace physical keys to sensitive facilities with state-of-the-art access devices, such as biometric systems, that are less susceptible to unlawful entry. Abraham also vowed to establish more consistent and realistic training methods for DOE security personnel.

In a related measure, in May 2003, the DOE issued a revised design basis threat (DBT), which is the government's assessment of the credible, but challenging, threats confronted by nuclear facilities. Abraham, in his May 2004 speech, said that the DOE would examine the DBT annually to make sure it meets evolving and emerging threats.

Yet the DOE took almost two years after September 11 to revise the DBT. In April 2004, the Government Accountability Office (GAO) warned that the "DOE's deadline to meet the requirements of the new DBT by the end of fiscal year 2006 is probably not realistic for some sites."[11] After publication of the April 2004 GAO report, congressional criticism and additional intelligence information prompted the DOE to again revise its DBT in October 2004. The DOE has a deadline of 2008 to implement fully this revised security plan. In July 2005, the GAO spotlighted an area where the DOE needs to make further urgent improvements. Specifically, the GAO focused on weapons-grade nuclear material at the five sites of the DOE's Energy, Science, and Environment Office.[12]

In October 2005, the DOE inspector general issued a special report concerning the implementation of the revised DBT. This report found too much reliance on "costly interim measures, such as increased protective forces overtime, to meet safeguards and security requirements." Moreover, the inspector general discovered, "As of June 2005, the Department had not fully evaluated the effectiveness of either the interim measures it had implemented or planned measures to meet the DBT requirements; and since May 2003, the Department had not completed comprehensive inspections of the security posture at all of the NNSA sites that have special nuclear material."[13]

Fourth, Abraham proposed consolidating weapons-usable nuclear materials into fewer locations. Doing so would save security costs and would leave fewer sites to defend against attack. In particular, he called for:

♦ removing HEU fuel from the Sandia Pulsed Reactor over a three-year period;

♦ speeding up the construction of the HEU Materials Facility at the Y-12 National Security Complex in order to combine the two existing HEU storage facilities at Y-12;

♦ relocating all of the most dangerous nuclear materials from Technical Area 18 (TA-18) at Los Alamos National Laboratory;

♦ moving "essential defense-related research" and other nuclear material at Lawrence Livermore National Laboratory to another, more secure site; and

♦ examining the feasibility of converting about 100 metric tons of HEU to non-weapons-usable form.

Concerning the last initiative, Secretary Bodman, as mentioned earlier, set aside 200 metric tons as excess to defense needs, but only 20 metric tons of this amount are slated for conversion. While the DOE has made some progress in accomplishing the other initiatives, much greater consolidation, and thus security improvements, can be achieved.

On the positive side, the DOE announced in November 2005 that it had completed removing the most dangerous nuclear materials out of TA-18 to a more secure site. However, at the Y-12 site, which contains hundreds of tons of HEU, the DOE inspector general issued a report in June 2005 that pointed out that "foreign construction workers, using false documents, had, in fact, gained access to the Y-12 site on multiple occasions. Specifically, sixteen foreign construction workers were found to have been illegal aliens. Some of these workers acquired facility access badges and were, as a result, permitted access to the main Y-12 site."[14] Admiral Mies's independent review concluded that the DOE "lacks an enterprise-wide plan for consolidation of special nuclear material."[15]

Consolidating weapons-usable materials can result in significant cost savings. The independent Project on Government Oversight estimated that "shrinking the number of facilities from 13 to 7" could result in "a cost savings of nearly $3 billion over three years."[16] Recommending even more far-reaching consolidation, the secretary of energy's advisory board in July 2005 called for "most optimally" reducing "to a single location."

While there would be significant upfront costs, the advisory board concluded that "the long-term cost savings are approximately twice the near-term cost increases."[17]

BE ON GUARD FOR
UNINTENDED CONSEQUENCES

The dominant security paradigm is that more security forces equal more security. However, Stanford University professor Scott Sagan has challenged this traditional thinking by raising three concerns.[18]

1. The insider threat can actually increase with more guards. Although there is a small overall probability that guards would act subversively, each new guard raises that probability. Concerning background checks, Sagan cautions, "Unfortunately, organizations that pride themselves on high degrees of personnel loyalty can be biased against accurately assessing and even discussing the risk of insider threats and unauthorized acts." Once a background check is completed on a guard, that person can become the target of foreign or domestic terrorist cooption through extortion or other means of influence.

2. Guard "redundancy can backfire . . . when diffusion of responsibility leads to 'social shirking.'" Social psychology has documented how, in certain situations, individuals in a group tend to assume that others "will take up the slack." Sagan cites examples of social shirking even in elite military units. He points out that there appears to be little recognition of this phenomenon in nuclear security operations.

3. Increasing the number of guards can lead to overconfidence that the security system is stronger than it really is. The unintended consequence is that "improvements in safety and security [can] lead individuals to engage in inherently risky behavior—driving faster, flying higher, producing more nuclear energy, etc." In this situation, the "expected increases in system reliability could be reduced or even eliminated." Sagan cautions, "Predicted increases in nuclear security forces should not be used as a justification of maintaining inherently insecure facilities or increasing the numbers of nuclear power plants, storage sites, or weapons facilities."

RECOMMENDATIONS

To prevent nuclear terrorism, the United States must lead by example. It needs to demonstrate that it has done all it can do to improve the security of its own nuclear weapons and weapons-usable nuclear materials. A terrorist group that acquired these weapons or materials inside the U.S. homeland would not have to surmount the barrier of crossing borders or entering ports where radiation detection equipment might spot radioactive components of nuclear explosives.[19]

The most effective defense efforts to prevent nuclear terrorism are to secure, consolidate, and eliminate these materials. Consequently, in addition to the urgently needed international efforts outlined earlier, the United States should rapidly take action in the following domestic security areas:

14.1. ISSUE A POLICY THAT DELEGITIMIZES HIGHLY ENRICHED URANIUM IN THE CIVILIAN SECTOR. Congress should reenact the 1992 Schumer amendment restrictions on exporting HEU.

14.2. EXPAND THE GLOBAL THREAT REDUCTION INITIATIVE PROGRAM TO INCLUDE ALL HEU-POWERED CIVILIAN REACTORS. Speed up conversion of U.S. research reactors from HEU to non-weapons-usable uranium.

14.3. EXPAND THE AMOUNT OF U.S. HIGHLY ENRICHED URANIUM SLATED FOR CONVERSION TO NON-WEAPONS-USABLE FORM. Accelerate the conversion of HEU already scheduled for conversion. The United States could set aside this converted material as a strategic nuclear fuel reserve.

14.4. DO NOT PURSUE PLUTONIUM REPROCESSING METHODS THAT WOULD LEAD TO SEPARATED WEAPONS-USABLE PLUTONIUM.

14.5. INCREASE CONSOLIDATION OF WEAPONS-USABLE MATERIALS IN THE U.S. NUCLEAR COMPLEX. Work toward the secretary of energy's advisory board recommendation to move these materials to one highly secure site. Further consolidation could pay off in billions of dollars of cost savings.

14.6. THE DEPARTMENT OF ENERGY AND THE NATIONAL NUCLEAR SECURITY ADMINISTRATION SHOULD DEVELOP A COMPREHENSIVE STRATEGIC SECURITY PLAN. Such a plan must be based on frequently tested performance and not just on compliance with security requirements. The DOE and the NNSA should coordinate their security efforts with the Department of Defense. To protect against the most likely route for terrorists or criminals to gain access to weapons-usable materials, the DOE and the NNSA should increase vigilance against the insider threat to nuclear facilities.

15. The Perils of Neglecting America's Waterfront

The controversy that erupted in February 2006 over Dubai Ports World taking over five American container terminals was fueled more by politics than by real concern within Congress for port and cargo security. Elected leaders on both sides of the aisle were engaged in a combination of hyperbole and demagoguery when they warned of dire security consequences should a foreign company with a Middle Eastern home office be allowed to operate marine terminals on U.S. soil. But the political firefight over the ports deal has had an important and salutary effect: It has drawn long-overdue attention to the appalling state of maritime transportation and supply chain security.

Take the case of the harbor shared by Los Angeles and its neighbor Long Beach, arguably America's most important seaport. Its marine terminals handle over 40 percent of all the ocean-borne containers shipped to the United States.[1] Its refineries receive daily crude oil shipments and produce one-quarter of the gasoline, diesel, and other petroleum products that are consumed west of the Rocky Mountains. It is a major port of call for the $25 billion ocean cruise industry.[2] Just three bridges handle all the truck and train traffic to and from Terminal Island where most of the port facilities are concentrated.[3] In short, it is a tempting target for any adversary intent on bringing its battle to the U.S. homeland.

Yet there is no one in the Pentagon who sees it as their job to protect Los Angeles and the nation's other busiest commercial seaports from terrorist attacks. Oakland, Seattle, Newark, Charleston, Miami, Houston, and New Orleans are America's economic lifelines to the world, but the U.S. Department of Defense does not view them as national security priorities. Because these ports do not deploy "defense critical infrastructure"—that is, ships, troops, munitions, and supplies needed for overseas combat operations—the Defense Department has decided that the responsibility for safeguarding them is not its job.

It is the Department of Homeland Security that has been tasked with assuring that there is credible security along America's long-neglected waterfront. But the new department lacks both the resources and the White House mandate to undertake this critical mission. This is because the Office of Management and Budget sees port security as primarily the responsibility of state and local governments and of the private companies that operate marine facilities.

The 2002 National Strategy for Homeland Security sets forth principles to guide the federal outlays for homeland security. It maintains that all levels of government must "work cooperatively to shoulder the cost of homeland security."[4] It also hands much of the tab for protecting critical infrastructure to the private sector. "The [federal] government should only address those activities that the market does not adequately provide—for example, national defense or border security. . . . For other aspects of homeland security, sufficient incentives exist in the private market to supply protection."[5]

So when it comes to port security, the buck stops outside Washington, D.C. Since seaports in the United States are locally run operations where port authorities typically play the role of landlord, issuing long-term leases to private companies, it falls largely to those companies to provide for the security of the property they lease.

In the case of Los Angeles, this translates to the security of 7,500 acres of facilities that run along forty-nine miles of waterfront being provided by low-wage, private security guards and a tiny port police force of under one hundred officers.[6] The situation in Long Beach is even worse, with only twelve full-time police officers assigned to its 3,000 acres of facilities and a small cadre of private guards provided by the port authority and its tenants. The command and control equipment to support a new joint operations center for the few local, state, and federal law enforcement authorities that are assigned to the port will not be in place until 2008.

In the four years following September 11, 2001, Los Angeles and Long Beach received less than $40 million in federal grants to improve the port's physical security measures. That amount is equivalent to what American taxpayers spend in a single day on domestic airport security.[7]

But the fallout from a terrorist attack on any one of the nation's major commercial seaports would hardly be a local matter. For instance, should al Qaeda or another organization succeed in sinking a large ship in the Long Beach channel, auto-dependent southern California would literally run out of gas within two weeks. This is because, as Hurricanes Katrina and Rita highlighted, U.S. petroleum refineries are operating at full throttle and their products are consumed almost as quickly as they are made. If the crude oil shipments stop, so too would the refineries—and there exists no excess capacity or refined fuels to cope with a long-term disruption.[8]

But the most serious threat comes from the possibility that terrorists could smuggle a weapon of mass destruction into one of the over nine million forty-foot cargo containers annually shipped to U.S. seaports. The September 11, 2001, attacks on New York and Washington, the March 11, 2004, attacks on Madrid, and the July 7, 2005, attacks on London highlight that transport systems have become favored targets for terrorist organizations. Cargo containers have long been exploited to smuggle narcotics, migrants, and stolen property, such as luxury automobiles. Their vulnerability is highlighted by the billions of dollars in cargo losses derived from theft each year. A typical cargo container that is shipped from Asia will pass through over a dozen transportation waypoints before it is loaded on a ship destined for the United States. Most are "secured" only with a fifty-cent lead seal passed through the padeyes on the container doors.

The potential for the cargo container to be exploited for an act of terror was demonstrated not long ago in Israel in a sparsely reported event that took place shortly after the train bombings in Madrid. On March 14, 2004, two Palestinian suicide bombers were intercepted before they reached their intended targets of several fuel and chemical storage tanks in the port of Ashdod. The Palestinian militants killed themselves along with ten Israelis, and wounded eighteen others. They reportedly evaded the security at the port facility's gate by being smuggled from Gaza in a container outfitted with a secret compartment and an arms cache.[9]

It is just a question of time before terrorists with potentially more destructive weapons breach the superficial security measures that have been put in place to protect the ports, the ships, and the millions of intermodal containers that link global producers to consumers. Should that breach involve a "dirty bomb," the United States will likely raise the port security alert system to its highest level while investigators sort out what happened and establish whether or not a follow-on attack is likely. In the interim, the flow of all inbound traffic would slow to a point that the entire intermodal container system, and the millions of tons of goods it carries, would grind to a halt. In economic terms, the costs associated with managing the attack's aftermath would substantially dwarf any actual destruction from the bomb attack. Those costs will be borne internationally, which is why transportation and trade security must be not only a U.S. homeland security priority but also an urgent global priority.

The good news is that there are pragmatic measures that the U.S. government can be pursuing right now that would substantially enhance the integrity and resilience of our ports and the global trade lanes. Further, this agenda can be advanced by making modest up-front investments that enhance transportation visibility and accountability and will have commercial benefits that go beyond security. By constructing the means to better monitor the flow of legitimate goods through complex international supply chains, companies will be able to better manage the choreography of global logistics, which will improve their bottom lines.

A BRITTLE SYSTEM

While advocates for more open global markets have rarely acknowledged it, when it comes to converting free trade from theory to practice, the now ubiquitous cargo container deserves a great deal of the credit. On any given day, millions of containers, each carrying up to thrity-two tons of goods, are being moved by trucks, trains, or ships. These movements have become remarkably affordable, efficient, and reliable, with the result that manufacturers and retailers have constructed increasingly complex global supply chains and operate with razor-thin inventories. From a commercial standpoint, this has been all to the good. But there is a problem: As their dependence on the intermodal transportation system rises, enterprises become extremely vulnerable to the consequences of that system being disrupted.

Indeed, multiple port closures in the United States and elsewhere would quickly throw this system into chaos. Container ships already destined for the United States would be stuck in anchorages unable to unload their cargo. Ships would be delayed in overseas loading ports as the maritime industry and its customers try to sort out how to redirect cargo. Marine terminals would have to close their gates to all incoming containers since they would have no place to store them. Trucks and trains would not be allowed into the terminal. If they are carrying perishable goods, their cargo would spoil. Also, the trucks and trains would not be able to recirculate to pick up new shipments until they can get rid of the old ones. Goods for export would pile up at factory loading docks with no place to go. Imports to support just-in-time deliveries would not arrive. Soon factories would idle and retailers' shelves would go bare.

In short, a catastrophic terrorist event involving the intermodal transportation system could well lead to unprecedented disruption to the global trade system.

What Has Been Done?

The possibility that terrorists could compromise the maritime and intermodal transportation system has led several U.S. agencies to pursue initiatives designed to manage this risk. The U.S. Coast Guard chose to take primarily a multilateral approach by working through the London-based International Maritime Organization to establish new international standards for improving security practices on ocean-going vessels and within ports, called the International Ship and Port Facility Security (ISPS) code.[10] As of July 1, 2004, each member state was obliged to certify that the ships that fly their flag or the facilities under their jurisdiction are compliant. The Coast Guard also requires that ships destined for the United States provide a notice of their arrival a minimum of ninety-six hours in advance, including a description of their cargoes and a crew and passenger list.[11] The agency then assesses the potential risk the vessel might pose and, if the available intelligence indicates that a pre-arrival boarding might be warranted, it arranges to intercept the ship at sea or as it enters the harbor in order to conduct an inspection.

The new U.S. Customs and Border Protection Agency (CBP), which was created when the Department of Homeland Security was launched by combining inspectors from the former U.S. Customs Service and the U.S. Immigration and Naturalization Service, has pursued a mix of unilateral, bilateral, and multilateral approaches.[12] First, U.S. Customs authorities mandated that ocean carriers electronically file cargo manifests, which outline the contents of containers, for all ships destined for the United States twenty-four hours in advance of their being loaded in an overseas port. These manifests are then analyzed against the intelligence and other data bases at CBP's new National Targeting Center to determine if the container may pose a risk. If the answer is yes, that container will likely be inspected overseas before it is loaded on a U.S.-bound ship under a new protocol called the Container Security Initiative (CSI).[13] As of November 2005, there were forty-one CSI port agreements in place, wherein host countries permit U.S. Customs inspectors to operate within their jurisdiction and agree to conduct pre-loading inspections of any containers.[14]

Decisions about which containers will *not* be subjected to an inspection are informed by an importer's willingness to participate in another post–September 11 initiative known as the Customs-Trade Partnership Against Terrorism (C-TPAT).[15] C-TPAT importers and transportation companies voluntarily agree to conduct self-assessments of their company operations and supply chains and then put in place security measures to address any vulnerabilities they find. At the multilateral level, U.S. Customs authorities have worked with the Brussels-based World Customs Organization on establishing a new non-binding trade security framework that all countries are encouraged to adopt.

In addition to these Coast Guard and Customs initiatives, the U.S. Department of Energy and Department of Defense have developed their own programs aimed at the weapons of mass destruction threat. They have been focused primarily on developing the means to detect and intercept nuclear weapons, the fissile ingredients such as plutonium and highly enriched uranium used in their construction, and "dirty bombs" (a conventional explosive device containing radioactive material). The Energy Department has been funding and deploying radiation sensors in many of the world's largest ports as part of a program called the Megaport Initiative.[16] These sensors are designed to detect radioactive material within containers on passing trucks. The Pentagon has undertaken a counter-proliferation initiative that involves obtaining permission from seafaring countries to allow specially trained navy boarding teams to conduct inspections of a foreign flag vessel on the high seas when there is intelligence that points to the possibility that smuggled nuclear material or a weapon may be part of the ship's cargo.

Finally, in September 2005, the White House weighed in directly on container security as a part of its new National Maritime Security Strategy.[17] The strategy creates an interagency process to oversee the development of eight supporting plans. These include an International Outreach and Coordination Strategy, a Maritime Transportation System Security Plan, and a Maritime Infrastructure Recovery Plan. The stated objective of the strategy and these plans is to "present a comprehensive national effort to promote global economic stability and protect legitimate activities while preventing hostile or illegal acts within the maritime domain."

A HOUSE OF CARDS

On its face, the flurry of U.S. government initiatives since September 11 suggests substantial progress is being made in securing the global trade and transportation system. Unfortunately, all this activity should not be confused with progress. The approach has been piecemeal, with each agency pursuing its signature program or programs with little regard for the other initiatives. There are vast disparities in the resources that agencies have been allocated, ranging from an $800 million budget for the Department of Energy's Megaport Initiative to no additional funding for the Coast Guard to support its congressionally mandated compliance oversight of the ISPS Code. Perhaps even more problematic are some of the questionable assumptions about the nature of the terrorist threat that underpin these programs.

Further, in an effort to secure funding and public support, agency heads and the White House have oversold the contributions these new initiatives are making toward addressing a very complicated and high-stakes challenge. Should a terrorist attack on the intermodal transportation system occur, the public is likely to be highly skeptical of official assurances after its unrealistic expectations are deflated. In such an environment, a public backlash could ultimately lead the White House and Congress to impose draconian inspection protocols that dramatically raise costs and disrupt cross-border trade flows.

The new "risk management" programs advanced by the Customs and Border Protection Agency (CBP) are especially vulnerable to being discredited should terrorists succeed in turning a container into a poor-man's missile. Before stepping down as commissioner in late-November 2005, the agency's head, Robert Bonner, repeatedly stated in public speeches and in congressional testimony that his inspectors "inspect all high risk cargo containers."[18]

Former Commissioner Bonner is correct that only a tiny percentage of containers pose any potential security risk. However, CBP's risk-management tools are not capable of identifying which containers make up that small percentage that pose a security risk.

The fact is that there is very little counterterrorism intelligence available to support the agency's targeting system. That leaves customs inspectors to rely primarily on past experience in identifying criminal or regulatory misconduct to determine if a containerized shipment might potentially be compromised for nefarious purposes. This should not inspire confidence, given the fact that the U.S. Congress's watchdog, the Government Accountability Office (GAO), and the Department of Homeland Security's own inspector general have documented glaring weaknesses with the methodology, underlying assumptions, and execution of Customs targeting practices.[19]

Prior to September 11, the cornerstone of the risk assessment framework used by Customs inspectors was to identify "known shippers" that had an established track record of being engaged in legitimate commercial activity and playing by the rules. Since September 11, the agency has built on that model by extracting a commitment from shippers to follow the supply chain security practices outlined in the Customs-Trade Partnership Against Terrorism.[20] As long as there is not specific intelligence to tell inspectors otherwise, shipments from C-TPAT companies are viewed as presenting little risk.

The problem is that measures that may have made sense for combating crime do not automatically translate for combating determined terrorists. Private companies can put in place meaningful security safeguards that can deter criminals from exploiting legitimate cargo and conveyances for illicit purposes, but a terrorist attack involving a weapon of mass destruction would differ in three important ways. First, it is likely to be a one-time operation and most private company security measures are not designed to prevent single-event infractions. Second, terrorists are likely to find it particularly attractive to target a legitimate company with a well-known brand name precisely because they can count on these shipments entering the United States with only a cursory look or no inspection at all. Third, terrorists would be more willing than criminals to exploit the supply chains of well-established companies because they understand that, if a weapon of mass destruction entered the United States via a trusted shipper, the Customs system would come under paralyzing scrutiny.

The International Ship and Port Facility Security code would contribute to the problem of managing the aftermath of a terrorist attack involving an established importer. This is because all containers arriving in a U.S. port today are handled by marine terminals and carried aboard vessels that have been certified by their host governments as compliant with the code. There are no exceptions because if the loading facility or ship were not so certified, it would be denied permission by the Coast Guard to enter a U.S. port. Accordingly, the credibility of the ISPS code as a risk management tool is not likely to survive the aftermath of a terrorist attack involving a maritime container.

America's container security initiatives are not posing a meaningful barrier to determined terrorists. Neither are the radiation sensors being deployed by the U.S. Department of Energy. The technology currently being deployed around the world is not up to the task of detecting a nuclear weapon, a lightly shielded dirty bomb, or highly enriched uranium. Nuclear weapons are well shielded so that they can be readily handled, and give off very little radioactivity. Dirty bombs give off more radiation, but if terrorists were to place them in a box lined with lead, sensors are unlikely to detect sufficient levels of radioactivity to register an alarm. Finally, highly enriched uranium, which can be used in the construction of a nuclear weapon, has such a long half-life that it emits too little radiation to be readily detected.[21]

This leaves the Pentagon's counter-proliferation initiative, where boarding teams are sent on container ships at sea to determine if they are carrying weapons of mass destruction.[22] Even if there were enough trained boarding teams to perform these inspections on a regular basis—and there are not—there is the very practical problem that inspecting the contents of cargo containers at sea is nearly impossible to do. Containers are so closely packed into a container ship that they are simply not accessible to inspectors. This fact combined with the number of containers—upward of 3,000 per ship—guarantees that, in the absence of very detailed intelligence, inspectors will be able to perform only the most cursory of examinations.

In the end, the container security measures being pursued by the U.S. government resemble a house of cards. If the next terrorist attack occurs on U.S. soil and involves a maritime container, it will most likely have come in contact with most—or even all—of these new security protocols. That is, the container likely came from a C-TPAT company that originated or has been transshipped through a CSI port, has been handled in an ISPS-compliant marine facility, and has crossed the ocean on an ISPS-compliant ship. It will have passed through a radiation sensor and gone undetected. The ship may even have been examined by a navy boarding team. As a consequence, when the attack happens, the entire security regime will be implicated, generating tremendous political pressure to abandon it.

THE WAY AHEAD

We can do better. With relatively modest investments and a bit of ingenuity, the international intermodal system can have credible security while simultaneously improving its efficiency and reliability. What is required are a series of measures that collectively enhance visibility and accountability within global supply chains.

As a starting point, the United States should work with the Association of Southeast Asian Nations (ASEAN) and the European Union (EU) in authorizing third parties to conduct validation audits of the security protocols contained in the International Ship and Port Facility Security code and the World Customs Organization's new framework for security and trade facilitation. The auditing companies carrying out these inspections should be required to post a bond as a guarantor against substandard performance and be provided with appropriate liability protections should good-faith efforts prove insufficient to prevent a security breach. A multilateral auditing organization made up of experienced inspectors and modeled on the International Atomic Energy Commission should be created to periodically audit the third-party auditors. This organization also should be charged with investigating major incidents and, when appropriate, recommending changes to established security protocols.

To minimize the risk that containers will be targeted by terrorist organizations between the factory shipping the goods and the final destination, the next step must be for governments to create incentives for the speedy adoption of new technical standards, to be developed by the International Standards Organization, for tracking a container and monitoring its integrity. By knowing the exact location of a container at any time, and whether it has been entered in an unauthorized manner, security officials can be easily directed to potential problem containers. The Radio Frequency Identification (RFID) technologies now being used by the Department of Defense for the global movement of military goods can provide a model for such a regime.[23]

Washington should embrace and actively promote the widespread adoption of a novel container security project being sponsored by the Container Terminal Operators Association (CTOA) of Hong Kong. Starting in late 2004, every container arriving in two of the busiest marine terminals in the world has been passing, at average speeds of fifteen kilometers per hour, through a gamma ray machine to scan its contents, a radiation portal to record the levels of radioactivity found within the container, and optical character recognition cameras, which photograph the numbers painted on the top, back, and two sides of the container. These scanned images, radiation profiles, and digital photos are then stored in a database for customs authorities to immediately access if and when they want.[24]

The marine terminals in Hong Kong have invested in this system for three reasons. Most importantly, they are hoping that this 100 percent scanning regime will deter a terrorist organization from placing a weapon of mass destruction in a container passing through their port facilities. A second reason for making this investment is to minimize the potential disruption associated with targeting containers for inspection at the loading port. Third, by maintaining a record of the contents of every container entering their terminal, the port is able to provide government authorities with a forensic tool that can support a follow-up investigation should a container still slip through with a weapon of mass destruction.

This low-cost system of inspection is being carried out without impeding the operations of these very busy marine terminals. It could be put in place in every major container port in the world at a cost of $1.5 billion, or approximately $15 per container. The system could be paid for by authorizing ports to collect user fees that cover the costs associated with purchasing the equipment, maintaining its upkeep, and investing in upgrades when appropriate. Once such a system is operating globally, each nation would be in a position to monitor its exports and to spot-check its imports against the images first collected at the loading port.[25]

The total cost of third-party compliance inspections, deploying "smart" containers, and operating a cargo scanning system such as the one being piloted in Hong Kong would likely reach $50 to $100 per container depending on the number of containers an importer has and the complexity of its supply chain. Such an investment would allow container security to quickly move from the current "trust, but don't verify" system to a "trust, but verify" one. Even if the final price tag came in at $100 additional cost per container, it would raise the average price of cargo by only .06 percent.[26]

Happily, developing the means to track and verify the status of containers provides benefits that go beyond security. This is because there is also a powerful commercial case for constructing this capability. When retailers and manufacturers can monitor the status of all their orders, they can confidently reach out to a wider array of suppliers to provide them what they need at the best price.

Transportation providers will benefit from greater visibility as well. Terminal operators and container ships that have earlier and more detailed information about incoming goods can develop load and unload plans for outbound and inbound vessels in advance, and can direct truck movements with greater efficiency.

Greater visibility also brings potential benefits for dealing with insurance issues. Knowing precisely where and when a theft takes place makes it easier to decipher the nature of the threat and to identify what breaches, if any, contributed to the loss. When there is damage, it is much easier to track down the responsible parties. In short, rather than spreading the risk across the entire transportation community, insurance premiums can be more accurately tailored. This dynamic, in turn, creates a stronger market incentive for all participants in the supply chain to exercise greater care.

Even if there were no terrorist threat, there are ample reasons for individual governments, ASEAN, the EU, the WTO, and other regional and international organizations to place port, border, and transportation security at the top of the multilateral agenda. Enhanced controls within the global trade lanes will help all countries reduce theft, stop the smuggling of drugs, humans, and counterfeit goods, crack down on tariff evasion, and improve export controls.

RECOMMENDATIONS

In addition to a sustained and systematic effort to bolster the security of the global intermodal transportation system, Washington must simultaneously invest in securing America's neglected waterfront, which serves as the on-ramp and off-ramp for that system.

There are seven steps that must be taken right away.

15.1. OVER THE NEXT EIGHTEEN MONTHS, THE DEPARTMENT OF DEFENSE MUST WORK CLOSELY WITH THE COAST GUARD (NOW PART OF THE DEPARTMENT OF HOMELAND SECURITY) AND WITH LOCAL AUTHORITIES IN ORGANIZING AND PARTICIPATING IN EXERCISES THAT INVOLVE SIMULATED ATTACKS ON THE NATION'S LARGEST COMMERCIAL SEAPORTS.

15.2. THE DEPARTMENT OF DEFENSE NEEDS TO TAKE THE LEAD ON FUNDING AND SETTING UP JOINT OPERATIONS CENTERS IN ALL MAJOR U.S. COMMERCIAL PORTS: to outfit them with advanced information and communications technology that supports surveillance and data sharing; and to provide the necessary training to the local, state, and federal agency participants. This should be completed by 2007.

15.3. THE U.S. NAVY SHOULD REPOSITION ONE OF ITS TWO SALVAGE SHIPS IN NORFOLK, VIRGINIA, TO THE WEST COAST AND TAKE THE LEAD IN DRAWING UP COMMERCIAL SALVAGE CONTRACTS TO SUPPORT DOMESTIC HARBOR CLEARANCE. Over the next five years, the Navy should double its salvage fleet from four vessels to eight, and base two of them on the West Coast, two on the Gulf Coast, and two on the East Coast. The remaining two can be deployed overseas to support navy operations.

15.4. THE NATIONAL OCEANOGRAPHIC AND ATMOSPHERIC ADMINISTRATION (NOAA) HYDROGRAPHIC RESEARCH VESSELS SHOULD RECEIVE ADDITIONAL FUNDING TO COMPLETE BOTTOM SURVEYS OF ALL MAJOR U.S. COMMERCIAL SEAPORTS. This baseline information is indispensable in quickly spotting mines, should an adversary deploy them.

15.5. THE COAST GUARD NEEDS TO SEE ANNUAL FUNDING DOUBLED TO $2 BILLION TO REPLACE ITS ANCIENT FLEET OF VESSELS AND AIRCRAFT, and to bring its command and control capabilities into the twenty-first century. Many of its cutters, helicopters, and planes are operating long beyond their anticipated service life and are routinely experiencing major breakdowns. Under the current delivery schedule, it will be thirty years before the Coast Guard has the kind of assets it needs today to perform its mission. This could leave a two-decade gap in capability as the existing fleet becomes too decrepit and dangerous to operate.[27]

15.6. CONGRESS SHOULD AUTHORIZE THE REALLOCATION OF ALL SEAPORT DUTIES AND FEES BACK INTO THE PORTS TO SUPPORT SECURITY UPGRADES AND INFRASTRUCTURE IMPROVEMENTS. Currently, ports are the only transportation sector where the federal government is "parasitic." That is, unlike airports and highways, the federal treasury takes more money away than it returns. According to the Coast Guard, seaports need to invest upward of $5 billion to put in place minimal access control and physical security measures.[28] Neither the ports nor their city or state governments have such resources.

15.7. THE FEDERAL GOVERNMENT NEEDS TO DEVELOP A NATIONAL PORT PLAN THAT TAKES INTO ACCOUNT LONG-TERM TRADE AND SECURITY TRENDS. Relying on a patchwork quilt of locally based decisions for managing this critical infrastructure is just not acceptable.

◆ ◆ ◆

In the end, as our dependency on global trade grows and the catastrophic terrorist threat persists, Washington must start acting as though our commercial seaports are the critical national security assets that they are. There are few more urgent priorities than making sure America's ports and related transportation systems are secure. Together, they are responsible for moving the overwhelming majority of world trade, and together they must possess adequate capacity, redundancy, and resiliency to meet the daunting challenges that lie ahead.[29]

16. RECREATING OUR BORDERS

In 2002, a Web site utilized by al Qaeda noted that "in 1996, 254 million persons, 75 million automobiles, and 3.5 million trucks entered America from Mexico. At the 38 official border crossings, only 5 percent of this huge total is inspected. . . . These are figures that really call for contemplation."[1] Border security presents an especially vexing series of policy dilemmas, because while the permeability of our nation's borders bolsters our economy and diversifies our society, it also places the country at risk.

The flow of people and goods across the northern and southern borders lies at the heart of the country's prosperity.[2] Yet this flow has also served as a conduit for terrorists and their weapons. In 1997, the Palestinian Ghazi Ibrahim Abu Mezer was apprehended on three occasions crossing the Washington–British Columbia border. He was later discovered attempting to build a bomb in New York City. In 1999, Lucia Gaofalo was arrested for attempting to smuggle suspected terrorists into the United States from Quebec. Later that year, an alert Customs inspector in Port Angeles, Washington, caught Ahmed Ressam, the "millennium bomber," trying to bring materials into the United States to blow up the Los Angeles Airport.

Despite these threats, in the decades preceding September 11, protecting America's 6,000 miles of land borders was not perceived as a national security issue. After September 11, new attention was devoted to the inadequate infrastructure, insufficient staffing, stove-piped organizations, and Byzantine immigration process along those borders. But secure borders remain a long way off: Crossing points are congested and technologies to detect individuals and materials entering the country illegally are seriously outdated. Personnel shortages along the border, coupled with a lack of interagency intelligence sharing, has further undermined our ability to vigilantly police the border, and immigration databases are currently unable to effectively keep track of individuals entering and leaving the country, much less locate and deport those who succeed in entering or overstaying illegally.

To be sure, cross-border trade is critical to the economic well-being of the United States, and the demands of this legitimate policy interest must be calibrated with any effort to secure the border. Total trade between the United States and Mexico has grown from just over $100 billion in 1994, the first year of NAFTA, to over $236 billion in 2003.[3] To the extent that the border can be strengthened without creating undue shipping delays and economic damage to border communities, these kinds of approaches should be pursued. But while the American economy relies on access to inexpensive labor and the unfettered movement of goods, economic dictates are not absolute, and a secure homeland—which starts with a secure border—is a precondition for economic prosperity, and a cornerstone of America's national interest.

In a recent poll conducted by Hart Research, U.S. voters echoed this point by rating security and protection of U.S. borders as their top homeland security concern.[4] On November 30, 2005, Secretary of Homeland Security Michael Chertoff announced a multi-year plan to address the border, the Secure Border Initiative (SBI). The plan fails to deal with the border in the context of the terrorist threat we face. The ad hoc redeployment of resources and the failure to start with a rigorous analysis of the scope of the border security problem are symptomatic of the Bush administration's remedial and piecemeal efforts to secure the nation's frontlines.

At the time of publication, President Bush announced a new strategy to secure the border as part of his immigration reform agenda. The administration's proposal calls for $1.9 billion to fund both new surveillance technologies and a larger border patrol. Under this plan, up to six thousand National Guard troops would be deployed along the border as a stopgap until new border patrol personnel have been hired, trained, and assigned. The president's initiative, which emerged in the context of a gathering political storm over immigration, has met with strong resistance. Governors, including Arnold Schwarzenegger (R-CA), have criticized the plan as haphazard and incomplete. It provides little guidance to state capitals on the precise missions the National Guard troops would carry out; it also scants the problem of an increasingly vulnerable northern border. These shortcomings are to be expected when the impetus for action is political necessity, rather than strategic vision.

What is needed is not efforts to build fences, block immigrants, and deploy popular technologies, but a fundamental reassessment of where the problems of border security lie. The Bush administration has allowed itself to be completely distracted by the immigration debate. Although immigration and border security are related in a number of ways, the immigration debate should not be confused with efforts to secure our borders against the threat of terrorist infiltration. The paramount concern must be preventing terrorists from crossing our borders to do our nation harm. The first step toward achieving such a comprehensive border security strategy is the systematic reevaluation of border security. Here we divide the issue into four categories: personnel, technology and infrastructure, weapons of mass destruction, and illegal immigration. By assessing each of these categories in turn, and by considering the ramification of changes in policy, we will be better able to manage our borders.

PERSONNEL

When the Department of Homeland Security was created, the traditional roles played by agriculture inspectors in the Department of Agriculture, Customs agents and inspectors in the Treasury Department, Border Patrol agents, immigration inspectors, and interior enforcement agents from the Department of Justice were all shifted into the Department of Homeland Security in an effort to streamline border security efforts. The new agencies that emerged were to follow a simple formula: Customs and Border Protection (CBP)—to include Border Patrol—were to maintain the day-to-day operations of the border, managing security and all inspections. Immigration and Customs Enforcement (ICE) was to serve as the chief investigative unit of the new department and track down major cases that had managed to slip through the cracks. Customs and Immigration Services would take over the major paperwork efforts of processing visa requests and payment of tariffs. Almost immediately after the plan was announced, problems arose.

The bureaucratic reshuffling did not go smoothly. Immigration and Customs Enforcement originally stood for "Investigations and Criminal Enforcement," but the FBI fought and won a turf battle over use of the word "investigations." In the meantime, Detention and Removal Operations (DRO), which are responsible for illegal aliens inside the United States, was shifted to the new department, while the immigration judges who determine the fate of these individuals were left in the Department of Justice.[5] Up and down the border, all agencies reported personnel shortages. ICE and DRO were faced with significant budget shortfalls that resulted in hiring freezes.[6] The traditional missions of various agencies took a backseat to the new priority of locating terrorists and preventing attacks on the homeland. Yet new money and training for this formidable task were elusive and remain so today. To cut costs, the new department set performance and capability standards for the new organizations to the lowest common denominator of legacy agencies. When Immigration and Naturalization Services (INS) and Customs were combined, for instance, the INS requirement that agents speak Spanish was dropped because Customs agents were not required to have language skills. Directives like this from Washington abounded but in many cases undermined the clear strategy heralded by the new department's press releases. When Congress inserted into the Patriot Act a requirement for more agents along the northern border, for example, the Office of Homeland Security moved agents from the southern border, thereby increasing the vulnerability in the south, and undermining the intentions of Congress.[7] The failure to develop an integrated strategy in the wake of September 11 is perhaps best illustrated by the continued lack of a nationwide threat and vulnerability assessment as ordered by the Homeland Security Act of 2002.

Some incremental progress has been made in augmenting the numbers of border security personnel: In the 2006 Homeland Security Appropriations Bill, funding was provided for an additional 1,000 Border Patrol agents. With these new hires, Border Patrol will increase by nearly 3,000 agents since September 11. Increased funding will allow ICE to add roughly 250 new criminal investigators, 400 new immigration enforcement agents, and 100 new deportation officers—the first additions since the department was created.[8] But there is no way to determine whether these numbers are sufficient. More individuals are being added to accomplish a task that is still unclear. In 2004, Congress appropriated funding to do a comprehensive assessment of personnel requirements on the northern and southern borders to determine how many people are needed to manage the flow of traffic and enforce border areas between ports of entry. This assessment has yet to be completed, leaving the Strategic Border Initiative shortsighted.

To protect the border, a comprehensive border personnel assessment must be completed to identify how many individuals will be needed to monitor the entire U.S. border, twenty-four hours a day, seven days a week. The resulting strategy must include a clear command and control structure to ensure proper intelligence sharing among all agencies. It must also supply border crossings, DRO facilities, and border communities with the immigration and customs specialists needed to ensure adequate screening of all individuals and products entering the country without hindering the flow of traffic.

TECHNOLOGY AND INFRASTRUCTURE

In addition to personnel, new technologies and a functional, dynamic infrastructure will be enormously important in securing our borders. To date, various technologies have been employed along our borders to detect and keep track of materials and individuals in transit, but these measures have been implemented in an ad hoc, inconsistent manner, and many of the technologies currently in use appear ill-suited to the task at hand. At busy border crossings, radiographic machines are used to screen only a fraction of vehicles for smuggled drugs or hidden people. Multiple database technologies are used to identify individuals who legally and illegally cross the border. Between ports of entry, multiple technologies are employed. Border Patrol uses cameras and sensors and acts on information gathered from tethered balloons and unmanned aerial vehicles (UAVs) maintained by the Department of Defense. Quarter-century-old sensors typically used to monitor seismic activity have been utilized to detect individuals attempting to cross the border. Sensors are activated when individuals step on them, but are also triggered by animals and blowing brush. This results in so many false alarms that the sensors are routinely ignored by short-staffed Border Patrol offices. In just one sector along the southern border, more than 30,000 hits were reported in just one month. Cameras are also used, but staffing shortages have reduced their effectiveness, with one agent often responsible for the activity logs and response deployment for over twenty-six cameras.[9]

Tethered radar balloons are deployed along the southern border to detect low-flying air traffic. The balloons have impressive results for smuggler interception, but cost almost $2 million to purchase and more than $3 million to maintain annually. The tethered balloons are operated and maintained by the Department of Defense and are available to DHS only when the Department of Defense does not need them. When they are available, the balloons often fail in bad weather. Despite these shortcomings, the balloons are considered among the best capabilities being employed to protect our borders.

In 2003, DHS announced the creation of the Arizona Border Control Initiative and began actively employing Defense UAVs to detect individuals attempting to cross the Arizona desert. No significant study has been completed by the administration to determine the efficacy of UAVs in preventing illegal immigrants or shipments from entering the country, yet in fiscal year 2006, the Bush administration will spend an additional $10 million on the technology.

As these cases indicate, the deployment of various technologies to monitor the border since September 11 has been inconsistent, and large investments are being made without first assessing the comparative advantages of various devices. Hundreds of miles go unpatrolled every day, despite the fact that technology exists to monitor the entire border. In SBI, Secretary Chertoff has committed to creating an integrated border security system "including more Unmanned Aerial Vehicles (UAVs), aerial assets, Remote Video Surveillance camera systems, and sensors" to be deployed beginning in 2007. However, the department has not come up with a comprehensive research and development (R&D) program to inform this step, despite recommendations to do so from independent investigators.[10] In the past, technologies intended for other purposes have been employed on the border and have met with mixed results. Before dedicating scarce dollars to buying existing technologies, it is imperative that research and assessments be conducted to ensure that the men and women on the frontlines of our nation's security are as well equipped as the men and women this country sends into combat. Specifically, equipment purchased for monitoring the border should not be bought "off the shelf" and modified. Rather, a set of standards and requirements should be developed that will inform the production of new equipment to meet the needs of border enforcement. In addition, these systems—currently stove-piped within old agencies, and often confined to a specific geographic area—should be combined into a nationwide system to allow for integrated and constant monitoring.

WEAPONS OF MASS DESTRUCTION

To a smuggler of nuclear weapons, the miles of unpatrolled border and congested ports-of-entry provide countless opportunities. The vital task of preventing a nuclear attack from within the United States currently falls to equipment which is insufficient and to border personnel who are overextended and, in many cases, who are not trained to detect nuclear material in transit. Again, our national efforts to address this problem suffer from a decentralized approach, with inadequate or nonexistent interagency coordination, a resulting duplication of efforts, widespread use of inappropriate technologies that have been retooled for the task at hand, rather than designed for it, and the conspicuous absence of any overall government plan to confront the problem.[11]

At ports of entry, CBP officers use portable radiation detectors (PRDs) and radiation portal monitors to screen trucks and trains for weapons of mass destruction. Hand-held devices are also used to screen some but not all vehicles. The employment of this equipment is determined by how many individuals are on a shift at a given time, who is trained to use the equipment, and whether the equipment is working. At the same time, CBP inspectors are looking for drugs, smuggled individuals, and other contraband, all while trying to ensure that the flow of traffic is not impeded, and often with a language barrier and no intelligence to direct efforts.

CBP has issued over 9,400 PRDs to agents and inspectors at a cost of nearly $1,200 each.[12] These are small, pager-like devices worn by individual inspectors to detect radiation. They are not intended to be detection devices for containers or vehicles, because they have to be in close proximity to the nuclear or radiological source in order to detect it. Despite this, CBP continues to deploy the devices. The Government Accountability Office (GAO) expressed concern that "DHS has not yet deployed the best available technologies for detecting radiological and nuclear materials at U.S. border crossings and ports of entry. Specifically, we have found that CBP's primary radiation detection equipment—radiation pagers—have certain limitations and may be inappropriate for the task."[13]

More than 470 radiation portal monitors have been deployed throughout the United States.[14] This equipment allows a vehicle to be driven through and reviewed for radiological material. Although the equipment is in the field, government investigators have found that the way the equipment is used has reduced its effectiveness: Sensitivity is often reduced to eliminate alarms and trucks are run through the monitors too quickly to produce accurate readings.[15]

On April 13, 2005, the president issued National Security Presidential Directive 43 (NSPD-43/HSPD-14) to create the Domestic Nuclear Detection Office (DNDO) to be housed in the Department of Homeland Security. Despite expressing doubts in the mission and effectiveness of this office, Congress allotted nearly $200 million for the development of a system to detect and report terrorist attempts to transport or use radiological or nuclear materials.[16] Despite efforts at integrating multiple agencies in this process, DNDO lacks the organizational power within the DHS to compel agencies to act according to its recommendations. Currently, the Department of Defense is testing radiation monitors for deployment on U.S. military bases. It is unclear to what degree their findings have been shared or implemented by other agencies, and how DNDO will remedy such problems.[17]

If it is to be effective, the president should strengthen DNDO and compel all U.S. agencies involved in the detection and prevention of nuclear materials to operate under its authority. DNDO should have budget authority over activities of all national labs for research and development on emerging technologies and establish requirements, rather than recommendations, for deployment of technologies.

IMMIGRATION

In recent years, the immigration system has received the attention of the Bush administration and Congress, in terms of both the nation's security and its economic dependence on immigrant labor. These questions are critical, and given the political nature of the issue, will be revisited numerous times in the future. While the immigration debate is perhaps as old as the country itself, the fact that several of the September 11 hijackers were present in the country on lapsed visas has added a new urgency and a new dimension to that debate, and traditional questions about whom we admit to this country must be reevaluated in light of the threat of foreign terrorists operating within our borders.

When the late Congresswoman Barbara Jordan (D-TX) chaired the bipartisan Commission on Immigration Reform in 1994, she noted in her first report to Congress that immigration and border policy can be measured by a simple yardstick:

- people who should get in, do get in;
- people who should not get in, are kept out; and
- people who are judged deportable, are required to leave.[18]

These criteria are in tension with one another—regulations that promote one may end up undermining another—but using Johnson's yardstick, the current system is failing overall and in each individual area.

In the first case, academic institutions, scientific organizations, and U.S. businesses report continued difficulties in obtaining visas for students and professionals.[19] The problem is that academic institutions and businesses have the least incentive to assist the government in monitoring compliance to immigration laws. To mitigate this problem, every U.S. institution interested in sponsoring a visa or in employing a foreign national must have at least one individual per every one hundred foreign nationals certified in understanding immigration processes. By mandating training, organizations will be able to be held accountable for failing to comply with immigration law.

To complicate this problem, while people who should be able to enter the country are often excluded, people who should be excluded are often able to enter. The United States Visitor and Immigrant Status Indicator Technology (US-VISIT) is the system being implemented at airports, seaports, and land borders to comply with statutory mandates to track the arrival and departure of foreign visitors. Since its development, it has been plagued with difficulties from database management to international distrust. At this point, the administration has met requirements for tracking individuals who enter the United States, ensuring that every person who enters the country is tracked—with the exception of individuals presenting Canadian or Mexican documentation. But in light of the fact that most people entering the country via a land border do have Canadian or Mexican documentation, this means that only 22 percent of all border crossings into the United States are tracked through the system.[20] The exit component of the program is virtually nonexistent: No system is in place to inform law enforcement of individuals who failed to leave by the designated time. The biggest challenge of US-VISIT, however, is the sheer volume of individuals passing through the system. To properly implement US-VISIT, a significant investment in infrastructure must take place. Staffing and equipment to track individuals leaving the country are needed. Databases must be fully functional and provide real-time actionable intelligence. One of the failures that enabled the September 11 hijackers to carry out their deadly attacks was the fact that they were able to overstay their visas. In the current configuration of US-VISIT, this systemic vulnerability endures.

The biometric technology (fingerprint and photographic indentification) included in US-VISIT and other systems is not a panacea for the border security problem. Law enforcement efforts must be in place to remove individuals caught entering the United States illegally. Detention and Removal Operations are tasked with providing custody management to support the removal of illegal immigrants through the immigration courts and to enforce their departure from the United States. To fulfill this mission, the DRO facilities feed, house, and provide medical attention to the detainees until their hearings before election judges. Historically, the DRO has been severely underfunded. More than 1.2 million illegal immigrants were apprehended in fiscal year 2005.[21] The DRO, however, is capable of detaining only 200,000 illegal immigrants a year, and is funded to maintain only 19,444 beds annually. Through overcrowding of detention centers and cutting funds from equipment budgets, DRO has managed to add an additional 2,000 beds annually to that number. As a result, the DRO releases non-criminal aliens into the United States on their own recognizance and schedules them for deportation hearings—a practice known as "catch and release." Eighty to 90 percent of these individuals never appear in court and are left to work and live in the United States.[22]

In the Strategic Border Initiative, the Bush administration has made clear that it understands the danger of this practice, but to date the administration has done little to provide the funding to solve it. The administration has pledged to completely eliminate the practice, pledging to develop the capability to return every single illegal entrant amenable to removal—no exceptions. The goal is to achieve significant progress on this capability in less than a year. This will be achieved through greater efficiencies in the removal process, cooperation with foreign governments, increasing detention capacity, and expanding expedited removal.[23]

Despite this commitment, the Homeland Security Appropriations Bill contained funds that will enable DRO to pay for the additional 2,000 beds it currently provides only by cutting into other appropriations, and will not allow DHS to further expand detention capacity. Even with this increased funding, DRO will not keep pace with the increased number of individuals being captured along the U.S. border. In Brownsville, Texas, the Border Patrol reported that out of the 14,000 non-Mexicans apprehended through May of fiscal year 2004, 9,500 were released into the United States due to lack of DRO capacity. Furthermore, while the Bush administration claims that cooperation for deportation with foreign countries will allow for an expedited process, some nations refuse to accept individuals who have made it to American shores, including Vietnam, China, Iraq, Iran, Nigeria, and Eritrea.

The immigration challenge will not be met unless the basic tracking and deportation processes are in place. For the purposes of homeland security, the ability of individuals to work in the United States is less important than the necessity that exists for U.S. officials to know the true identities of every individual entering, residing, or leaving the country. To ensure legitimate travelers are allowed to enter, the Bush administration must complete the exit portion of US-VISIT and ensure all databases are interoperable, so visitors can be tracked regardless of how or where they attempt to enter the United States. For those who are caught entering illegally, steps must be taken to ensure they are returned to their countries and not released into the United States. To meet this need, an assessment of the needs of all of the agencies involved in the detention and removal operation—including immigration judges, prosecutors, and detention guards—must be taken. In addition to efforts to look for creative ways to monitor individuals awaiting deportation, the United States must make it clear to foreign governments that refusing to accept the return of their citizens who illegally attempted to enter the United States will have meaningful consequences.

INVESTMENT WITHOUT VISION

While the Bush administration has taken steps to increase border security, these efforts have been ad hoc; they do not reflect any serious, integrated vision of the full scope of the border security issue, and as such their impact has been minimal. One critical lesson of the past several years is that appropriations—while desperately needed—are not enough. Until a comprehensive review of threats and vulnerabilities is undertaken, even the recent $2 billion in proposed spending by the administration will fail to provide any measurable amount of security.

A case in point is the administration's much lauded Arizona Border Control (ABC) Initiative. Created in 2004 to patrol the most vulnerable part of the U.S. border, the ABC Initiative borrowed UAVs from the Department of Defense and redeployed agents from other overburdened sectors to catch illegal immigrants and smugglers. The project yielded thousands of arrests and seizures. However, it also caused significant problems for other border areas. By stemming the flow of traffic in one area of the border, traffic increased elsewhere, causing governors to declare a state of emergency while neighboring border agents and state law enforcement officials complained about a lack of attention from the Department of Homeland Security.[24] To compensate for failures of the federal government to solve this problem, the state of New Mexico was forced to spend almost $2 million in state revenue to secure border communities. Volunteer militia groups assembled to try to stem the flow of illegal immigrants. Deaths increased by more than 25 percent and violence was rampant.[25] This was the result of a $10 million investment intended to allow the government to take "operational control of the border."[26] The clear lesson of this debacle is that investment in the absence of strategy or analysis will leave us worse off than if we had not acted at all.

CONCLUSION

Bush administration policies have failed to secure America's porous border. To accomplish this task, the United States needed a comprehensive border security strategy. Secretary of Homeland Security Michael Chertoff's plan provides no baseline for progress, because no assessment of what is needed has been conducted on any of the major areas of concern. Strategies being introduced by the Department of Homeland Security will continue to be tactical and ad hoc if comprehensive reviews of staffing requirements, immigration priorities, and technologies are not completed.

National security now depends on our ability to prevent terrorists from crossing the border. It depends on the well-being of the communities and individuals who live and work along the border, where the concept of "two countries—one community" has been the central pillar of the good relations between the United States and our neighbors to the north and south. Those who serve our nation on our borders deserve nothing less than a well-researched and reasoned plan backed with adequate funding. No longer can we ignore the needs of our border regions. Our terrorist enemies will not wait, and neither can we.

RECOMMENDATIONS

Even in the absence of a comprehensive assessment, several imperatives are clear:

16.1. SECURITY FROM THE THREAT OF TERRORISM SHOULD BE THE PRIMARY FOCUS OF U.S. BORDER EFFORTS. Strong physical barriers on the border with Mexico are essential. Approximately 150,000 "OTMs," or other-than-Mexican illegal immigrants, crossed this border in 2005, and are able to blend into American society and pose a serious security threat once inside our borders.

16.2. UTILIZING TECHNOLOGY AND PERSONNEL, THE ENTIRE U.S. NORTHERN AND SOUTHERN BORDER MUST BE CONTINUALLY MONITORED. Capability must be developed to respond to the detection of illegal crossings.

16.3. ELIMINATE "WHACK-A-MOLE" RESPONSES, SUCH AS THE ARIZONA BORDER CONTROL INITIATIVE, THAT SIMPLY RELOCATE MAJOR CROSSING POINTS WITHOUT REDUCING OVERALL FLOW. The practice of redeployment to targeted areas should be ended and focus placed instead on augmenting capabilities.

16.4. U.S. VISA AND ASYLUM PROCESSES MUST BE MADE TO CONFORM WITH THE MEXICAN AND CANADIAN SYSTEMS, SO THAT, EXCEPT IN RARE CASES, ALL THREE COUNTRIES AGREE ON WHO IS ADMITTED.

16.5. DEVELOPMENT AND DEPLOYMENT OF COUNTERFEIT-PROOF VISITOR IDENTIFICATION FOR GUEST WORKERS AND PERMANENT ALIENS.

16.6. WORKPLACE ENFORCEMENT OF IMMIGRATION RULES MUST BE DONE ON A CONTINUAL BASIS. Sponsoring institutions must have personnel certified in understanding the immigration process and documentation.

16.7. DETECTION OF RADIOACTIVE SOURCES MUST BE PRIORITIZED AND INEFFECTIVE PERSONAL RADIATION DETECTORS SHOULD BE REPLACED BY RADIATION PORTAL MONITORS AND X-RAY SYSTEMS.

◆ ◆ ◆

Some of these measures are as controversial as they are necessary. To the degree that a guest worker program or amnesty initiative might take some of the sting out of these proposals, the administration and Congress ought to consider them seriously.

17. LAND OF SWEET LIBERTIES

It was all but inevitable that on September 12 there would be outraged Americans willing, as Benjamin Franklin had feared over two centuries earlier, to "trade liberty for security." A week after September 12, President Bush, speaking to a joint session of Congress, told Americans that the terrorists hated us because we stood for freedom. Federal authorities then began taking a series of steps in the name of security that restricted that freedom, and in doing so repeatedly stretched and violated domestic and international law.

The list of worrisome developments is long: electronic surveillance of Americans in the United States without court order; the order to use military tribunals to try U.S. citizens as enemy combatants; long-term, open-ended detention of captives; the use of torture techniques in interrogations of detainees; heavy reliance on secret renditions of suspects to the security services of foreign governments; and the creation of hermetically sealed virtual penal colonies like Guantanamo Bay. Many Americans also expressed concern with what they feared might be abuses related to government mining of data, ethnic profiling, video surveillance, the requisitioning of private data without court review, and the shielding of executive branch actions from congressional oversight.

Americans miss something important if they focus on these measures expanding federal power only as discrete affronts to civil liberties sensitivities. The problem with the way government authorities are now seeking to balance civil liberties and national security goes beyond the substantive objections we might have to a particular action or policy. Rather, we have not developed a considered framework for striking a balance when fundamental values collide—a balance, that is, between our desire for security and our dedication to a free society.

Without such a framework there cannot be broad public agreement on what actions are needed to increase our security from terrorism at

217

home. This lack of consensus has made it difficult for both the federal government and local jurisdictions to pursue a number of measures that would enhance security, such as:

- implementing the Real ID Act with state-of-the-art, foolproof driver's licenses issued only to users whose identity has been reliably confirmed;
- the creation of a trusted traveler program in which citizens voluntarily carry identity cards and submit to background investigations;
- a requirement for background investigation prior to employment in sensitive, critical infrastructures such as private security firms, chemical plants, railroads, biological laboratories, electric power systems, and others;
- the expansion of the use of smart, closed-circuit television cameras (intelligent CCTV) for surveillance of public spaces;
- the establishment or enhancement of intelligence capabilities within city or state police departments;
- the random screening of backpacks and other bags in subways and other mass transit systems; and
- the use of "tip" programs for citizens to provide information on suspicious activities that they believe might be related to terrorism.

These and other programs do have the potential to infringe on citizen rights and lead innocent people to fear government, but if they are accompanied by carefully devised safeguards, they could significantly enhance our security. Unfortunately, broad national backing for these measures is unlikely now, given the performance of the administration to date and the mistrust it has engendered among many citizens. The government's aggressive approach to counterterrorism at home has stiffened public resistance to otherwise reasonable security measures. A serious effort to recalibrate the balance between civil liberties and security is overdue.

WHERE IS THE DEBATE?

Americans appear broadly to agree that it is reasonable to strike an appropriate balance between security and freedom, and not simply sacrifice one for the other. Yet despite a general consensus that the events of September 11 and afterward require us to weigh the competing values, understand the tradeoffs, and define the right balance, most of those engaged in public debate essentially deny that any real choices need to be made. This is true of both the administration and its critics, whenever one side or the other sorties out to defend or oppose a particular policy.

The administration, for example, will posit that many of the grants of new authority it has gained (or desires) are not actually being used, and therefore should be of no practical concern to civil liberties advocates. Consider only the legislative provision that would authorize the government to collect information from public institutions, such as libraries, without a warrant, if the government asserts that the information was necessary for a terrorism investigation.[1] The administration defended its call for the renewal of this provision not by discussing the contributions this substantive authority had made to the detection and prosecution of terrorists, but by claiming that the concerns of paranoid librarians were inconsequential, since the Justice Department had not yet used its new authority to gather such information. In this way, an important policy debate was sidestepped by the claim that there was, in fact, nothing really worth debating at all.

A second stratagem used by those supporting wider authority for the government might be called the "status quo" argument. According to this line of argument, the balance struck years, even decades, ago in other criminal justice contexts is intrinsically well suited to the new and different threat environment. In other words, the powers that the government is seeking are nothing new—just technical extension of prior practice—and therefore should not warrant any new concern. The administration's congressional allies, for example, slipped into an intelligence authorization bill a provision that would expand the FBI's power to demand financial records, without a judge's approval, from car dealers, travel agents, pawnbrokers, and other businesses—a dramatic shift in the traditional obligations of businesses regarding financial transactions. Yet worries about the potential of this provision for abuse were waved off. The explanation of one senior congressional staff member was typical: "This is meant to provide agents with the same amount of flexibility in terrorism investigations that they have in other types of investigations . . . this was really just a technical change."[2] This airy assertion was inaccurate and perhaps even somewhat disingenuous. The new legislation dramatically expands the potential subjects of such investigations. Its sponsors clearly understood it to be a departure from previous practice, which is why they wanted the change in the law—and also why the change was hidden in an omnibus intelligence authorization bill. It was not merely a technical revision that did not warrant debate.

The debate surrounding the administration's highly controversial use of military tribunals provides a particularly vivid example of this political strategy. A Department of Defense Web site regarding the use of these tribunals asserts a long history and tradition within the United States of trying "enemy combatants" before military tribunals—without acknowledging that it is precisely the designation of the prisoners (including Americans) as "enemy combatants" that is a source of concern.[3] Nor is there any discussion of whether a military tribunal is appropriate to the kind of enemy the United States is facing—irregular, non-uniformed personnel—especially since civilian courts have been used for previous cases. Nonetheless, federal authorities would have us believe that this momentous policy departure simply revives prior practice, has already been decided within the bowels of the executive branch, and does not warrant further debate outside.

In each of these examples, the administration used a variety of dismissive assertions—that its actions were "nothing new," signified only a "technical change," were "simply updating the law," had "long history," or reflected "controlling precedent"—to short-circuit debate on recalibrating the balance between security and liberty, and to suggest that the balance as codified pre–September 11 was unaffected by the administration's actions and new congressional grants of police power to federal authorities. This is hardly the way to engage the public in a frank and informed debate.

Many critics of administration policy are likewise culpable. Vigilant as they are to defend the inviolability of American freedom, they too tend to deny that any new balance need be struck—or even mooted. According to some on this side of the divide, new police powers would not materially assist the government in its fight against terrorism. Others argue that the powers in place before September 11 were adequate to counter the jihadists' new threat of terrorism. On the first argument, the champions of civil liberties who assert that the proponents of national security have created a false debate have it wrong. It may be true that some intrusive measures have been wholly irrelevant to security, including such highly contentious post–September 11 program failures as "voluntary interviews" of Arab immigrants that proved not only unsuccessful in eliciting useful information but also alienated an entire community; but some sacrifice of traditional privacy expectations can surely empower government to detect and thwart terrorist plots—in which case the "debate" between liberty and security is not "false." The second argument is just as flawed and, perhaps like the administration's assertions that nothing has changed, a touch disingenuous. It posits that federal law as understood on September 10, 2001, provided authorities with sufficient power to combat terrorism, and that it was a dysfunctional bureaucracy, stove-piping of intelligence, a prosecution-oriented FBI, and lack of leadership that left the door open to the terrorist attacks.[4] There is in fact evidence to support this contention, but the argument ignores how the law compounded these problems, in part by drawing a line between the intelligence community and FBI that impeded the sharing of foreign intelligence.[5] Arguably, the administration's delay in deploying military forces to maintain order in New Orleans when Hurricane Katrina sent water crashing through the levees was due in part to the legal confusion arising from post-Reconstruction law circumscribing the appropriate role of the military in homeland security.[6]

The absence of any successful terrorist attack in the United States since 2001 has also drained the energy of the debate over the tradeoffs between civil liberties and expanded executive national security powers (although the current debate about the National Security Agency's intercept program may yet be an exception). Citizens could reasonably conclude that the government's actions had kept us safe and that it would be unwise to "mess with success." Yet the counterterrorism agenda can hardly be seen as complete in the absence of serious discussion about these tradeoffs. The reprieve from jihadist attack that Americans have enjoyed on their national territory since late 2001 should make it easier to have this debate, since civil liberties advocates should be less vulnerable to the charge of undermining security when we are not actually under fire on our own soil.

This discussion—which is only beginning to gather momentum— must address three important questions.[7]

First, how are our democratic institutions faring, given the concession of new and exceptional powers to the executive branch? To a very real extent, this question hinges on the existence, or absence, of robust, independent oversight by the judiciary and Congress. Even at its best, judicial oversight can be a long, drawn-out process. While it can protect individuals' constitutional rights against abusive exercise of governmental power, judicial review often results in vague definitions of principles. Such oversight is necessary, despite the judiciary's deference to executive assertions of power in the name of national security; but even in the best of circumstances, it is unlikely to offer comprehensive results in the near term.[8] Congressional oversight, on the other hand, is often viewed as too dysfunctional and—when controlled by partisans of the executive authority—too docile and uninquisitive to be effective. The 9/11 Commission, for example, concluded that the diffusion among congressional committees of oversight and budgetary responsibility for issues of terrorism and homeland security made effective oversight unworkable; Congress, however, has proved incapable of reforming its own management in any significant way.[9]

Those responsible for oversight must assess, with some transparency, the extent to which security provisions—whether new, permanent, or subject to sunset clauses—are jeopardizing Americans' privacy and liberty, compared to how they demonstrably increase public safety. Furthermore, they must do so without inadvertently disclosing classified information or compromising ongoing investigations. In making their assessment, congressional overseers should consider:

- the degree to which the measure is actually used;
- assumptions, clearly delineated, that are invoked to justify the measure;
- the plausibility of such assumptions;
- the extent to which other countries, particularly democracies, have used, adopted, or debated such measures; and
- the degree and type of oversight appropriate to specific measures.

Such oversight may be conducted by a special commission, a special congressional committee, or a standing committee. Oversight panels need to recognize that changes in the government's legal powers have indeed occurred, that new ones may be necessary, and that they are not without consequences. In short, a functioning system of accountability is essential if the country is to honor its commitment to divided, shared powers and to our constitutional system of checks and balances.

The nation also needs to understand the content of and sources for the laws under which it is acting against terrorism. These include laws duly enacted by Congress; international treaty law negotiated by the executive branch and ratified with the consent of two-thirds of the Senate; and executive orders issued by the president under his authority to faithfully execute the laws. This leads to a series of questions that have always been considered fundamental to U.S. democracy.

LAW OR DECREE? Should the legislature adopt laws to provide for new powers, or, in a War on Terrorism, does the president have inherent authority to adopt a new measure?

Legislation is always the most desirable and the most certain course of lawmaking action, both on solid constitutional grounds and because the legislative process fosters political and public participation. Certainly the president still has authority within the parameters of congressional enactments to determine how best to implement the laws. And in a novel assertion of executive authority, the argument is advanced that in time of "war" (however determined) the president also has an inherent authority as "commander-in-chief" not only to direct the disposition of the armed forces, but also to provide for security more broadly. In the security versus liberties debate, the expansive reading of this "inherent" authority, which the administration has invoked to defend its warrantless domestic surveillance, leaves little room for effective oversight by the legislative branch. When executive powers can be created secretly, disclosed minimally, and insulated from public debate, a bypassed legislature can scarcely impose oversight. When executive measures threaten to undermine and even blatantly contravene legislated restraints, the dangers to democratic accountability and constitutionality are compounded. This is why the space for executive decree should be extremely narrow and subject to full disclosure to the appropriate committees of Congress. The security risks entailed by disclosure are low: While the disclosure of a specific undertaking or individual could handcuff a specific counterterror action, the disclosure of a general policy or procedure is most unlikely to have adverse consequences. Indeed, even if specific operations cannot always be transparent, the system can and should be transparent.

DOES THE PUBLIC NEED TO KNOW? To what extent ought new counterterrorist policies or measures be disclosed to the public? Even if executive and legislative decisionmakers agree that in a particular case public disclosure is not warranted, to what extent will unauthorized disclosure of the policy or measure (a reasonable likelihood in a free society) undermine the policy and the authority on which it is based? A useful guide in answering these questions might well be found in an old intelligence community truism: If a policy or program cannot withstand unauthorized disclosure, then it may not be worth authorizing—or doing.

HOW LONG IS TOO LONG? Should the period of time that new powers are in force be limited? Given the nature of the jihadist threat, it is difficult to say when, if ever, this rhetorically, but not legally, declared "war" on terrorism will end. This uncertainty might be seen to justify permanent weaving of expansive police measures into America's legal and constitutional order. But it is not idle speculation to argue that such powers could be turned against other "enemies of the state" (or of a future administration) long after the jihadist threat has faded. The dangers that this would pose for American democracy and Americans' freedom make limits on the duration of these provisions vitally important. New authority should include a sunset or reauthorization provision that would allow enough time for the use of the new powers to respond to the jihadist emergency, with the presumption that the new powers will lapse unless an affirmative vote by lawmakers renews them. The burden should be on the executive branch to justify the renewal of such authorities to Congress. In a similar vein, new powers that a president asserts by executive order under existing statutory or constitutional authority should also be limited in duration, though as a practical matter reliable control over them will be almost impossible without some form of external oversight, for example, the annual executive branch review and reauthorization of covert action, which is reported to the congressional intelligence committees. Vigilant congressional oversight may be hardest to effect in these cases—arguably the cases where it is most needed; Congress needs to assert firmly its broader statutory and budgetary authority over the executive agencies to keep counterterrorism powers initiated within the executive branch inside appropriate bounds. Judicial review is the slowest but ultimately most authoritative curb on possible abuse of executive power.

Finally, Americans must consider how leaders and publics of other countries view the practices and policies the United States adopts to counter the threat of terrorism. International support is indispensable to success in the suppression of Islamic terrorism: The United States must rely on other countries' intelligence services, their surveillance of suspects within their borders, their prosecutors indicting terrorist plotters, their judges extraditing terror suspects, and their political leaders allowing U.S. military forces to operate from bases on their territory.

America's international partners, in the democratic world most of all, care deeply about the rule of law and scrupulous adherence to international law. U.S. practices secretly sanctioned by executive decree that contravene international law create a popular backlash that makes many foreign governments' cooperation with Washington politically toxic. The secret rendition of suspects without judicial review, allegations of U.S. abduction of suspects on European territory, indefinite detentions without appeal at Guantanamo, and torture at Abu Ghraib have all taken a heavy toll on America's credibility and on other governments' willingness to collaborate with it.

In contemplating new legal authorities, much less any extra-legal actions, policymakers must consider whether their actions may contravene international treaty law or undermine international norms. Beyond alienating allies whose cooperation U.S. authorities need, American disregard for international law governing human rights and treatment of prisoners invites less democratic states—as well as jihadist adversaries—to justify abuses based on the policies that U.S. officials have embraced. The administration's condoning of torture, distilled in the widely distributed images of Abu Ghraib, and revelations rocking Europe about extraordinary renditions to Arab governments that are even less embarrassed about torture, have helped al Qaeda to recruit new waves of jihadist fighters and to justify its own targeting of civilians.

U.S. government agencies have warned that some actions, such as the executive's dismissal of the "quaint" Geneva Conventions in some instances, may well result in greater danger to Americans' own interests, especially jeopardizing the safety of military personnel. Our actions have also been used as an excuse by other states to avoid compliance with the obligations of international human rights law, or to stonewall Washington's insistence that they halt other abusive practices. The measures the United States employs can also be models for repressive regimes to intensify harsh controls, and also undermine long-term American goals of promoting political, religious, and economic freedoms abroad.[10]

RECOMMENDATIONS

Ultimately, Americans need to construct a new framework for assessing the cost and benefits of a range of specific security powers—from data-mining, profiling, eavesdropping, and sharing information among agencies, to listening in at religious or political institutions, detention and interrogation of "enemy combatants," and rendition of suspects to foreign governments. Such a framework is the only way Americans, as a nation, can hope to strike a judicious balance between security and civil liberty. It is the only way Americans can have a real debate, despite the desire of some to deny the need for one or to avoid its occurrence. It is also the only way that we can honestly confront difficult balancing issues sure to arise in the future debate about long-term strategy against terrorism, issues that we have not even thought of today. If there is another significant terrorist attack in the United States, there will likely be a rush to adopt whatever measures, ill-conceived or not, that will sate a public demanding security. There will be, as after September 11, little time for real debate.

17.1. IT IS VITAL TO SPARK A STRUCTURED NATIONAL DISCUSSION NOW ABOUT THE TRADEOFF BETWEEN SECURITY AND LIBERTY. The Civil Liberties Protection Board, created by executive order of the president in August of 2004, could lead the effort. Forums could be held online, on television, in newspapers, and in regional centers. This discussion should create support for appropriate congressional oversight and enhanced transparency, in order to reduce risks to civil liberties.

17.2. GOVERNORS AND BIG-CITY MAYORS SHOULD CONSIDER APPOINTING REGIONAL LIBERTY PROTECTION BOARDS TO WORK WITH STATE AND LOCAL LAW ENFORCEMENT AUTHORITIES. This is appropriate because many of the recently enhanced security measures are often carried out at the state or city level. Moreover, the liberty protection boards can engage many more Americans in the national discussion. Local boards could share information and experiences with each other through a national coordinating forum. The boards should be asked to provide advice to state officials and regional offices of federal agencies about the implications for privacy and civil liberties of security programs; recommend safeguards; and perform civil liberties oversight of ongoing programs (with due regard for operational security).

17.3. LOCAL LIBERTY PROTECTION BOARDS SHOULD SPONSOR OUT-REACH AND EDUCATIONAL ACTIVITIES IN SCHOOLS, CIVIC ORGA-NIZATIONS, PLACES OF WORSHIP, AND LOCAL MEDIA. The purpose of their outreach would be to combine messages about due vigilance with reminders to citizens of why America's founding fathers thought it so necessary to restrict government powers and to enshrine rights and liberties in the federal Constitution. It would also foster an atmosphere of civic trust regarding existing procedures and institutions as well as laws that might be used inappropriately to erode citizens' rights.

17.4. THE NATIONAL CIVIL LIBERTIES PROTECTION BOARD SHOULD ISSUE A YEARLY REPORT on its activities and on threats to American freedoms, brief Congress on the report (including classified annexes if necessary), and convene an annual national conference to review its report.

17.5. THE BOARD SHOULD FILE A CIVIL LIBERTIES IMPACT STATE-MENT WITH THE EXECUTIVE BRANCH AND CONGRESS ON ANY PROPOSED MEASURE OR PROGRAM THAT MAY RAISE PUBLIC CON-CERN ABOUT POTENTIAL ABUSES OF LIBERTY. Such statements should be unclassified, although they may, if necessary, have classified annexes. The chairmen and ranking minority members of the committees on the judiciary of the U.S. Senate and House of Representatives should each be authorized to initiate a review leading to an impact statement, upon their request to the board.

◆ ◆ ◆

Such bold steps would create an ongoing process to shore up civil liberties when security threats in America raise doubts about protecting the rights of persons in suspect groups. Such steps are necessary, and not only because sweeping assertions of executive power have undermined confidence in federal authorities' willingness to defend civil liberties or even respect the courts. Without a renewed consensus on civil liberties, the American political community will become ever more polarized, shattering the national unity required to strengthen our security and defeat terrorism at home. Such steps are necessary because the infringement of the civil liberties of some Americans could begin a process leading to the erosion of values that underpin our unique nation.

18. PAYING FOR IT

T he budget request for homeland security for fiscal year 2006 does contain some positives: (1) an overall funding increase of $3.9 billion, or 8.6 percent, to $49.9 billion; (2) a shift toward allocating funds to states and localities based on their relative risks and needs; and (3) an increased use of user fees to fund operations. However, more than four years after September 11, several key priorities still remain severely, and dangerously, underfunded. These shortfalls occur in seven major areas and amount to about $23 billion. In effect, a prudent budget for homeland security would be at least $73 billion as opposed to $50 billion.

CRITICAL INFRASTRUCTURE PROTECTION

The disparity between funding to protect military bases and civilian infrastructure (transportation, food systems, energy) has grown wider: $8.7 billion will protect the bases, an increase of $1.1 billion; $2.8 billion will protect critical civilian infrastructure, an increase of $200 million.[1] Since September 11, Washington has provided only $516 million toward the $5.6 billion that the Coast Guard estimates U.S. ports need to make them minimally secure.

While inadequate funding is part of the problem, another major contributing factor is the Bush administration's belief that voluntary action on the part of the private sector will be adequate to ensure the security of critical infrastructure. According to President Bush's National Strategy for Homeland Security, "The government should only address those activities that the market does not adequately provide—for example, national defense or border security. . . . For other aspects of homeland security, sufficient incentives exist in the private market to supply protection." This misguided ideology has left U.S. citizens vulnerable to terrorism at privately owned chemical and nuclear plants.

CHEMICAL PLANTS

According to the Government Accountability Office (GAO), "the extent of security preparedness at U.S. chemical facilities is unknown . . . [because] no federal requirements are in place to require chemical facilities to assess their vulnerabilities and take steps to reduce them . . . [and] no federal oversight or third-party verification ensures that voluntary industry assessments are adequate and that necessary corrective actions are taken."[2] The GAO, the Department of Homeland Security (DHS), and the Environmental Protection Agency (EPA) all agree that a national strategy is necessary "to require chemical facilities to expeditiously assess their vulnerability to terrorist attacks and, where necessary, require these facilities to take corrective action."[3] The proposed Chemical Security Act would require companies to perform vulnerability assessments, implement security enhancements, be subject to audits, and actively pursue alternative approaches to the way they manufacture their products. The Congressional Budget Office estimated the government cost of the proposal at $80 million over five years, or about $16 million a year.[4]

NUCLEAR POWER PLANTS

Nuclear power plants were not designed to withstand aircraft crashes or explosions, and the federal government still does not require nuclear plants to be secure from an aircraft attack. An April 2005 study by the National Academy of Sciences concluded that nuclear plants in thirty-one states containing fuel storage pools are vulnerable to such attacks, which could trigger raging fires and the release of deadly radiation. The U.S. Nuclear Regulatory Commission (NRC) has resisted congressional efforts for additional security regulation.

Several European nations have placed all spent fuel older than five years into thick-walled, dry-storage modes. The cost of such hardening would be about $7 billion over the next ten years, or $700 million a year.

TRANSPORTATION SECURITY

Much of the post–September 11 focus has been on passenger airplane security, and there have been some significant improvements there. Yet air cargo remains virtually unmonitored and rail security and public transit security remain underfunded and lacking in overall strategic frameworks for pursuing security.[5]

The American Public Transportation Association estimates it would cost $6 billion to secure the nation's transit systems, which serve approximately 32 million Americans every day.[6] Since September 11, however, only $155 million has been appropriated by Congress for this effort—which is about 1 percent of the funding appropriated for aviation security, even though every day sixteen times as many people travel by public transportation as by air. A block grant program of $6 billion aimed at commuter rail, subways, and Amtrak should be used to address these vulnerabilities.

CONTAINER AND PORT SECURITY

Homeland security requires border security, and effective border security requires "smart borders" that don't begin at the water's edge, but begin at the ports and departure points of origin. This requires effective cooperation with other countries and with the private sector to provide the resources, personnel, and technology adequate to the task. Although the CIA has concluded that the most likely way weapons of mass destruction would enter the United States is by sea, the federal government is spending more every three days to finance the war in Iraq than it has provided over the past three years to prop up the security of all 361 U.S. commercial seaports.

Container security is the primary focus of two initiatives: the Customs-Trade Partnership Against Terrorism (C-TPAT) and the Container Security Initiative (CSI). C-TPAT is a public-private partnership aimed at securing the supply chain from point of origin through entry into the United States. It includes trade other than that conducted with containers, but a large part includes container shipments. CSI is a Customs and Border Protection (CBP) program stationing CBP officers in foreign seaports to target and inspect marine containers before they are loaded onto U.S.-bound vessels.

In the proposed fiscal year 2006 budget, the CSI is scheduled for an increase of $5.4 million over 2005 levels and C-TPAT an increase of $8.2 million. But both remain funded at orders of magnitude well below what is needed to ensure adequate inspection. Only an estimated 4–6 percent of cargo containers are inspected each year. *ABC News* has twice successfully smuggled depleted uranium in a container without it being recognized. Customs officials abroad lack adequate training and resources. The GAO has raised issues concerning both the CSI and C-TPAT programs including: systematic human capital plans, performance measures for accountability and program achievement, and a long-term strategic plan to successfully manage the two programs. There needs to be an effort to more systematically monitor and track containers throughout the supply chain process and for ports to be able to use the top-of-the-line radiation-detection portals and container-scanning equipment, which cost an estimated $1 million per unit.[7]

Security at ports themselves is another critical area. Since 2002, the DHS's Port Security Grant program has provided support to address immediate security needs and assessments. But federal money allocated in the first four rounds of the program—about $565 million—accounted for only about one-sixth of what seaports identified as needs, while a fifth round of grants totaling $150 million has yet to be made available to ports.[8] At the same time, the Coast Guard has estimated that ports would have to spend $5.4 billion over ten years to meet mandated security enhancements.[9] That is on top of the more than $3 billion they already spend annually on infrastructure improvements and operations, maintenance and personnel expenses, just to keep pace with burgeoning world trade. Furthermore, the fiscal year 2006 budget eliminates targeted port security funds, consolidating all funds in a targeted infrastructure protection program and thereby making it difficult to ensure adequate direct funding. Bringing port security and container security to acceptable levels will require an increase of about $2.4 billion a year ($0.5 billion for port security and $1.9 billion for container security).

First Responders

Overall funding for key first responder programs would be cut by $510 million, from $3.27 billion in fiscal year 2005 to $2.76 billion in fiscal year 2006.[10] Although interoperable communications systems remain a critical need for the first-responder community, the budget requests zero dedicated funding for this effort.[11] In addition, the Science and Technology Directorate will no longer receive funding from other federal agencies—a cut of $11 million—for operations of Project SAFECOM, which coordinates all federal interoperable communication efforts.

A 2003 Council on Foreign Relations Task Force, chaired by former Senator Warren Rudman, focused specifically on emergency response to a catastrophic attack and found that "[i]f the nation does not take immediate steps to better identify and address the urgent needs of emergency responders, the next terrorist incident could have an even more devastating impact than the Sept. 11 attacks." The task force called for increasing spending on police, fire, medical, and other first responders—approximately $100 billion over five years, which would also have substantial immediate benefits for day-to-day emergency response unrelated to terrorist attacks. Using that metric, the United States will fall approximately $98.4 billion short of meeting emergency responder needs over the next five years if current funding levels are maintained.[12]

These shortfalls in funding translate into dangerous vulnerabilities, given the scope and character of the terrorist threat. For example: Only 10 percent of fire departments nationwide have personnel and equipment to handle a building collapse; police departments throughout the United States do not have protective gear required to secure a site after a weapons of mass destruction (WMD) attack; public health laboratories in most states do not have the basic equipment to adequately respond to chemical or biological attacks; and most cities do not have the equipment needed to determine which hazardous agents emergency responders are facing following an attack.[13] Curing the funding shortfalls for the first responders will require an increase of at least $4 billion a year.

PUBLIC HEALTH

The anthrax attacks in the United States during 2001 showed what a relatively mild bioterrorist attack could do in terms of sparking fear and taxing the public health infrastructure. Yet the Bush administration's proposed budget actually cuts funds for critical public health infrastructure. The proposed fiscal year 2006 budget cuts nearly 7 percent—or $530 million—from the allocation for the Centers for Disease Control and Prevention (CDC). This includes a cut of approximately 9 percent to core CDC programs and at least a $260 million cut to state and local public health programs. These cuts include:

- elimination of the $130 million Preventive Health and Health Service block grants that have routinely been awarded to states;
- a 12.6 percent cut to CDC's bioterrorism preparedness fund, representing nearly $147 million, despite repeated reports that indicate that the country is still not adequately ready to respond to a biological or chemical terror attack;
- CDC building and facilities funds, which include money for upgrading or modernizing research and testing capabilities, were cut by 88 percent, nearly $240 million; and
- elimination of funding for the Metropolitan Medical Response System which helps local first responders prepare for radiological, chemical, and other terrorist attacks.[14]

These cuts come on the back of decades of reduced funding for public health. The Public Health Foundation estimates that an infusion of an additional $10 billion would be necessary to bring the public health system up to an acceptable level of preparedness.[15] With respect to homeland security concerns in particular, there are other major vulnerabilities. According to the Trust for America's Health, nearly one third of states cut their public health budgets in fiscal years 2003 and 2004 and federal

TABLE 18.1. PROPOSED CHANGES TO HOMELAND SECURITY BUDGET

HOMELAND SECURITY PROGRAM	ADMINISTRATION FY 2006 REQUEST, IN BILLIONS	PROPOSED CHANGE, IN BILLIONS
Nuclear plant hardening	0.00	0.70
Chemical plant security	0.00	0.02
Port security	2.00	0.50
Public transit security		6.00
Public health infrastructure	2.28	10.00
First responders	2.76	4.00
Container security	0.19	1.90
TOTAL HOMELAND SECURITY FUNDING	49.90	23.12

Source: "Report of the Task Force on a Unified Security Budget for the United States, 2006," Center for Defense Information, May 2005, p. 8, available online at http://www.cdi.org/pdfs/unified-security-budget-2006.pdf

bioterrorism funding decreased by over $1 million per state in 2004, while states still do not have adequate resources to address their preparedness gaps.

Only five public health labs report capabilities (facilities, technology, and/or equipment) to adequately respond to a chemical terrorism threat, and only one-third of states report that they have sufficient bioterrorism lab response capabilities (facilities, technology, and/or equipment).

Although planning for a flu pandemic (often viewed as requiring a similar response to a bioterrorism attack) has improved, twenty states still do not have publicly available plans in place, and, based on model estimates, an outbreak would still have dire consequences.[16] Bringing public health funding to an acceptable level will require an increase in homeland security funding of about $10 billion.

SOLUTIONS

Table 18.1 displays the additions necessary to cure the major defects in homeland security. To see how the nation might pay for these necessary additions, it is important to look at the total national security spending.

There are two major components of national security spending: an offensive component, which is funded primarily in the Department of Defense; and a defensive component, which is funded through the Department of Homeland Security. Since September 11, the Bush administration has increased spending on both components. On September 11, 2001, the United States was spending $327 billion on the combined offensive and defensive components of national security. Four years later, in September 2005, these components consumed $482 billion, an increase of $155 billion, or 47 percent.

However, the majority of the increased funding has gone to the Department of Defense. In 2001, the defense budget was $306 billion. Four years later, in the fiscal year 2006 budget (for the fiscal year which began on October 1, 2005), the baseline defense budget was $442 billion. Moreover, very little of the Defense budget goes to homeland defense (less than $10 billion in 2006).

Spending on the other component of national security has also risen but not nearly as much as that of the Department of Defense. In 2002, spending on the twenty-two agencies that were put into the DHS amounted to $21 billion. The 2006 budget for homeland security will be $40 billion, exclusive of what the Pentagon spends, an increase of only $19 billion—or $117 billion less than the increase in Department of Defense spending.

There are three possible ways to deal with the homeland security spending shortfall. First, increase overall government spending. Given that the federal deficit for 2005 will be over $300 billion, without counting funding for the wars in Iraq or Afghanistan or for rebuilding the areas hit by Hurricanes Katrina and Rita, this is an unlikely prospect.

Second, the federal government could raise taxes. After all, the Global War on Terrorism is the first war in our history in which we have not raised taxes or instituted a draft. In fact, the Bush administration has decreased taxes since September 11, primarily on the wealthy. But, given the fact that neither the president nor the Republican leadership have even broached the subject of tax increases, and are still debating whether to make the earlier tax cuts permanent, this too is an unlikely prospect.

The third alternative is to adjust the balance between the offensive and defensive components of national security spending. As noted above, spending on the regular defense budget, as opposed to the supplementals that fund the wars in Afghanistan and Iraq, is now $442 billion. Even controlling for inflation, this is more than the defense budgets of 1960, 1970, 1980, or 1990, and is more than the rest of the world combined. Transferring $23 billion from the Department of Defense to the Department of Homeland Security would leave the United States with a regular Defense budget that is three times as much as China and Russia combined. These funds can be taken from defense without jeopardizing national security or undermining the Global War on Terrorism, primarily by eliminating Cold War–era weapons and weapons systems that do not work, and slowing down the development of weapons experiencing technical problems.[17] Specifically, here are areas where reductions could be made in ways that would strengthen the nation's security against the threat of terrorism.

Ballistic Missile Defense (BMD)

There's no doubt that this nation needs to be concerned about ballistic missile attacks against our troops in the field (Theater Missile Defense, or TMD) or against U.S. territory (National Missile Defense, or NMD)—and indeed it is. Since President Reagan gave his speech twenty-two years ago that urged the nation to develop a defense against Soviet intercontinental ballistic missiles, this nation has spent about $150 billion in a vain attempt to construct such a defense.

President Bush, who in his 2000 campaign promised to deploy a national missile defense before the end of his first term, has spent nearly $40 billion toward that goal since taking office. Indeed, one of his first acts after taking office was to double the size of Clinton's ballistic missile defense budget—from $5 billion to $10 billion—and withdraw from the anti-ballistic missile (ABM) treaty on the grounds that the agreement, negotiated by President Nixon, would preclude the United States from developing and deploying an effective missile defense. For 2006, the administration is seeking $10.5 billion for the missile defense program.

Using the funds already allocated, the Bush administration has already placed eight missile interceptors at launch sites in Alaska and California and expects to have twenty-seven ground- and sea-based interceptors in place by the fall of 2005. If the 2006 budget is approved, the administration would add sixteen more interceptors next year. Eventually, the Bush administration would like to deploy a large layered system that will include space-based interceptors. The total cost of the Bush plan over the next twenty years will exceed $200 billion.

There are two problems with the Bush approach. First, the system is not ready for deployment. It has not been successfully tested in over three years. Moreover, to fulfill Bush's campaign promise, the Pentagon took a number of shortcuts that put schedule ahead of performance. The shortcuts included insufficient ground tests of key components, a lack of specifications and standards, and a tendency to postpone the resolution of difficult issues. Finally, there is increasing evidence that no matter how much money is spent and no matter how long we continue to test it, the system can never work effectively.

Second, even if missile defense were to work perfectly, and that is by no means assured, it is still addressing a low-priority threat. Enemy nations can deliver nuclear weapons in many cheaper, more reliable, and more accurate ways (for example, placing a nuclear weapon in a container rather than firing a long-range missile with a return address). The entire BMD program can be reduced from $10.5 billion to $3 billion. This would allow the Pentagon to continue testing NMD and provide sufficient funding for such TMD programs as the Patriot (PAC-3) program, which protects the troops in the field.

INVESTMENT PROGRAMS

During the 2000 presidential campaign, President Bush promised to transform the military from a force designed to fight the Soviet military on the plains of Europe to a smaller, more agile force capable of dealing with the challenges of the twenty-first century. As part of this transformation, then-governor Bush promised to cancel a large number of weapons systems designed to refight the Cold War. The wars in Afghanistan and Iraq demonstrated how inappropriate these Cold War relics are to fighting the Global War on Terrorism.

Yet since taking office, President Bush has cancelled only two of these systems, the Army's Crusader artillery system and the Comanche helicopter program. Consequently, a large portion of the $160 billion investment program in the 2006 budget is still being spent on systems that deal with threats from a bygone era. Moreover, the cost of those systems will continue to grow in the future unless steps are taken now.

By 2011, the investment budget is expected to grow to about $200 billion. But that figure is really a lowball estimate. The Bush administration has $1.5 trillion worth of weapons systems in various stages of development. And that number assumes that the Pentagon can successfully meet its current cost goals for new weapon systems, something it has not been able to do in this administration. In the past four years alone, the top five weapon systems under development have increased in cost from $281 billion to $521 billion—an increase of $240 billion, or 85 percent.

The Pentagon can reverse this trend by taking the following steps. First, cancel outright the following weapon systems: the F/A-22 Raptor fighter attack aircraft; the SSN 774 Virginia Class attack submarine; the DD(X) Destroyer; the V-22 Osprey Tilt Rotor transport aircraft; and the C-130J transport aircraft. Second, slow down the development of the joint strike fighter and the Future Combat System programs.

THE RAPTOR. The Raptor is the most unnecessary weapon system currently being built by the Pentagon. It was originally designed to achieve superiority over Soviet fighter jets that were never built. Back in 1985, the Air Force claimed it could build about 750 of these stealth fighter jets for $35 million each or at a total cost of $26 billion. Over the last twenty years, the total cost of the program has continued to grow even as the number of planes to be purchased has declined. Just a year ago the Air Force said it could purchase 275 Raptors for $72 billion, or about $262 million per aircraft. At the current time the Pentagon says it can buy 178 planes for $64 billion. Assuming no further cost growth, this will mean spending about $360 million per plane for an unnecessary aircraft, a $100 million increase in the unit cost in just one year.

The performance of the current generation of Air Force fighters in Afghanistan and Iraq, as well as in the first Persian Gulf War, makes it clear that the Air Force already has the capability to achieve air superiority easily and quickly against any enemy or nation. To put it bluntly, the Taliban, al Qaeda, and Iraqi insurgents do not have jet fighters for the Raptor to conquer.

The Air Force has recognized this and has added a ground attack or bombing mission to the Raptor. But using the world's most expensive fighter, which travels at twice the speed of sound, for attacking ground targets is neither cost-effective nor technically feasible. Instead the Air Force should cancel the F/A-22.

To prevent an excess of aging in the aircraft fleet, the Pentagon should buy upgraded F-16, "block sixty" planes. Cutting the 2006 request for twenty-four Raptors will save $4.3 billion. About $1 billion of this could be allocated to purchasing thirty upgraded F-16s, resulting in a net savings of $3.3 billion.

SSN-774 VIRGINIA CLASS SUBMARINE. Like the Raptor, the primary role of the Virginia Class submarine was to combat the next generation of Russian submarine which, we now know, will never be built. The Navy plans to buy thirty of these boats to replace the SSN-688 Los Angeles Class submarines at an estimated cost of $94 billion, or more than $3 billion for each submarine. For 2006, the Navy is asking Congress to appropriate $2.6 billion for one boat and plans to build one vessel per year through 2011 and increase to two per year beginning in 2012.

As these Virginia Class submarines are built, the Navy plans to retire the existing Los Angeles Class submarines early—that is, before their normal service life is reached. Canceling the Virginia Class and refueling the reactors of the Los Angeles Class can save $2.3 billion in 2006.

DD(X) DESTROYER. The proposed DD(X) is a new class of surface combatant that is substantially larger than any existing surface ship—that is, cruiser or destroyer—and is sized more for open ocean warfare against another naval superpower than its stated mission of providing fire support in crowded, dangerous, close-in coastal areas for forces ashore. The program, begun in 1996, has been beset by technological and cost difficulties. The projected unit price has already risen from $2.7 billion to $3.3 billion and, at the current rate, the Navy will probably spend about $20 billion for the first five ships. Canceling the program will save $1.8 billion in 2006. Moreover, the Navy's Littoral Combat Ship, which is already under development and will cost $12 billion for sixty ships, or about $200 million each, is better suited for actual operations ashore.

V-22 OSPREY. The Pentagon began development of the Osprey, which takes off and lands like a helicopter and, once airborne, flies like a plane, about twenty years ago. It was originally supposed to be a joint service program, but the Army dropped support for the program in the late 1980s. In 1991, then-Secretary of Defense Richard Cheney canceled the program because of cost concerns and continuing technical problems.

Cheney's decision was overridden by Congress and, with the support of Presidents Clinton and George W. Bush, the Department of Defense has now spent $15 billion on the program. Yet the Osprey is still in a test phase and nowhere ready for operational deployment. Moreover, several accidents, three of which resulted in fatalities, have occurred during this time. Finally, the cost of the program has risen from about $30 billion to over $50 billion.

Under current plans, the Pentagon intends to buy 458 of these aircraft at a cost of over $100 million each. This assumes that the Pentagon can get costs under control and solve the technical problems. Even if this unlikely scenario comes to pass, the Osprey will be only marginally more capable than existing helicopters in terms of speed range and payload, yet cost at least five times as much. Canceling the V-22 and buying an equivalent number of existing helicopters will save $1.6 billion in 2006.

C-130J. The Pentagon has already spent $2.6 billion to purchase fifty C-130J transport aircraft. But none of these planes has met commercial contract specifications. It has 168 deficiencies that could cause death, severe injury, or illness. Consequently the C-130J cannot perform its intended mission of transporting troops and equipment into combat zones and can be used only for training. Secretary of Defense Rumsfeld is so concerned about the aircraft that he has considered canceling the program. And during the 1990s, when Congress had appropriated more funds for the aircraft than the Pentagon requested, the Air Force contended it did not need the planes. And yet in 2006, the Pentagon is requesting $1.6 billion to buy twelve more of these aircraft, and the Air Force now contends that it needs the plane. If the Air Force has its way, it would purchase one hundred planes at a total cost of $16.4 billion, or about $164 million per plane. Canceling the C-130J will save $1.6 billion in 2006.

F-35 JOINT STRIKE FIGHTER. The F-35 joint strike fighter (JSF) is an ambitious program to build three related but slightly different aircraft for the Air Force, Navy, and Marine Corps. Current plans call for building 2,458 planes at a total cost of $257 billion, or slightly more than $100 million per plane.

This aircraft should be built. It is more cost-effective to produce the new JSF platform than to upgrade older systems, which by 2010 will need to be replaced. Moreover, since all of these variants use common parts and are manufactured on a single and large-scale production line, it is more affordable than allowing each of the services to develop its own unique aircraft. Finally, since so many allied countries are willing to purchase the fighter, the joint strike fighter will improve our interoperability with allied forces.

However, given the technological challenges of trying to build three fairly different planes from one design, the program should not be rushed. This country's overwhelming numerical and qualitative advantage in tactical aircraft will not soon be challenged. Therefore, the JSF program can afford to slow down and be reduced from the requested $5.2 billion in 2006 to $1.5 billion.

FUTURE COMBAT SYSTEM (FCS). The Future Combat System is an army program to build a family of eighteen combat vehicles and other systems, including unmanned aerial vehicles and sensors, which will be linked together into an integrated and very complex system. The army intends to begin equipping its first units with the future combat system in 2011, and eventually will equip about one-third of its troops at a cost of at least $99 billion. The FCS is necessary for the Army because it will make units more deployable, lethal, and survivable. However, its current schedule is far too ambitious, given the complexity of the program. Of the network of fifty-three crucial technologies, fifty-two are unproven. Therefore, the $3.4 billion requested in 2006 should be reduced to $1 billion.

Table 18.2. Changes in Investment Programs

Weapon System	FY 2006 Request, in Billions	Proposed Changes, in Billions	Savings, FY 2006 in Billions
BMD	10.5	3.0	7.5
F/A-22	4.3	1.0	3.3
SSN-774	2.6	0.3	2.3
DD(X)	1.8	0.0	1.8
V-22	1.8	0.2	1.6
C-130(J)	1.6	0.0	1.6
F-35	5.2	2.0	3.2
FCS	3.4	1.0	2.4
Total	31.2	7.5	23.7

Source: Lawrence Korb, "The Korb Report: A Realistic Defense for America," Business Leaders for Sensible Priorities, Table 2, available online at http://www.sensiblepriorities.org /pdf/korb_report_finalb.pdf.

◆ ◆ ◆

As indicated in Table 18.2, these savings would add up to $23.7 billion, more than enough to pay for the programs needed in the homeland security area without raising taxes or adding to deficit, and would make us more secure in the process.

19. Moving Forward to Secure America at Home

We have found that almost five years after September 11, America is still substantially at risk of catastrophic terrorist attack. Significant vulnerabilities have not been mitigated. We concur with the 9/11 commissioners that further terrorist attacks in the United States are not a matter of if, but a matter of when. Nonetheless, we believe that there are ways to increase the likelihood that such attacks might be disrupted. We also believe that there are ways to improve government's capabilities to assist citizens during a crisis, and to recover after such attacks.

In the broadest terms, our review has three major conclusions. First, metropolitan areas should be the major focus of domestic security, including metropolitan response plans, medical systems, policing and intelligence efforts, and transportation security. Second, working with the private sector, government must increase security and reduce risk at privately owned facilities, attacks against which could create mass casualties or disrupt the operation of the economy. Third, there are certain functions that the federal government must perform better than it does today, including border and port security, aviation security, national-level intelligence, and catastrophic event response.

The steps to better security can be taken without additional governmental expenditures, and certainly at a cost lower than we have incurred to secure another nation, Iraq. The recommended measures will require, however, a reallocation of funding at the federal, and to a lesser extent, at the state and local level. They will also require that some regulated industries pass on additional security costs to consumers. The federal government must ignore regulatory options for ideological reasons when market forces have largely failed to provide necessary security risk management measures. By using smart regulation that specifies end-states rather than micromanaging means, the federal government can encourage innovation and reduce the cost of required security measures.

245

Securing America at home will involve tradeoffs within federal spending on security. Congress has required the Pentagon to perform a Quadrennial Defense Review to articulate a strategy, determine capability requirements, and plan funding for a multi-year program to achieve the necessary capabilities. So, too, Congress should require such an exercise for homeland security. The review should propose clearly articulated goals for achieving specific capabilities by precise dates, and the review process should be sufficiently transparent so that Congress may make choices, stretching out some programs and accelerating others.

The administration should then be required to perform a Synoptic Security Review encompassing both Pentagon programs and domestic security requirements. The review should present tradeoffs and choices so that Congress can determine, for example, whether the cost of maintaining three aircraft carrier battle groups (out of the current twelve) improves our security better than programs meant to enable us to control our maritime approaches, ports, and borders. We believe it is both intellectually dishonest and damaging to our nation's overall security to divide artificially Pentagon spending from other federal funding of security measures. The bottom line: Homeland security is national security.

The measures we propose also can be accomplished without infringing on constitutionally protected civil liberties. Indeed, they can be accomplished even as we reverse the erosion of civil liberties that has already occurred, including illegal wiretapping, declaring Americans to be enemy combatants, and extending the authority of federal agents to demand material without court review. We believe that civil liberties oversight should be incorporated at the program level in the federal government and should be present at the state and local levels of government.

Our recommendations can be accomplished with minimal further reorganization of federal departments and agencies. The creation of the Department of Homeland Security (DHS) and the director of national intelligence (DNI), as well as a plethora of new centers and task forces, caused bureaucratic confusion, diverted energies and attention from implementation, and often gave political appointees responsibilities that would have been served far better by professional managers. In the interest of consolidation, we are reluctant to propose further organizational turmoil. Therefore, we are recommending only one major change to reduce the size of DHS and an adjustment to the executive office of the president to restore White House leadership in key areas. Specifically, we propose that the Federal Emergency Management Agency (FEMA) should once again be a separate agency, apart from DHS. Within the White House, we propose the elimination of the Homeland Security Council structure, merging it within the National Security Council system (NSC) as envisioned in the original legislation creating the NSC. Within the NSC, there would be a deputy national security adviser for homeland security, and subordinate to that official, a special assistant to the president for emergency preparedness and a special assistant to the president for cyber security. There would also be a deputy national security adviser for crisis management, for both domestic and international events.

In sum, we believe there is much to be done to secure America at home and that these measures should be considered neither optional nor deferrable. Fortunately, our domestic security agenda is well within our capabilities as a nation and pales by comparison to the challenges overcome by previous generations of Americans. Overall government security spending need not be increased. Nor do we need to trade liberty for security. For too long we have lacked a focused agenda, sustained presidential leadership, bipartisan cooperation, and competent professional management. Without those qualities, even as we "fight them over there," we will continue to have a forgotten homeland.

SUMMARY OF RECOMMENDATIONS

In this section we offer a summary of task force recommendations. Like the report itself, the recommendations are divided into three parts. The first set of recommendations highlights the efforts necessary to better prepare our cities for the lead role they must play in preventing and responding to acts of terrorism. The second set of recommendations focuses on how to engage the private sector in homeland security. These recommendations aim to create a different relationship between the public and private sectors to secure our infrastructure, leverage private sector resources for the homeland security mission, and show how individual industries have dealt with or must deal with the homeland security challenge. The third set of recommendations addresses the role of the federal government in homeland security, including its role in protecting our civil liberties and paying for homeland security.

I. A METROPOLITAN APPROACH TO HOMELAND SECURITY

METROPOLITAN AREAS SHOULD BECOME THE PRIMARY UNIT FOR PLANNING, FUNDING, AND TRAINING FOR HOMELAND SECURITY. Every metropolitan area must complete vulnerability and mitigation assessments for every major component of security: First responders must be supplied with and trained in the use of personal protective equipment; interoperable communications must be established for all major metropolitan areas; realistic training and preparedness exercises must be conducted; evacuation routes and shelter-in-place plans must be developed and tested.

METROPOLITAN AREAS MUST MOVE FROM BEING FIRST RESPONDERS TO BEING FIRST PREVENTERS. Congress should establish a COPS II first preventers program to hire and train local law enforcement to do counterterrorism and gather intelligence. Regional networks for information sharing must be established and integrated with state and local intelligence fusion centers for coordinating prevention, preparedness, and response activities with the states and municipal areas. All law enforcement officers and civilian analysts dedicated to counterterrorism and intelligence operations must be cleared at the top secret level to achieve adequate information exchange with their federal counterparts.

THE SECURITY OF PUBLIC TRANSPORTATION SYSTEMS MUST BE BOLSTERED WHILE MAINTAINING EASE OF USE FOR PASSENGERS. Increasing the visibility of security personnel and the use of closed-circuit television systems is essential; making the public part of security efforts, as in the "if you see something, say something" campaigns, can provide a substantial increase in security. Interoperable communication systems and robust command and control systems must be built to work in subway systems. Federal funds should be made available to support capital improvements that would help prevent attacks, mitigate effects, and facilitate rapid post-attack recovery of the transit system.

PUBLIC HEALTH AND HOSPITAL PLANS SHOULD BE DEVELOPED IN EVERY MAJOR METROPOLITAN AREA AND FUNDING SHOULD BE TARGETED TO OUR LARGEST CITIES FIRST. Detection systems for chemical and biological releases must be installed in subways and metro stations, convention and athletic centers, and other public areas where large numbers of people congregate. A crash effort must be made to develop real-time biodetection sensors, and local agencies should have access to the data produced by the sensors. Syndromic surveillance systems should be established in all major metropolitan areas and linked to a federal network. Local agencies must have access to the SNS formulary, and the program should be expanded to include treatment for radiation sickness and additional all-hazards materials. The Vendor Managed Inventory should be extended to include food, water, and other basic supplies; and the distribution plans for SNS material must be developed and drilled on.

II. A NEW APPROACH TO THE PRIVATE SECTOR

THE OVERUSE OF "CRITICAL INFRASTRUCTURE" DESIGNATIONS MUST BE ELIMINATED AND NARROWER DEFINITIONS OF HIGH-IMPACT TARGETS AND ESSENTIAL SYSTEMS ADOPTED. Different standards of security should be set within each category, and different levels of federal support are appropriate. Infrastructure security plans that specify the end-state to be achieved, goals and milestones for achieving it, standards for implementation and compliance, and timelines for accomplishing intermediate actions should be set. Congress should pass the Chemical Facility Anti-terrorism Act with the Infrastructure Protection Regional Security and Area Security framework intact with amendments that will encourage companies to invest in passive security and inherently safer technologies. The act should mandate a design basis threat for security requirements for highest risk tier facilities, and security personnel at these facilities must be authorized to use deadly force when necessary. Facilities compliant with the act should receive liability protection and reductions in their insurance premiums; Congress must provide sufficient funding to enforce the act. Smart regulation on a sector-by-sector basis can be used to encourage the development and implementation of appropriate security measures. Congress should revamp the Terrorism Risk Insurance Act (TRIA) to promote risk mitigation and create a safe harbor against litigation following a terrorist attack where targeted companies have complied with government-approved security standards.

THE ENERGY INDUSTRY PROVIDES MANY EXAMPLES OF HOW SYSTEMS CAN BE MADE RESILIENT AND HOW COMPANIES CAN EFFICIENTLY RESPOND TO DISRUPTIONS. However, too many energy facilities could be targeted by terrorists to bring harm to local communities. The industry must work to eliminate these facilities. Where it is not possible, they must invest in better physical security measures. Our ailing energy infrastructure must be rebuilt and expanded, including federal support and assistance for infrastructure investments that have nationally critical import, such as a stockpile of critical, hard-to-replace equipment to improve system resiliency and service restoration speed. We must invest more in research, development, and deployment of designs and technologies that can make energy infrastructures and networks more resilient and resistant to failure. Finally, we must make a dedicated effort to increase energy efficiency and reduce our dependence on foreign energy sources.

CYBER SECURITY MUST BE MADE A NATIONAL PRIORITY, AND THE FEDERAL GOVERNMENT MUST USE ITS CONVENING POWER TO STANDARDIZE AND COORDINATE PRIVATE SECTOR EFFORTS. The White House must develop a new national information assurance policy directive to establish a framework for protecting critical cyber systems, clarify roles and responsibilities, and eliminate overlap. The number of committees nominally in charge of cyber security policy should be reduced to one under the reinstated position of cyber czar; Department of Defense indications and warnings efforts should be expanded into a national cyber attack sensing, warning, and response capability. Research and development efforts should be focused on the deployment of resilient networks; and sentencing guidelines for cyber crimes should be increased to reflect the damage they cause to our society and economy.

III. FIXING THE FEDERAL ROLE

**OUR DISASTER MANAGEMENT SYSTEM MUST BE REBUILT START-
ING WITH THE REESTABLISHMENT OF FEMA AS AN INDEPENDENT
CABINET-LEVEL AGENCY.** FEMA must be designated as the executive
agent for federal disaster planning and liaison and coordination with
state and local governments, and the lead agency for federal disaster crisis management in the field. FEMA must have the legal authority and
capability to take over control and operations when local authorities are
overwhelmed, disabled, or dispersed; it must help make cities "disaster-
resistant" by invigorating Project Impact to ensure that local authorities
have vital medical and interoperable mobile communications; and it
must involve the private sector in planning and preparation for catastrophic events.

**A RENEWED EFFORT TO FIX THE PROBLEMS THAT CONTINUE TO
PLAGUE OUR DOMESTIC INTELLIGENCE EFFORTS MUST BE MADE.**
The president should establish an intelligence transformation group of
the National Security Council, with delegation to the national security
advisor, to include the secretary of defense, the secretary of homeland
security, the attorney general, and the DNI. DHS should be given responsibility for assuring a two-way intelligence exchange with state and local
governments; the FBI's role in domestic intelligence must be clarified,
particularly in relation to DHS and its legislated role as an analytic and
fusion center; and the National Counterterrorism Center should become
the center for all analytic production.

**WHILE AVIATION SECURITY HAS SEEN BETTER FUNDING AND MORE
IMPROVEMENT THAN ANY OTHER HOMELAND SECURITY ACTIVITY,
THERE IS STILL MUCH TO BE DONE.** The Transportation Security
Administration (TSA) must bring Secure Flight online as rapidly as possible while providing protection for personal information; newer screening
technologies like backscatter and multi-view X-ray must be employed to
replace the first generation of technology purchased after September 11,
which is rapidly reaching the end of its service life; the Threat Image
Projection (TIP) program should be expanded to keep screeners alert; airports should be allowed to replace federal screeners with private contractor screeners, if doing so will increase efficiency and security; and in-line

explosive detection systems (EDS) should be built at the busiest passenger airports to screen checked baggage. All cargo that is shipped on passenger aircraft must be screened; continued reliance on known shipper methods is not sufficient. DHS research and development should focus on developing affordable and effective countermeasures against the threat of surface-to-air missiles; training flight crews in basic security measures and self-defense; expanding the transportation workers identification card to all passenger airports and major air cargo shipping ports.

PORT SECURITY EFFORTS MUST GO WELL BEYOND CONCERN OVER THE OPERATION OF MARINE TERMINALS. The security of the global intermodal transportation system must be bolstered and a national port plan developed that takes into account long-term trade and security trends. The Department of Defense and the Coast Guard joint operations centers should be set up in all major U.S. commercial ports for surveillance and data sharing and for training local, state, and federal participants. The navy salvage fleet should be doubled and the ships repositioned to the East and West coasts; Coast Guard fleet modernization annual funding should be increased to $2 billion; and all duties and fees collected in seaports should be allocated to fund security upgrades and infrastructure improvements.

OUR BORDER SECURITY CANNOT BE IGNORED WHILE THE POLITICS OF IMMIGRATION ARE SORTED OUT. Amnesty and guest worker initiatives may be necessary tradeoffs in order to gain control of our borders. While a comprehensive assessment of the border is necessary, five imperatives are already clear: We must have strong physical barriers on the border with Mexico and the capability to monitor both the southern and northern border continually; agreement must be reached among the United States, Canada, and Mexico on asylum policies; counterfeit-proof visitor identification for guest workers and permanent aliens must be developed and deployed; workplace enforcement of immigration rules is essential; and radiation detection must be prioritized.

WE MUST ENGAGE IN A STRUCTURED NATIONAL DISCUSSION ABOUT THE TRADEOFF BETWEEN SECURITY AND LIBERTY LED BY THE CIVIL LIBERTIES PROTECTION BOARD. Governors and mayors should consider appointing regional civil liberty protection boards to work with local police and other authorities; and outreach and educational activities in schools, civic organizations, places of worship, and local media should be undertaken. To ensure that the national Civil Liberties Protection Board is actively engaged in protecting civil liberties, it should issue a yearly report on its activities and on threats to civil liberties, brief Congress on the report, and hold an annual national conference to review its report. Moreover, the board should file a civil liberties impact statement with the executive branch and Congress on any proposed measure or program that may raise public concerns about potential abuses of liberty.

SECURITY FUNDING SHOULD NOT BE SEGMENTED BETWEEN "NATIONAL SECURITY" AND "HOMELAND SECURITY." The administration should be required to perform a Synoptic Security Review (SSR) encompassing both Pentagon and domestic security. Tradeoffs should be made between traditional defense spending and homeland security. Pentagon programs including the F/A-22 Raptor, the Virginia Class submarine, the DD(X) destroyer, the V-22 Osprey, and ballistic missile defense can be eliminated or scaled back. This would generate $23.7 billion for public health and first responders, transportation security, port security, chemical plant security, and other priorities.

APPENDIX: SUMMARY OF CHAPTER RECOMMENDATIONS

1. INTRODUCTION: BUILDING HOMELAND SECURITY IN OUR CITIES AND STATES

1.1 Every major metropolitan area should have complete vulnerability and mitigation assessments.

1.2 Every major metropolitan area should have personal protective equipment for all first responders.

1.3 Every major metropolitan area should have interoperable communications.

1.4 Every major metropolitan area should have a public health and biological/chemical/radiological surveillance system.

1.5 Every major metropolitan area should have an intelligence collection and sharing program.

1.6 Every major metropolitan area should conduct realistic training and preparedness exercises.

1.7 Every major metropolitan area should have closed-circuit television (CCTV) systems to secure infrastructure.

1.8 Every metropolitan area should have an enhanced security program for public transportation.

1.9 Metropolitan areas should create and periodically test evacuation/shelter-in-place plans.

2. A COUNTERTERRORISM POLICY FOR OUR OWN BACKYARD

2.1 Create COPS II first preventers program.

2.2 Build and inspire a culture of "first preventers."

2.3 The homeland security secretary should create a regional network integrated with state and local fusion centers for coordinating prevention, preparedness, and response activities with the states and municipal areas.

2.4   The Department of Homeland Security (DHS) should establish
        standards for collection, analysis, and reporting for state and
        local intelligence fusion centers.

2.5   Provide advanced prevention training and proper security clearances.

2.6   Ensure that prevention training and exercises include realistic
        adversarial play for scenarios involving both conventional
        attacks and weapons of mass destruction (WMD).

3. Security for a Nation in Motion

3.1   Increase visibility and frequency of personnel and increase use
        of CCTV systems.

3.2   Promote public engagement to foster security awareness.

3.3   Ensure interoperable communications systems and robust command
        and control systems are extended to ground transportation systems.

3.4   Conduct annual vulnerability assessments and review potential
        threats, vulnerabilities, and risks with local and federal officials.

3.5   Ensure adequacy of crisis management and communications
        plans, awareness of plans, readiness of equipment and person-
        nel, and accuracy of all contact information.

3.6   Continue development of new explosive and WMD detection
        and countermeasures. Allow the use of DHS grant money for
        deployment of canine detection until effective detection tech-
        nologies can be brought to bear.

3.7   Direct federal funding to support capital improvements that will
        help prevent attacks, mitigate their effects during an attack, and
        allow the transit system to be rapidly recoverable.

4. A Healthy Medical Response System

4.1   Metropolitan health and hospital plans should be developed
        based on federally set standards; federal funding initially should
        be targeted at our largest cities.

4.2   Detection systems for chemical weapons should be installed in
        subways and metro stations, convention and athletic centers, and
        other public areas where large numbers of people congregate.

4.3   BioWatch must be redesigned to include developing cooperative agreements for the maintenance of the systems and the use of the data; increasing the number of air monitoring stations in each city to 40 to 60; and the fast-tracking of research for real-time detection.

4.4   Building syndromic surveillance systems in all major metropolitan areas and tying them into a federal backbone should be a top priority of the Centers for Disease Control and the DHS.

4.5   The Strategic National Stockpile (SNS) should revert to the Department of Health and Human Services with a DHS liaison; the SNS formulary should be released to local officials with a legitimate need to know; the program should be expanded to include treatment for radiation sickness and additional all-hazards material; the Vendor Managed Inventory should be expanded to include food, water, and other basic supplies.

4.6   The CHEMPACK program should be redesigned to put the antidotes in mobile emergency units.

4.7   The Cities Readiness Initiative (CRI) should be redesigned based on input from the public health community; funding should be provided to hire a fulltime CRI coordinator for each metropolitan area with the goal of implementing a plan within one year.

4.8   Additional financial incentives and policy adjustments must be made to bring private sector interest to the BioShield program.

4.9   Decision makers at local, state, and national levels must prepare graduated quarantine measures; plans to carry out quarantine must be prepared and drilled; states that do not have the authority to quarantine should make necessary legal modifications.

4.10   Hospital surge capacity must be built, starting with the nation's largest metropolitan areas.

5. INTRODUCTION: A NEW APPROACH TO THE PRIVATE SECTOR AND HOMELAND SECURITY

5.1   Focus on securing high-impact targets and assuring continuity of essential systems over a blanket approach to critical infrastructure.

5.2   Establish joint planning committees for each HITS and ACES sector. Exercise authority under Section 871 of the Homeland Security Act of 2002 to exempt joint planning committees from FACA. Amend provisions of relevant anti-trust laws to exempt explicitly standard-setting discussions and planning sessions. Establish a congressional select committee to oversee joint planning.

5.3   Once established, these committees should develop infrastructure security plans that specify the security end-state to be achieved, goals and milestones for achieving it, standards for implementation and compliance, and timelines for accomplishing intermediate actions.

5.4   Integrate chief executive review into joint planning process; obtain approval and commitment to carry out plans according to agreed upon timelines.

5.5   Implement the Infrastructure Protection Regional Security and Area Security framework as set out in the Chemical Facility Anti-Terrorism Act of 2005.

5.6   Adopt smart regulation on a sector-by-sector basis to encourage the development and implementation of appropriate security measures.

5.7   Revamp the Terrorism Risk Insurance Act (TRIA) to promote risk mitigation and create a safe harbor against litigation following a terrorist attack where targeted companies have complied with government-approved security standards.

5.8   Develop a CEO-level system for managing resource allocations during recovery and reconstitution phases following a catastrophic national event to allow a coordinated effort with the federal government.

6. Financial Services: Learning from Success

6.1   Diverse and resilient communication channels are essential. Elements such as cell phones, wireless e-mail devices, landline phones, and the Internet are required.

6.2   The power grid must be considered among the most vital of critical infrastructures and needs investment to make sure it works across the nation.

6.3   Recognize the interdependencies among critical infrastructure sectors.

6.4   Recognize the dependency of critical infrastructures on software operating systems and the Internet.

6.5   As Hurricane Katrina has poignantly illustrated, establishing improved coordination procedures across all critical infrastructures and with federal, state, and local government is essential to rapid, coordinated, and effective response when events occur. To minimize the economic and social risks during a crisis, coordination in planning and response between the private sector and public emergency management must improve.

7. CHEMICAL PLANT SECURITY: PREVENTING A TERRORIST BHOPAL

7.1   Providing a stronger framework for developing regulations that will focus companies on investing in passive security over active security.

7.2   Using a "design basis threat" for developing security requirements for facilities in the highest-risk tier.

7.3   Giving security personnel at high-risk facilities the legal authority to use deadly force against attackers.

7.4   Establishing a training and certification program under which security professionals can conduct vulnerability assessments and establish security plans.

7.5   Providing liability protection and terrorism insurance premium reductions for facilities certified as being compliant.

8. PROTECTING ENERGY INFRASTRUCTURE

8.1   Relocate the most vulnerable assets, such as LNG terminals, away from population centers. Where this is not feasible, mandate increased security measures.

8.2   Increase the redundancy of our energy infrastructure to reduce vulnerability.

8.3   Increase system resiliency and recovery speed.

8.4   Strengthen other infrastructures and systems, those that both support and depend on energy systems.

8.5   Focus on energy security, that is, the long-term availability of reliable, affordable energy supplies to the nation.

8.6   Increase the use of small-scale distributed generation (including renewables and combined heat and power) close to energy users.

8.7   Increase investment in research, development, and deployment of designs that will make energy infrastructures and networks more resilient and resistant to failure.

9. CYBER SECURITY: A SILENT CATASTROPHE

9.1   A new national information assurance policy should formally establish a framework for protecting critical cyber systems.

9.2   The directive should clarify roles and responsibilities, eliminating overlapping responsibilities.

9.3   A single committee should replace the six that currently advise the federal government on cyber security and should reside in the White House.

9.4   The position of cyber czar should be reinstated and, among other duties, should head the committee.

9.5   Joint exercises involving the DHS and the Department of Defense, as well as key players in the private sector, should be held to test capabilities and coordination.

9.6   Defense Indications and Warnings efforts must be expanded and fully integrated into a national cyber attack sensing, warning, and response capability.

9.7   The position of assistant secretary for cyber security and telecommunications must be filled immediately.

9.8   A concerted effort must be made to develop and deploy resilient networks.

9.9   A synoptic, real-time view of the condition of key cyber nodes and systems throughout the United States should be developed.

9.10   Legislative changes concerning public-private partnerships and information sharing and protection should be made.

9.11   Legislative changes to the Wartime Production Act to bring those emergency powers into the information age should be made.

9.12 Increased sentencing guidelines that treat cyber crimes as real crimes and deter would-be hackers should be put in place.

9.13 In support of this directive, an annual report should be prepared for the president for his approval, including a requirements-driven multiyear budget, research and development plan, and roles and missions statements for all relevant agencies, including the Department of Defense, the FBI, the CIA, the National Security Agency, and the DHS.

10. INTRODUCTION: FEDERAL ROLES AND RESPONSIBILITIES

10.1 Abolish the Homeland Security Council and strengthen homeland security policy and functionality within the National Security Council.

10.2 Establish DHS domestic regions to push disaster management, infrastructure protection, and intelligence out to states and localities. These should be based on the eight existing Federal Emergency Management Agency (FEMA) regions.

10.3 Reestablish FEMA as an independent cabinet-level agency.

10.4 Resist structural solutions to functional problems.

10.5 Provide adequate funding for homeland security missions under an integrated homeland security budget strategy.

10.6 Push for congressional reform to limit the number of committees with jurisdiction over homeland security operations.

11. EMERGENCY RESPONSE: RESTORING DISCARDED STRATEGIES THAT WORKED

11.1 Reestablish FEMA as an independent cabinet-level agency.

11.2 Review existing authorities for federal management of disasters when local authorities are overwhelmed.

11.3 Make FEMA once again an international leader in emergency management and use the agency as a tool of public diplomacy.

11.4 Establish two new White House positions: deputy assistant to the president for crisis management; and special assistant to the president for emergency preparedness.

11.5   Designate FEMA as the executive agent for federal disaster planning and liaison and coordination with state and local governments and the lead agency for federal disaster crisis management in the field, whether in support of state and local efforts or as the overall controlling organization.

11.6   Invigorate Project Impact and ensure that local authorities have the medical and interoperable mobile communications capabilities to spur development of "disaster-resistant" cities.

11.7   Develop communication strategies for informing the public and inspiring confidence in crises, while avoiding undue risk to law enforcement or intelligence collection efforts.

11.8   Focus on making the Homeland Security Advisory System useful.

11.9   Create law enforcement response teams (LERTs) to help reestablish order following catastrophic incidents.

11.10   Involve the private sector in planning and preparation for catastrophic terrorist attack.

12. AN INTELLIGENCE APPROACH TO DOMESTIC SECURITY

12.1   The president should establish by executive order an intelligence transformation group (ITG)—or its functional equivalent—of the National Security Council, chaired by the president with delegation to the national security advisor, to include the secretary of defense, the secretary of homeland security, the attorney general, and the director of national intelligence.

12.2   Resist structural buildup. The hasty establishment of the TTIC and National Counterterrorism Center (NCTC) taught us that the resistance encountered to these centralized models was in part the result of legitimate leadership concern about degrading critical capabilities needed in an increasingly decentralized intelligence community.

12.3   Strengthen the DHS's intelligence role. The president should publicly, as well as in his leadership of the ITG, make clear his support for DHS as an intelligence assessment and sharing center. Under this arrangement, the FBI must share information with DHS and, through DHS, state and local authorities. A joint DHS-FBI committee on intelligence chaired by the White House would ensure that sharing of information became a reality.

12.4 Use regional offices for information sharing. The DHS second-stage review should be revised to give the secretary responsibility for assuring a two-way intelligence exchange with state and local governments—as well as with the twenty-two agencies incorporated into DHS.

12.5 Clarify the FBI's particular role in domestic intelligence. The FBI, its fifty-six field stations, and its growing network of Joint Terrorism Task Forces (JTTFs) have a part to play in the development of a national intelligence capability, which in an ideal world would be a collaborative and not a leading role. We should, once and for all, lower expectations of the Bureau's intelligence role. The FBI should not be expected to produce at a local level either the authoritative analysis or the integrated collection assessments that it cannot provide nationally.

12.6 Clarify departmental roles and responsibilities. The president and the ITG should work urgently to clarify roles and responsibilities of key agencies with responsibilities for intelligence and homeland security missions. The NCTC, the DHS, the Department of Defense (especially Northern Command), the CIA, and the FBI, while understandably enlarging their missions, are bumping into each other in the integration of foreign and domestic intelligence, and colliding in establishing working relationships with state and local governments. This is a manageable problem if caught early, but a serious issue with implications for preparedness, response, and civil liberties if ignored.

12.7 Promote government-wide information sharing. The program director for information sharing, a position given government-wide authorities by statute, should be placed in the National Security Council (NSC), not under the DNI, where it recently has been placed by the White House at least partly on the misguided recommendation of the WMD Commission.

12.8 Make the National Counterterrorism Center (NCTC) work. The NCTC, now a key institution, will continue to struggle to establish itself as the dominant provider of terrorism analysis because of the long-standing and growing pressures for decentralization of analytic production in the intelligence, defense, and law enforcement communities.

12.9   Support the director of national intelligence, but hold him accountable. The president and the ITG should actively support and carefully monitor the implementation of the director of national intelligence's agenda to reform management, to professionalize the intelligence service, and to improve intelligence collection and analysis.

12.10   Clarify the CIA's role under the director of national intelligence (DNI).

12.11   Push congressional reform. On domestic intelligence, it appears that some overseers are more protective of the FBI than they are disappointed with its post–September 11 performance. None of this has changed the inadequate oversight of the intelligence committees or otherwise gone far enough to align, in any lasting way, executive and legislative branch priorities for intelligence community reform.

13. Losing Focus on Aviation Security

13.1   Passenger screening

- The Transportation Security Agency (TSA) needs to bring Secure Flight online as rapidly as possible. The TSA must assure passengers that their personal information will be strictly safeguarded from unauthorized use, and will be used only for the purposes of distinguishing high-risk from low-risk passengers. The TSA may also consider segmenting the passenger population into travelers who are willing to give extra personal information for Secure Flight and those who are not willing to provide information.

- Several technologies may potentially help to improve passenger screening at security checkpoints. One option is the multiview X-ray, which provides screeners with much higher resolution images that can be rotated on the screening monitor in order to improve detection rates. A second and more traditional option is to expand the canine explosive detection teams to operate at security checkpoints.

- To keep screeners sharp and alert, the TSA should expand the use of the Threat Image Projection (TIP) program.

- Biometric identity verification is the obvious next step to enhancing screening effectiveness. The TSA's Registered Traveler pilot program, which uses iris and fingerprint verification, was completed on September 30, 2005, and seems to have been a widespread success. The TSA should aim for a quick review and expansion of this program to all major airports.

13.2   Checked baggage security

- The TSA should develop a plan to rapidly deploy in-line EDS systems at the busiest passenger airports, and ultimately at all passenger airports.

- Screeners should have access to ongoing training and every Online Training Center should be available by high-speed Internet so that trainers can access and complete training courses more rapidly. TSA should also systematically monitor and document the completion of required screener training.

13.3   Air cargo security

- The TSA should screen all of the cargo that travels by passenger aircraft with canine explosives detection teams and machines.

- Cargo containers should also be sealed with tamper-evident tape, which offers a visual indication of tampering at a very low cost.

- The use of hardened unit loading devices (HULDs) should also be explored more vigorously.

- The TSA should make the Known Shipper Program mandatory for air carriers and should develop strict monitoring procedures to verify that shippers in the database are actually securing their cargo according to TSA standards.

13.4   Shoulder-fired missile threat

- The TSA should vigorously explore and test countermeasures for airlines against these weapons. Countermeasures should contribute to a layered defense, including securing a perimeter around airports that would prevent an attacker from firing within range of the missile system.

13.5   In-flight and crew member security

- The TSA should fund and monitor mandatory self-defense and security training for flight crews rather than relying on air carriers to train their own flight crews according to varying standards.

- The TSA should explore the development and installation of special visors on cockpit windows whose light-blocking properties would be activated only when a laser threat is detected—technology already in development by the Department of Defense.
- The TSA should mandate that federal air marshals establish a standard procedure for compiling, analyzing, and responding to mission reports of security incidents.

13.6   Aviation worker screening

- The TSA should aggressively pursue development of biometric verification for all aviation workers. The Transportation Workers Identification Card is a good start and should be expanded to include all passenger airports and major air-cargo shipping ports.

14. PREVENTING NUCLEAR TERRORISM

14.1   Issue a policy that delegitimizes highly enriched uranium in the civilian sector. Congress should reenact the 1992 Schumer amendment restrictions on exporting highly enriched uranium (HEU).

14.2   Expand the Global Threat Reduction Initiative program to include all HEU-powered civilian reactors. Speed up conversion of U.S. research reactors from HEU to non-weapons-usable uranium.

14.3   Expand the amount of U.S. highly enriched uranium slated for conversion to non-weapons-usable form. Accelerate the conversion of HEU already scheduled for conversion. The United States could set aside this converted material as a strategic nuclear fuel reserve.

14.4   Do not pursue plutonium reprocessing methods that would lead to separated weapons-usable plutonium.

14.5   Increase consolidation of weapons-usable materials in the U.S. nuclear complex. Work toward the secretary of energy's advisory board recommendation to move these materials to one highly secure site. Further consolidation could pay off in billions of dollars of cost savings.

14.6 The Department of Energy (DOE) and the National Nuclear Security Administration (NNSA) should develop a comprehensive strategic security plan. Such a plan must be based on frequently tested performance and not just on compliance with security requirements. The DOE and the NNSA should coordinate their security efforts with the Department of Defense. Protecting against the most likely route for terrorists or criminals to gain access to weapons-usable materials, the DOE and the NNSA should increase vigilance against the insider threat to nuclear facilities.

15. THE PERILS OF NEGLECTING AMERICA'S WATERFRONT

15.1 Over the next eighteen months, the Department of Defense must work closely with the Coast Guard (now part of the Department of Homeland Security) and with local authorities in organizing and participating in exercises that involve simulated attacks on the nation's largest commercial seaports.

15.2 The Department of Defense needs to take the lead on funding and setting up joint operations centers in all major U.S. commercial ports: to outfit them with advanced information and communications technology that supports surveillance and data sharing; and to provide the necessary training to the local, state, and federal agency participants. This should be completed by 2007.

15.3 The U.S. Navy should reposition one of its two salvage ships in Norfolk, Virginia, to the West Coast and take the lead in drawing up commercial salvage contracts to support domestic harbor clearance. Over the next five years, the Navy should double its salvage fleet from four vessels to eight, and base two of them on the West Coast, two on the Gulf Coast, and two on the East Coast. The remaining two can be deployed overseas to support navy operations.

15.4 The National Oceanographic and Atmospheric Administration (NOAA) hydrographic research vessels should receive additional funding to complete bottom surveys of all major U.S. commercial seaports. This baseline information is indispensable in quickly spotting mines, should an adversary deploy them.

15.5   The Coast Guard needs to see annual funding doubled to $2 billion to replace its ancient fleet of vessels and aircraft, and to bring its command and control capabilities into the twenty-first century. Many of its cutters, helicopters, and planes are operating long beyond their anticipated service life and are routinely experiencing major breakdowns. Under the current delivery schedule, it will be thirty years before the Coast Guard has the kind of assets it needs today to perform its mission. This could leave a two-decade gap in capability as the existing fleet becomes too decrepit and dangerous to operate.

15.6   Congress should authorize the reallocation of all seaport duties and fees back into the ports to support security upgrades and infrastructure improvements.

15.7   The federal government needs to develop a national port plan that takes into account long-term trade and security trends. Relying on a patchwork quilt of locally based decisions for managing this critical infrastructure is just not acceptable.

16. RECREATING OUR BORDERS

16.1   Security from the threat of terrorism should be the primary focus of U.S. border efforts. Strong physical barriers on the border with Mexico are essential. Approximately 150,000 "OTMs," or other-than-Mexican illegal immigrants, crossed this border in 2005, and are able to blend into American society and pose a serious security threat once inside our borders.

16.2   Utilizing technology and personnel, the entire U.S. northern and southern border must be continually monitored. Capability must be developed to respond to the detection of illegal crossings.

16.3   Eliminate "whack-a-mole" responses, such as the Arizona Border Control Initiative, that simply relocate major crossing points without reducing overall flow. The practice of redeployment to targeted areas should be ended and focus placed instead on augmenting capabilities.

16.4   U.S. visa and asylum processes must be made to conform with the Mexican and Canadian systems, so that, except in rare cases, all three countries agree on who is admitted.

16.5   Development and deployment of counterfeit-proof visitor iden-
        tification for guest workers and permanent aliens.
16.6   Workplace enforcement of immigration rules must be done on a
        continual basis. Sponsoring institutions must have personnel
        certified in understanding the immigration process and docu-
        mentation.
16.7   Detection of radioactive sources must be prioritized and inef-
        fective personal radiation detectors should be replaced by radi-
        ation portal monitors and X-ray systems.

17. LAND OF SWEET LIBERTIES

17.1   It is vital to spark a structured national discussion now about
        the tradeoff between security and liberty. The Civil Liberties
        Protection Board, created by executive order of the president in
        August of 2004, could lead the effort.
17.2   Governors and big-city mayors should consider appointing
        regional liberty protection boards to work with state and local
        law enforcement authorities.
17.3   Local liberty protection boards should sponsor outreach and
        educational activities in schools, civic organizations, places of
        worship, and local media.
17.4   The national Civil Liberties Protection Board should issue a
        yearly report on its activities and on threats to American free-
        doms, brief Congress on the report (including classified annexes
        if necessary), and convene an annual national conference to
        review its report.
17.5   The board should file a civil liberties impact statement with the
        executive branch and Congress on any proposed measure or
        program that may raise public concern about potential abuses
        of liberty.

NOTES

CHAPTER 1

1. "Emergencies and Disasters: First Responders," Department of Homeland Security, available online at http://www.dhs.gov/dhspublic/interapp/editorial/editorial_0197.xml.

2. "Emergency Responders: Drastically Underfunded, Dangerously Unprepared," Report of an Independent Task Force Sponsored by the Council on Foreign Relations, June 2003.

3. David Howe, "Planning Scenarios: Executive Summary," Homeland Security Council, July 2004, available online at http://www.globalsecurity.org/security/library/report/2004/hsc-planning-scenarios-jul04.htm.

4. "Handouts for Homeland Security," *60 Minutes,* April 10, 2005, available online at http://www.cbsnews.com/stories/2005/03/31/60minutes/main684349.shtml.

5. Congressional Research Service, "State and Local Homeland Security: Unresolved Issues for the 109th Congress," June 9, 2005.

CHAPTER 2

1. "Facts and Figures 2003: Counterterrorism," Federal Bureau of Investigations, available online at http://www.fbi.gov/libref/factsfigure/counterterrorism.htm.

2. Jill Wagner, "Intelligence Community's Arabic Challenge," *NBC News,* October 19, 2004.

3. "New York Nuclear Bomb Scare Kept Secret for Months," AFP, March 3, 2002.

4. Kevin Johnson, "Police Executives: Budget Cuts Would Be Devastating," *USA Today,* March 4, 2004.

5. Van Harl, "Cops Are People Too," Air Force Security Police Association, Chapter Update, May 8, 2005, available online at http://afspaeagle.com/News Public/Update050509.htm.

6. Kelly, Raymond, "May the Force Be with You," *Gotham Gazette,* May 10, 2004. Available online at http://www.gothamgazette.com/article/20040510 /202/973.

7. James Gordon Meek and Grey Gittrick, "Al Qaeda Plot Targets US," *New York Daily News,* August 2, 2004.

8. For more on red teaming, see the Defense Science Board Task Force, "On The Role and Status of DoD Red Teaming Activities," September 2003, and the "National Strategy for Homeland Security," available online at http:// www.whitehouse.gov/homeland/book/nat_strat_hls.pdf.

CHAPTER 3

1. This chapter is drawn from Daniel B. Prieto, "Mass Transit Security after the London Bombings," Testimony Before the Commonwealth of Massachusetts Joint Committee on Public Safety and Homeland Security, August 2005.

2. Congressional Research Service, "Transit Security," memo to Homeland Security Committee Democratic staff, August 28, 2003.

3. Daniel B. Prieto, Harvard University, analysis of Memorial Institute for the Prevention of Terrorism (MIPT), Terrorism Knowledge Base, July 2005. Casualties are defined as the average number of injuries and fatalities per incident.

4. Information on the London system can be found at http://www.tfl.gov.uk/tfl/.

5. Bill Gertz, "Terrorists Said to Seek Entry to U.S. via Mexico," *Washington Times,* April 7, 2003, A1.

6. Thomas H. Kean et al., "Final Report on 9/11 Commission Recommendations," 9/11 Public Discourse Project, December 5, 2005, available online at http://www.9-11pdp.org/press/2005-12-05_report.pdf.

7. Eric Lipton, "Senators Clash on Security Cost," *New York Times,* July 15, 2005.

8. Ibid.

9. National Research Council, *Making the Nation Safer: The Role of Science and Technology in Countering Terrorism* (Washington, D.C.: National Academies Press, 2002), p. 220.

10. Sara Kehaulani Goo, "Marshals to Patrol Land, Sea Transport: TSA Test

Includes Surveillance Teams on Metro System," *Washington Post,* December 14, 2005, p. A1. Available online at http://www.washingtonpost.com/wp-dyn/content /article/2005/12/13/AR2005121301709.html.

11. Government Accountability Office, *Mass Transit: Federal Action Could Help Transit Agencies Address Security Challenges,* GAO-03-263 (Washington, D.C.: GAO, December 2002), p. 2.

12. Ibid., p. 12.

13. Staff of the House Select Committee Survey, "America at Risk: Closing the Public Transportation Security Gap," Democratic Staff Report, Select Committee on Homeland Security, U.S. Congress, May 2004.

CHAPTER 4

1. The Monterey Institute of International Studies maintains a terrorism database that tracks pertinent statistics from public data sources. Monterey Terrorism Database, accessed October 11, 2005.

2. Guy Gugliotta and Gary Matsumoto. "FBI's Theory on Anthrax Is Doubted, Attacks Not Likely Work of 1 Person, Experts Say," *Washington Post,* October 28, 2002, p. A1.

3. Bruce Taylor Seeman, "U.S. Ill-Prepared for Flu Pandemic, Experts Fear," Newhouse News Service, July 20, 2005, available online at http://www.new housenews.com/archive/seeman072005.html.

4. "Ready or Not? Protecting the Public's Health from Diseases, Disasters, and Bioterrorism, 2005," Trust for America's Health, December 2005.

5. Ibid., p. 7.

6. Health care providers can find guidance at: "Recognition of Illness Associated with Intentional Release of a Biologic Agent," *MMWR* 50, no. 49 (October 19, 2001): 893–7.

7. Homeland Security Subcommittee Hearing on Overview of the FY05 Science and Technology Budget and Information and Infrastructure Protection Budget: Testimony of the Honorable Charles E. McQueary, Under Secretary for Science and Technology, Department of Homeland Security, March 2, 2004.

8. For more information on state-of-the-art practices, see http://www.syndromic .org.

9. "Ready or Not? Protecting the Public's Health from Diseases, Disasters, and Bioterrorism, 2005," December 2005, p. 50.

10. Government Accountability Office, "Information Technology: Federal Agencies Face Challenges in Implementing Initiatives to Improve Public Health Infrastructure," GAO-05-308, June 2005.

11. "The Strategic National Stockpile," Centers for Disease Control and Prevention, January 20, 2005. See http://www.bt.cdc.gov/stockpile/.

12. Mimi Hall, "Cities Fret over How to Quickly Deliver Vaccines," *USA Today,* August 1, 2005.

13. "Ready or Not? Protecting the Public's Health from Diseases, Disasters, and Bioterrorism, 2005," p. 46.

14. "CHEMPACK Project, Operational Protocol," Strategic National Stockpile, Office of Terrorism Prevention and Emergency Response, Centers for Disease Control and Prevention, June 14, 2004, p. 2.

15. See http://www.bt.cdc.gov/cri/.

16. Mimi Hall, "Cities Fret over How to Quickly Deliver Vaccines."

17. The Senate passed S.19, the BioShield Improvement and Treatment for Americans Act, on May 19, 2004; the House of Representatives passed HR 2122, the Project Bioshield Act, on July 14, 2004; and President George W. Bush signed the bill into law on July 21, 2004. See Public Law 108-276.

18. Amy Smithson, conversations with representatives of pharmaceutical and biotechnology companies dating to the inception of the BioShield concept. See also Marc Kaufman, "Company Criticizes HHS BioShield Effort," *Washington Post,* September 28, 2005, p. A19.

19. For more on the adoption of the Model State Public Health Act, see http://www.publichealthlaw.net/Resources/Modellaws.htm.

20. "Ready or Not? Protecting the Public's Health from Diseases, Disasters, and Bioterrorism, 2005," p. 34.

21. See http://www.hhs.gov/ophep/npgs.html.

CHAPTER 6

1. K. C. Jones, "DHS Completes Cyber-Security Tests," *TechWeb News,* February 10, 2006. Available online at http://www.informationweek.com/security /showArticle.jhtml?articleID=180200486&subSection=Government+Security.

2. BITS is a nonprofit consortium of 100 of the largest financial institutions in the United States. BITS works as a strategic brain trust to provide intellectual capital and address emerging issues, acting quickly as needs arise. BITS' activities are driven by the CEOs and their direct reporters—CIOs, CTOs, vice chairmen, and executive vice

president-level executives of the businesses. See http://www.bitsinfo.org.

3. Homeland Security Presidential Directive 7, "Critical Infrastructure Identification, Prioritization, and Protection," Washington, D.C.: December 17, 2003.

4. The BITS Crisis Communicator expedites response and recovery processes and is also used to discuss consistent messaging that will maintain consumer confidence during times of crisis.

5. Available online at http://www.bitsinfo.org/p_publications.html.

6. See numerous reports, including FSSCC's action plan for 2005 at http://www.fsscc.org.

7. Written testimony of Donald F. Donahue, Chairman, Financial Services Sector Coordinating Council for Critical Infrastructure Protection and Homeland Security, before the Committee on Government Reform Subcommittee on Government Management, Finance and Accountability, United States House of Representatives, September 26, 2005.

8. Scott Parsons, Deputy Assistant Secretary for Critical Infrastructure Protection and Compliance Policy, the U.S. Department of the Treasury. Testimony before U.S. House of Representatives Committee on Government Reform, Subcommittee on Government Management, Finance, and Accountability, September 26, 2005.

9. For more information on work of FSSCC and Financial and Banking Information Infrastructure Committee see http://www.treas.gov/offices/domestic-finance/financial-institution/cip/.

10. "Potential Terrorist Attacks: Additional Actions Needed to Better Prepare Critical Financial Market Participants," GAO-03-251, Government Accountability Office, February 2003.

11. See Government Accountability Office, "Financial Market Preparedness: Improvements Made, but More Action Needed to Prepare for Wide-Scale Disasters," GAO-04-984, Washington, D.C.: September 14, 2004.

12. See briefing on ChicagoFIRST at http://www.infragard.net/library/congress_05/financial_sec/chicago_first_exp.ppt.

CHAPTER 7

1. "Security Fact Sheet," American Chemistry Council, available online at http://www.americanchemistry.com/s_acc/sec_mediakits.asp?CID=258&DID=63 2.

2. Ashok S. Kalelkar, "Investigation of Large Magnitude Incidents: Bhopal as a Case Study," Arthur D. Little, May 1988.

3. Carl Prine, "Chemical Sites Still Vulnerable," *Pittsburgh Tribune Review,* November 16, 2003.

4. "U.S. Plants Open to Terrorists," *60 Minutes,* June 13, 2004.

5. "FBI: We're Not Worried about Terrorist Cyberattack," Reuters, December 7, 2005.

6. Eric Lipton, "U.S. Lists Possible Terror Attacks and Likely Tolls," *New York Times,* March 16, 2005.

7. "Annual Energy Review 2004," Energy Information Administration, DOE/EIA-0384(2004), August 2005, available online at http://www.eia.doe.gov/emeu/aer/contents.html.

8. Government Accountability Office, "Voluntary Initiatives Are Under Way at Chemical Facilities, but the Extent of Security Preparedness Is Unknown," GAO-03-439, March 2003.

9. Chemical Facilities Security Act of 2003, S.994, 108th Congress (2003).

10. Testimony of Tim Felt, President and CEO, Explorer Pipeline, On Behalf of the American Petroleum Institute and the Association of Oil Pipe Lines, Before the Subcommittee on Energy and Air Quality of the House Committee on Energy and Commerce, April 27, 2006.

11. Interview with Malcolm Wolfe, Minority Counsel, Environmental and Public Works Committee, March 5, 2004.

CHAPTER 8

1. Energy Information Administration, *Electric Power Annual,* 2004, November 2005, available online at http://www.eia.doe.gov.

2. National Academy of Sciences, "Safety and Security of Commercial Spent Nuclear Fuel Storage: Public Report," April 2005.

3. North American Electric Reliability Council, "2005 Long-Term Reliability Assessment," September 2005.

4. NERC CIP-002-009, also called NERC 1300 standards.

5. Reuters, December 7, 2005.

6. Trusted Network Technologies survey, reported by Robert Ciampa, "Expect Breach of Critical Energy Systems, Feel Pain of SOX & NERC Compliance," *Fortnightly's Spark,* September 2005.

7. Energy Information Agency, *Electric Power Annual,* 2004.

8. Ibid.

9. Ibid.

10. Association of Oil Pipe Lines and American Petroleum Institute.

CHAPTER 9

1. Qiao Liang and Wang Xiangsui, *Unrestricted Warfare: China's Master Plan to Destroy America* (Pan American, 2002).

2. Alan Sayre, "Big Easy Launches Free Wireless System," Associated Press, November 29, 2005.

3. As of this writing, the national infrastructure protection plan is in draft form.

CHAPTER 10

1. Thomas H. Kean et al., "Report on the Status of 9/11 Commission Recommendations, Part II: Reforming the Institutions of Government," October 20, 2005, available online at http://www.9-11pdp.org/press/2005-10-20_report.pdf.

CHAPTER 11

1. Prepared testimony of James Lee Witt, "The Homeland Security Department's Plan to Consolidate and Co-locate Regional and Field Offices: Improving Communications and Coordination," Before the House Government Reform Committee Subcommittee on Energy Policy, Natural Resources, and Regulatory Affairs and the Subcommittee on National Security, Emerging Threats, and International Relations, March 24, 2004.

2. The group was originally mandated by President Reagan, when it was dubbed the "Coordinating Sub-Group" of the principals' committee, i.e., the national security cabinet chaired by the assistant to the president for national security. During the Clinton administration the CSG was renamed the Counterterrorism Support Group and was chaired by the national coordinator for

counterterrorism and security, a new position created by Clinton to coordinate policy and manage crises—foreign or domestic—arising from terrorist attack.

3. "Ridge Tries to Calm America's Nerves," CNN, February 14, 2003.

CHAPTER 12

1. Multilevel security is a critical priority for homeland security and domestic intelligence. The best work done on this, among several initiatives, is by the Markle Task Force on National Security in the Information Age. See Zoe Baird and James Barksdale, Chairmen, Markle Task Force, "Creating a Trusted Network for Homeland Security," New York, Markle Corporation, 2003.

2. *The 9/11 Commission Report: Final Report of the National Commission on Terrorist Attacks upon the United States* (Washington, D.C.: U.S. Government Printing Office, 2004). See especially chapters 3, 7, and 13.

3. For an informative assessment of New York's impressive counterterrorism initiatives since September 11, see William Finnegan, "The Terrorism Beat: How Is the NYPD Defending the City?" *New Yorker,* July 25, 2005, pp. 58-71.

4. *The Commission on the Intelligence Capabilities of the United States Regarding Weapons of Mass Destruction: Report to the President of the United States* (Washington, D.C.: U.S. Government Printing Office, 2005), chapter 10.

5. *9/11 Commission Report,* pp. 102–107.

6. Assistant Director of Central Intelligence for Analysis and Production, *Strategic Investment Plan for Intelligence Community Analysis,* Washington, D.C.: Central Intelligence Agency, 2000 (available on the Web).

7. One of the most eloquent voices against military encroachment into civilian government responsibilities is former Virginia Governor James Gilmore, a homeland security expert who headed the Gilmore Commission. Hear, for example, Gilmore's speech to the National Homeland Defense Symposium, Broadmoor Conference Center, Colorado Springs, Colorado, October 26, 2005. Available on compact disc from the National Homeland Defense Foundation through its Web site.

8. Former DHS senior officials have begun to go public with their criticism of the White House. See Michael Grunwald and Susan B. Glasser, "Prelude to Disaster: The Making of DHS," a two-part series, *Washington Post,* December 22–23, 2005, p. A1.

9. John Mintz, "At Homeland Security, Doubts Arise over Intelligence," *Washington Post,* July 21, 2003. The story recounts heavy bipartisan criticism of DHS for failing to resource its new intelligence directorate.

10. See prepared statement of John Gannon, former CIA deputy director for intelligence and staff director of the House Homeland Security Committee, to the 9/11 Public Discourse Project (9/11PDP) forum, "CIA and FBI Reform," June 6, 2005, available online at http://www.9-11pdp.org/ua/2005-06-06.htm.

11. See John Brennan, "Is This Intelligence? We Added Players but Lost Control of the Ball," *Washington Post,* November 20, 2005, p. B1. Brennan, the just-retired acting head of the National Counterterrorism Center, stated that: "What's still missing is a coherent framework of reform. The confusion over responsibilities sown by the rush of initiatives has produced the equivalent of a soccer game played by 7-year-olds—departments and agencies cluster around topical issues, bumping into each other and leaving important areas of the intelligence field dangerously unattended."

12. Walter Pincus, "Pentagon Expanding Its Domestic Surveillance Activity," *Washington Post,* November 27, 2005, p. A6. On allegations of NSA surveillance of U.S. citizens, see James Risen, *State of War: The Secret History of the CIA and the Bush Administration* (New York: Free Press, 2006), pp. 39–60.

13. A thoughtful and provocative analysis of options for domestic intelligence is contained in Richard Posner, "Remaking Domestic Intelligence," Hoover Institution Weekly Essays, June 16, 2006, available at http://www.hoover.org/pubaffairs/we/2005/posner06.html.

14. See June 30, 2005, statement of Congressman Frank Wolf, Chairman of the House Science-State-Justice-Commerce Appropriations Subcommittee, "FBI Making Progress Adapting to New Role, But More Needs to Be Accomplished," *Congressional Record,* Extension of Remarks, July 1, 2005.

15. See L. Britt Snider, "Congressional Oversight of Intelligence after September 11," in Jennifer E. Sims and Burton Gerber, editors, *Transforming U.S. Intelligence* (Washington, D.C.: Georgetown University Press, 2005), pp. 239–255.

CHAPTER 13

1. James Chow, James Chiesa, Paul Dreyer, Mel Eisman, Theodore W. Karasik, Joel Kvitky, Sherrill Lingel, David Ochmanek, and Chad Shirley, *Protecting Commercial Aviation Against the Shoulder-Fired Missile Threat,* RAND Corporation, 2005, p. 1.

2. U.S. Department of Justice, Office of the Inspector General, Audit Division, *Review of the Terrorist Screening Center's Efforts to Support the Secure Flight Program,* Audit Report 05-34, August 2005, p. ii.

3. Government Accountability Office, *Aviation Security: Screener Training and Performance Measurement Strengthened, but More Work Remains,* Report to the Chairman, Subcommittee on Aviation, Committee on Transportation and Infrastructure, House of Representatives, GAO-05-457, May 2005, p. 7.

4. Government Accountability Office, *Aviation Security: Progress Since September 11, 2001, and the Challenges Ahead,* Statement of Gerald L. Dillingham, Testimony before the Committee on Commerce, Science and Transportation, U.S. Senate, GAO-03-1150T, September 2, 2003, p. 1.

5. "Eleven Point Plan for U.S. Aviation Security," *Aviation Week and Space Technology,* August 23, 2004.

6. Bart Elias, William Krouse, and Ed Rappaport, *Homeland Security: Air Passenger Prescreening and Counterterrorism,* CRS Report to Congress, RL32802, March 4, 2005, p. 6.

7. Department of Homeland Security, Office of Inspector General, Office of Inspections, Evaluations, & Special Research, *Review of the Transportation Security Administration's Role in the Use and Dissemination of Airline Passenger Data,* OIG-05-12, March 2005, p. 12.

8. Bart Elias, *Aviation Security-Related Findings and Recommendations of the 9/11 Commission,* CRS Report to Congress, RL32541, March 30, 2005, p. 4.

9. Government Accountability Office, *Aviation Security: Secure Flight Development and Testing Under Way, but Risks Should Be Managed as System Is Further Developed,* Report to Congressional Committees, GAO-05-356, March 2005, p. 3.

10. CRS Report to Congress, RL32802, March 4, 2005, p. 9.

11. Ibid., p. 10.

12. Government Accountability Office, *Aviation Security: Screener Training and Performance Measurement Strengthened but More Work Remains,* p. 3.

13. Bart Elias, *Air Cargo Security,* CRS Report for Congress, RL32022, January 13, 2005, p. 20.

14. Paul Hoversten, "TSA Sets June 20 as Launch Date for Nationwide Registered Traveler Program," *Homeland Security and Defense,* November 9, 2005.

15. Government Accountability Office, *Aviation Security: Better Planning Needed to Optimize Deployment of Checked Baggage Screening Systems,* Testimony Before the Subcommittee on Economic Security, Infrastructure Protection, and Cyber Security, Committee on Homeland Security, House of Representatives, Statement of Cathleen A. Berrick, GAO-05-896T, July 13, 2005, p. 5.

16. Op. cit.

17. Ibid., p. 3.

18. Gary Kauvar, Bernard Rostker, and Russell Shaver, "Safer Skies: Baggage Screening and Beyond," RAND, White Paper, National Security Research Division, 2002, p. 1.

19. GAO-05-896T, July 13, 2005, p. 5.

20. Kauyar et al., p. 1.

21. GAO-05-896T, July 13, 2005, p. 3.

22. Ibid., p. 17.

23. Paul Hoversten, "TSA Mulls Use of Bomb-Sniffing Dog Teams to Inspect Cargo on Passenger Aircraft," *Homeland Security and Defense*, October 5, 2005.

24. CRS Report for Congress, RL32022, January 13, 2005, p. 1.

25. Government Accountability Office, *Aviation Security: Federal Action Needed to Strengthen Domestic Air Cargo Security*, GAO-06-76, October 2005, p. 11.

26. CRS Report for Congress, RL32022, January 13, 2005, p. 1.

27. Ibid., p. 4.

28. GAO-06-76, October 2005, p. 4.

29. Ibid., p. 6.

30. CRS Report for Congress, RL32022, January 13, 2005, p. 10.

31. GAO-06-76, October 2005, p. 13.

32. Chow et al., p. 4.

33. Op. cit.

34. Ibid., p. 1.

35. Op. cit.

36. CRS Report to Congress, RL32541, March 30, 2005, p. 15.

37. CRS Report for Congress, RL32022, January 13, 2005, p. 17.

38. CRS Report to Congress, RL32541, March 30, 2005, p. 14.

39. Government Accountability Office, *Federal Air Marshal Service Could Benefit from Improved Planning and Controls*, Report to the Honorable Peter A. DeFazio, House of Representatives, GAO-06-203, November 2005, p. 6.

40. Government Accountability Office, *Aviation Security: Flight and Cabin Crew Member Security Training Strengthened, but Better Planning and Internal Controls Needed*, GAO-05-781, September 2005, p. 5.

41. Bart Elias, *Lasers Aimed at Aircraft Cockpits: Background and Possible Options to Address the Threat to Aviation Safety and Security*, CRS Report for Congress, RS22033, January 26, 2005, p. 3.

42. CRS Report for Congress, RL32022, January 13, 2005, p. 16.

43. Ibid., p. 25.

44. CRS Report to Congress, RL32802, March 4, 2005, p. 4.

45. Op. cit.

46. Government Accountability Office, *Aviation Security: Measures for Testing the Impact of Using Commercial Data for Secure Flight Program,* Report to Congressional Committees, GAO-05-324, February 2005, p. 2.

47. U.S. Department of Justice, Office of the Inspector General, Audit Report 05-34, p. viii.

48. GAO-05-356, March 28, 2005, p. 11.

49. CRS Report to Congress, RL32541, March 30, 2005, p. 6.

50. GAO-05-457, May 2005, p. 4.

51. Ibid., p. 3.

52. CRS Report to Congress, RL32541, March 30, 2005, p. 5.

53. R. D. Shaver, Michael Kennedy, Chad Shirley, and Paul Dreyer, *How Much Is Enough? Sizing the Deployment of Baggage Screening Equipment to Minimize the Cost of Flying,* RAND, DB-412-RC, 2004, p. 5.

54. GAO-05-896T, July 13, 2005, p. 4.

55. Ibid., p. 3.

56. Kauver et al., p. 4.

57. Op. cit.

58. GAO-06-76, October 2005, p. 4.

59. Ibid., p. 6.

60. Op. cit.

61. CRS Report for Congress, RL32022, January 13, 2005, p. 12.

62. Ibid., p. 13.

63. Ibid., p. 23.

64. Op. cit.

65. Ibid., p. 25.

66. Chow et al., p. xi.

67. GAO-05-781, September 2005, p. 4.

68. Ibid., p. 5.

69. Ibid., p. 7.

70. CRS Report for Congress, RL32022, January 13, 2005, p. 17.

71. Government Accountability Office, *Federal Air Marshal Service Could Benefit from Improved Planning and Controls,* Report to the Honorable Peter A. DeFazio, House of Representatives, GAO-06-203, November 2005, p. 5.

72. CRS Report for Congress, RL32022, January 13, 2005, p. 15.

73. Department of Homeland Security, Office of Inspector General, Office of Audits, *Audit of Passenger and Baggage Screening Procedures at Domestic Airports*, OIG-04-37, September 2004, p. 3.

74. Ibid., p. 4.

75. Eric Lipton, "Significant Changes in Air Passenger Screening Lie Ahead," *New York Times*, December 1, 2005.

76. CRS Report for Congress, RL32022, January 13, 2005, p. 19.

77. Ibid., p. 18.

78. Chow et al., p. 13.

79. Ibid., p. 1.

80. CRS Report for Congress, RS22033, January 26, 2005, p. 4.

CHAPTER 14

1. Committee on Science and Technology for Countering Terrorism, National Research Council, *Making the Nation Safer: The Role of Science and Technology in Countering Terrorism* (Washington, D.C.: National Academies Press, 2002), p. 45.

2. See, for example, chapter 2 in *Making the Nation Safer: The Role of Science and Technology in Countering Terrorism*; Matthew Bunn and Anthony Wier, *Securing the Bomb 2005: The New Global Imperatives* (Washington, D.C.: Nuclear Threat Initiative and the Project on Managing the Atom, Harvard University, May 2005); Graham Allison, *Nuclear Terrorism: The Ultimate Preventable Catastrophe* (New York: Times Books, 2004); chapter 8 in Richard A. Clarke et al., *Defeating the Jihadists: A Blueprint for Action* (New York: Century Foundation, November 2004); and Charles D. Ferguson and William C. Potter, with Amy Sands, Leonard S. Spector, and Fred L. Wehling, *The Four Faces of Nuclear Terrorism* (New York: Routledge, 2005).

3. Robert S. Norris and Hans M. Kristensen, "U.S. Nuclear Forces, 2006," *Bulletin of the Atomic Scientists,* January/February 2006, pp. 68–71.

4. Robert S. Norris and Hans M. Kristensen, "U.S. Nuclear Weapons in Europe, 1954-2004," *Bulletin of the Atomic Scientists,* November/December 2004, pp. 76–77.

5. National Nuclear Security Administration, "NNSA's Reliable Replacement Warhead Program Will Enable Transformation of the Nuclear Weapons Complex," NNSA Press Release, 2005.

6. David Albright and Kimberly Kramer, "Fissile Material: Stockpiles Still Growing," *Bulletin of the Atomic Scientists*, November/December 2004, pp. 14–16.

7. Wade Boese, "U.S. Trims Nuclear Material Stockpile," *Arms Control Today*, December 2005, p. 29.

8. H.R. 6, Energy Policy Act of 2005. This bill passed the House on July 27, 2005, by 275–156, and the Senate on July 29, 2005, by 74–26. President Bush signed it into law on August 8, 2005.

9. Admiral Richard W. Mies (USN–Retired), Memorandum to NNSA Administrator, Ambassador Linton Brooks, "Independent NNSA Security Review," May 2, 2005.

10. Ibid.

11. Government Accountability Office, *Nuclear Security: DOE Needs to Resolve Significant Issues before It Fully Meets the New Design Basis Threat*, GAO-04-623, April 2004.

12. Government Accountability Office, *Nuclear Security: Actions Needed by DOE to Improve Security of Weapons-Grade Nuclear Material at Its Energy, Science and Environmental Sites*, Testimony before the Subcommittee on National Security, Emerging Threats and International Relations, Committee on Government Reform, House of Representatives, GAO-05-934T, July 26, 2005.

13. Department of Energy, Office of Inspector General, Office of Audit Services, "The National Nuclear Security Administration's Implementation of the 2003 Design Basis Threat," Special Report, DOE/IG-0705, October 2005, p. 2.

14. Department of Energy, Office of Inspector General, Office of Inspections and Special Inquiries, "Security Access Controls at the Y-12 National Security Complex," Inspection Report, DOE/IG-0691, June 2005, p. 1.

15. Mies memorandum, op. cit.

16. Project on Government Oversight, "U.S. Nuclear Weapons Complex: Homeland Security Opportunities," POGO Report, May 2005.

17. Secretary of Energy Advisory Board, U.S. Department of Energy, "Recommendations for the Nuclear Weapons Complex of the Future," Report of the Nuclear Weapons Complex Infrastructure Task Force, Draft Final Report, July 13, 2005.

18. Scott D. Sagan, "The Problem of Redundancy Problem: Why More Nuclear Security Forces May Produce Less Nuclear Security," *Risk Analysis: An International Journal*, August 2004, pp. 935–946. That article won Columbia University's Institute for War and Peace Studies prize for best paper in political violence for 2003.

19. In any case, radiation detection gear presents a relatively weak line of defense because nuclear-weapons-usable materials can be easily shielded. See Chapters 15 and 16.

CHAPTER 15

1. Randal C. Archibold, "Dockworkers' Union Calls for Cleaner Air at Seaports," *New York Times,* January 1, 2006.

2. "U.S. Public Port Facts," American Association of Port Authorities, available online at http://www.aapa-ports.org/industryinfo/portfact.htm.

3. Interview with the captain of the Port of Los Angeles and Long Beach, Captain Peter Neffenger, U.S. Coast Guard, on May 11, 2005.

4. *National Strategy for Homeland Security,* Office of Homeland Security, July 2002, p. 64, available online at http://www.whitehouse.gov/homeland/book /nat_strat_hls.pdf.

5. Ibid.

6. See http://www.portoflosangeles.org/about.htm.

7. Stephen E. Flynn, Interview with the captain of the Port of Los Angeles and Long Beach, Captain Peter Neffenger, U.S. Coast Guard, May 11, 2005.

8. Ibid.

9. John Schoen, "Ships and Ports Are Terrorism's New Frontier: As Airports Boost Security, Seaports Remain Vulnerable," MSNBC, June 21, 2005, available online at http://www.msnbc.com/id/5069435.

10. See http://www.imo.org/home.asp.

11. See http://usinfo.org/wf-archive/2003/030613/epf520.htm.

12. See http://www.cbp.gov/.

13. See http://www.cbp.gov/xp/cgov/border_security/international_activities/csi/.

14. See http://www.cbp.gov/xp/cgov/newsroom/press_releases/archives/2005_press _releases/0122005/12142005.xml.

15. See http://www.cbp.gov/xp/cgov/import/commercial_enforcement/ctpat/.

16. See http://www.nnsa.doe.gov/na-20/sld.shtml.

17. See http://www.dhs.gov/interWeb/assetlibrary/HSPD13_MaritimeSecurity Strategy.pdf.

18. Robert C. Bonner, Commissioner, Customs and Border Protection Agency, in remarks at the CBP Trade Symposium, Ronald Reagan Building, Washington, D.C., November 3, 2005.

19. Richard L. Skinner, testimony of acting inspector general of the U.S. Department of Homeland Security before the Committee on Commerce, Science, and Transportation, U.S. Senate, May 17, 2005. Available online at http://www.dhs.gov/interWeb/assetlibrary/OIG_SkinnerStatement_5-13-05.pdf.

20. See http://www.cbp.gov/xp/cgov/import/commercial_enforcement/ctpat/.

21. Stephen E. Flynn and Lawrence M. Wein, "Think Inside the Box," *New York Times,* November 29, 2005.

22. Paul McHale, assistant secretary of defense for homeland defense, testimony before the 108th Congress, Committee on Armed Services, U.S. Senate, March 25, 2004.

23. See http://www.defenselink.mil/news/Oct2005/20051007_2972.html.

24. Robert Block and Alex Ortoloni, "Keeping Cargo Safe From Terror, Hong Kong Port Project Scans All Containers; U.S. Doesn't See the Need," *Wall Street Journal,* July 29, 2005.

25. Stephen Flynn, *Addressing the Shortcomings of the Customs-Trade Partnership Against Terrorism* (C-TPAT) *and the Container Security Initiative,* Written testimony before a hearing of the Permanent Sub-Committee on Investigations Committee on Homeland Security and Governmental Affairs, U.S. Senate, May 26, 2005.

26. Ibid.

27. See http://www.icgsdeepwater.com/.

28. See http://www.house.gov/transportation/cgmt/08-25-04/flynn.pdf.

29. These recommendations have been adapted from Stephen Flynn, "U.S. Port Security and the Global War on Terror: Seven Specific Suggestions for Immediate Executive Action," *American Interest* 1, no. 1 (Autumn 2005): 92–96.

CHAPTER 16

1. Abu Ubayd al-Qurashi, "America's Nightmares," *Al Ansar* (Internet), February 13, 2002. In Anonymous, *Imperial Hubris* (Washington, D.C.: Brassey's, 2004), p. 84.

2. For the purpose of this report, the northern border spans 12 states and covers 4,121 miles, not including Alaska. United States Border Patrol does not patrol the Canadian-Alaskan border. The southern border is 1,940 miles.

3. Laredo Development Foundation briefing, February 18, 2004.

4. Hart Research poll on terrorism conducted June 5–6, 2005. Reprinted in July 21, 2005, edition of *National Journal.*

5. Susan B. Glasser and Michael Grunwald, "Department's Mission Was Undermined from Start," *Washington Post,* December 22, 2005.

6. Chris Strohm, "Hiring Freeze, Spending Restrictions Take Toll on Homeland Security Bureau," *Government Executive,* November 19, 2004.

7. Jerry Seper, "Border War" series, *Washington Times,* September 23–27, 2002.

8. DHS Press Release, "DHS Announces Long-Term Border and Immigration Strategy," November 2, 2005.

9. *Transforming the Southern Border,* p. 50.

10. GAO-05-573.

11. Government Accountability Office, "Combating Nuclear Smuggling: Efforts to Deploy Radiation Detection Equipment in the United States and Other Countries," GAO-05-840T, p. 1.

12. *Transforming the Southern Border,* a report by the Democrats on the U.S. House of Representatives Homeland Security Committee, September 2004, p. 59.

13. Government Accountability Office, "Homeland Security: Agency Plans, Implementation and Challenges Regarding the National Strategy for Homeland Security," GAO-05-33, pp. 50–51.

14. GAO-05-840T, p. 1.

15. GAO-05-840T, p. 8.

16. AAAS, "DHS Receives Modest R&D Boost in Final 2006 Budget," December 29, 2005.

17. GAO-05-840T, p. 8.

18. U.S. Commission on Immigration Reform, *First Interim Report: Immigration Policy: Restoring Credibility* (Washington, D.C., September 30, 1994.)

19. Edward W. Lempinen, AAAS News Release, "AAAS and Allied Science Groups See Dramatic Improvement in U.S. Visa System," April 5, 2005.

20. Jessica Vaughan, Center for Immigration Studies report, August 2005.

21. "CBP Border Patrol Overview," Department of Homeland Security Press Office, January 11, 2006.

22. *Transforming the Southern Border,* p. 98.

23. "DHS Announces Long-Term Border and Immigration Strategy," DHS Press Office, November 30, 2005.

24. Chris Strohm, "Southwestern States, Homeland Security at Odds over Border Controls," *Government Executive,* April 15, 2005.

25. Arizona Border Control Initiative Fact Sheet, undated, available online at http://www.dhs.gov/dhspublic/display?content=4029.

26. Undersecretary for Border and Transportation Security Asa Hutchinson quoted in Luke Turf, "$10M Boost to Border Security Effort," *Tucson Citizen,* March 17, 2004.

CHAPTER 17

1. See, for example, *The USA Patriot Act: The Basics* (New York: Century Foundation, 2004), at pp. 15–16 (discussing Patriot Act provision Section 215, which allows demands for personal records from libraries and the resulting controversy).

2. Eric Lichtblau, "FBI's Reach Into Records Is Set to Grow," *New York Times,* Nov. 12, 2003, p. A12.

3. See http://www.defenselink.mil/news/commissions.html.

4. For example, see the findings in *The 9/11 Commission Report: Final Report of the National Commission on Terrorist Attacks Upon the United States* (Washington, D.C.: U.S. Government Printing Office, 2004).

5. See the "Joint Inquiry into Intelligence Community Activities before and after the Terrorist Attacks of September 11, 2001" (released in December 2002), available online at http://www.gpoaccess.gov/serialset/creports/911.html.

6. David Sanger, "Storm and Crisis: Federal Response; Bush Wants to Consider Broadening of Military's Powers During Natural Disasters," *New York Times,* September 27, 2005, p. A18.

7. This part of this chapter is drawn mostly from Philip B. Heymann and Juliette N. Kayyem, *Protecting Liberty in an Age of Terror* (Cambridge, Mass.: MIT Press, 2005).

8. For example, despite the Supreme Court ruling in 2004 regarding the status of detainees at Guantanamo Bay, *Rasul v. Bush* (decided June 2004), the question of the exact process due to those being held is still being litigated over a year later.

9. *The 9/11 Commission Report,* p. 419.

10. These questions, from Heymann and Kayyem, are the result of tremendous research and insights by Paul Lettow, Harvard Law School, 2005.

CHAPTER 18

1. This replicates similar trends from previous years. See Stephen E. Flynn, "The Neglected Home Front," *Foreign Affairs,* September/October 2004. This analysis is drawn from the Center for Defense Information and Foreign Policy in "Report of the Task Force on a Unified Security Budget for the United States, 2006," *Focus,* May 2005.

2. Government Accountability Office, "Homeland Security: Voluntary Initiatives Are Under Way at Chemical Facilities, but the Extent of Security

Preparedness Is Unknown," GAO-03-439, March 2003, p. 30. Available online at http://www.gao.gov/cgi-bin/getrpt?GAO-03-439.

3. Ibid., p. 31. See joint statement by Secretary Ridge and EPA Administrator Christine Todd Whitman, October 2002, for DHS and EPA views.

4. Congressional Budget Office, *Cost Estimate for S.1602 Chemical Security Act of 2002,* As ordered reported by the Senate Committee on Environment and Public Works on July 25, 2002, www.cbo.gov/showdoc.cfm?index=3840 &sequence=0.

5. On rail security see Jack Riley, RAND Corporation, "Terrorism and Rail Security," testimony presented to the Senate Commerce, Science, and Transportation Committee on March 23, 2004, available online at http://www.rand.org/publications/CT/CT224/CT224.pdf.

6. See testimony of William W. Millar, President, American Public Transportation Association, before the Subcommittee on Homeland Security of the House Committee on Appropriations, April 9, 2004. Available online at http://www.apta.com/Government_Affairs/Positions/Aptatest/Documents /Testimony040409.pdf.

7. See Richard Clarke et al., *Defeating the Jihadists: A Blueprint for Action* (New York: Century Foundation, 2004), p. 125. Also see Henry H. Willis and David S. Ortiz, *Evaluating the Security of the Global Containerized Supply Chain,* RAND Corporation, 2004, available online at http://www.rand .org/pubs/technical_ reports/2004/rand_tr214.pdf; Henry H. Willis and David S. Ortiz, *Assessing Container Security: A Framework for Measuring Performance of the Global Supply Chain,* RAND Corporation, 2005, available online at http://www.rand.org/publications/rb/rb9095/rand_rb9095.pdf.

8. American Association of Port Authorities, "Authority Association Vice President Provides Written Testimony for TSA Budget Hearing," February 15, 2005, available online at http://www.aapa-ports.org/pressroom/feb1505.htm.

9. Coast Guard figures from Government Accountability Office, "Maritime Security: Substantial Work Remains to Translate New Planning Requirements into Effective Port Security," June 2004, p. 42, available online at http://www.gao.gov/new.items/d04838.pdf. These costs are for compliance with the Maritime Transportation Security Act. Total compliance costs for ten years (2003–2012) are estimated at $7.3 billion, of which $5.4 billion is for port security, $1.4 billion is for vessels, and about $500 million is for outer continental shelf facility and area maritime security and automatic identification system requirements. This report also suggests that the Coast Guard figures are likely low (or at least of uncertain accuracy), suggesting an actual range of $4.5–6.4 billion for the 2003–2012 period for port security, and of course do not include

expenses beyond 2012. They also assume relative low threat levels. Increases in threat levels would raise costs.

10. See *FY2006 Appropriations for State and Local Homeland Security,* Congressional Research Service, February 14, 2005, available online at http://www.ndu.edu/library/docs/crs/crs_rs22050_14feb05.pdf, and Staff Executive Summary of Key City Priorities in the President's FY 2006 Budget, U.S. Conference of Mayors, February 8, 2005, available online at http://www.usmayors.org/executivedirector/fy06budget.pdf.

11. See Lois M. Davis, K. Jack Riley, Greg Ridgeway, Jennifer E. Pace, Sarah K. Cotton, Paul Steinberg, Kelly Damphousse, and Brent L. Smith, *When Terrorism Hits Home: How Prepared Are State and Local Law Enforcement?* RAND Corporation, 2004, pp. 79, 199, available online at http://www.rand.org/pubs/monographs/2004/RAND_MG104.pdf.

12. See Richard Clarke et al., *Defeating the Jihadists,* p. 129.

13. See *Emergency Responders: Drastically Underfunded, Dangerously Unprepared,* Independent Task Force on Emergency Responders, Council on Foreign Relations, June 2003; Richard Clarke et al., *Defeating the Jihadists,* p. 129; and Stephen Flynn, *America the Vulnerable: How Our Government Is Failing to Protect Us from Terrorism* (New York: HarperCollins, 2004).

14. On the MMRS see *Tools for Evaluating the Metropolitan Medical Response System Program: Phase I Report, Institute of Medicine,* National Academy Press, 2001, available online at http://www.nap.edu/books/0309076471/html/R1.html.

15. "Public Health: Costs of Complacency," *Governing,* February 2004, available online at http://governing.com/gpp/2004/public.htm.

16. *Ready or Not: Protecting the Public's Health in the Age of Bioterrorism,* Trust for America's Health, December 2004, available online at http://healthyamericans.org/reports/bioterror04/BioTerror04Report.pdf.

17. Data for this section is drawn from the Center for Defense Information and Foreign Policy in Focus, *Report of the Task Force on a Unified Security Budget for the United States, 2006,* May 2005, and the Pentagon's *Selected Acquisition Records.*

INDEX

ABC (Arizona Border Control) Initiative, 208, 214, 215
ABC News, 40, 232
ABM (Anti-Ballistic Missile) treaty, 237
Abqaiq oil facility attack, Saudi Arabia, 96
Abraham, Spencer, 183, 184, 185
Abu Ghraib prison, Iraq, 5, 225
Abu Hafs al-Masri Brigade, 34
Abu Mezer, Ghazi Ibrahim, 203
ACC (American Chemistry Council), 85, 86
Accountability, intelligence, 155–156, 158–159
ACES (Assuring Continuity of Essential Systems), 61
Advanced Research and Development Agency, 123
Afghanistan, war in, 236, 240
Agriculture, 13, 205
Air cargo security, 164–165, 170–171, 173–174. *See also* Aviation security
Air Cargo Strategic Plan, 165
Air Force weapons programs, 239–240, 241–242
Air marshals, federal, 162, 171–172
Air quality monitoring, 47–48
Airport security. *See* Aviation security
al Qaeda. *See also* 9/11/2001 terrorist attacks, view from: 9/11/2001

attacks by, 149; border security, 203; chemical and biological weapons interest, 43; electrical power threats, 103; energy infrastructure attacks, 96; federal focus on, 26; and jihadism, 3–8; MAN-PAD threat, 166; transportation attacks (2005), 3, 4, 22, 34, 37, 38, 39, 191; U.S. torture and recruitment to, 225; as U.S. intelligence failure, 149
al-Sayid Umar, Midhat Mursi, 43
"All-hazards" management priorities, 138, 139, 140, 144
American Chemistry Council (ACC), 85, 86
American democracy, as jihadist motivation, 4
American Muslims, characteristics of, 5–6
American Public Transportation Association, 231
American Red Cross, 133, 136
Amsterdam, van Gogh murder, 4
Anthrax attacks (2001), 44, 143
Anti-Ballistic Missile (ABM) treaty, 237
Anti-Terrorism and Intelligence Reform Act, 129
Anti-Terrorism Intelligence Awareness Training Program, 31
Antidote stockpiles, 45, 49–51, 54–55